THIRD EDITION

THE CULTURAL ENVIRONMENT OF INTERNATIONAL BUSINESS

VERN TERPSTRA
International Business Department
The University of Michigan

KENNETH DAVID
Department of Anthropology
Michigan State University

SI87CA
PUBLISHED BY
SOUTH-WESTERN PUBLISHING CO.
CINCINNATI, OH

Publisher: James R. Sitlington, Jr.
Production Editor: Susan C. Williams
Production House: Beckwith-Clark, Inc.
Cover and Interior Designer: Joseph M. Devine
Marketing Manager: David L. Shaut

Library of Congress Cataloging-in-Publication Data

Terpstra, Vern.
    The cultural environment of international business / Vern
Terpstra, Kenneth David. — 3rd ed.
        p.   cm.
    "SI87CA."
    Includes bibliographical references and index.
    ISBN 0-538-80003-8
    1. International business enterprises—Social aspects.
I. David, Kenneth H.   II. Title
    HD2755.5.T47   1991
    306.3'6—dc20   90-61084
                                                       CIP

1 2 3 4 5 6 7 8 9 D 8 7 6 5 4 3 2 1 0
Printed in the United States of America

About the Authors

Vern Terpstra, Ph.D., is Professor and Chairman of the International Business program at The University of Michigan.

Dr. Terpstra received his bachelor's degree in economics and marketing, a master's degree in marketing and international business, and his doctoral degree in international business and marketing, all from The University of Michigan. Additional graduate study was conducted at the Free University of Brussels.

His professional experience includes several visiting professorships in China, Taiwan, England, and the Netherlands, as well as active membership in and past-presidency of the Academy of International Business. He has also served on editorial boards, including the *International Marketing Review, Journal of Business Research, Journal of Marketing,* and the *Journal of International Business Studies.*

Dr. Terpstra is the author of numerous articles, monographs, papers, and books.

Kenneth David, Ph.D., is Associate Professor of Social Anthropology and International Business at Michigan State University.

Dr. David received his bachelor's degree with honors from the College of Letters (Comparative Literature, Language, History, and Philosophy) at Wesleyan University of Connecticut, a master's degree and doctoral degree in social anthropology from the University of Chicago, and a master's degree in business administation from Michigan State University. Doctoral-level work on international business and business policy was done at The University of Michigan during a sabbatical year.

His teaching experience includes the University of London (School of Oriental and African Studies), the Vrije Universiteit of Amsterdam, the Hogeschool voor Economie en Management of Utrecht, the Indian Institute of Management at Ahmedabad, and Seoul National University.

Dr. David has presented major papers at the American Anthropology Association, the Academy of Management, and the Strategic Management Society. He has also published books and articles in anthropology and business.

Preface

This book represents an unusual collaboration between a business school professor and a professor of cultural and business anthropology. Our goal is to aid the reader in understanding the complexities of operating in foreign environments—a task crucial to success in international business. This new edition reflects changing global conditions and the growing awareness in the business community of the need for more sophisticated orientation to managing relationships between organizations from different cultures. The overall aim of the book, however, remains environmental: how should organizations orient themselves in order to respond to issues that stem from the differing logics and objectives of foreign organizations, associates, or regulators. Our epilogue, "Environments and Issues," provides an overview of this approach. Readers who favor structure before content might want to read it now.

The earlier editions of this book have been widely used in various international departments. Based on that experience and discussions with users, this third edition has been prepared. We do not assume that our readers are well prepared in either anthropology or international business administration.

The overall structure of the book is intended to provide an introduction to cultural anthropology adapted for business use. The epilogue provides background in business policy and international business. We have added an index and a general bibliography to facilitate further inquiry into the areas we address.

The structure of individual chapters has also been revised. We have inserted a focus case near the beginning of chapters to engage the reader's attention to the topic. The main body of each chapter consists of three parts. First, the cultural system is defined. Second, in the spirit of *learning how to learn* rather than encyclopedic completeness, we sketch major ways in which the cultural system differs in various societies and world regions. Third, we draw attention to policy implications (for countries as well as companies) of the cultural system. Exercises found at the end of chapters have been used by the authors to facilitate class discussions, short projects, or examinations. There are three types of exercises: questions designed to review aspects of material covered in the chapter, questions designed for further awareness raising about the cultural system covered, and exercises that can be assigned as brief projects. Further, we include mini-cases that can be used either for in-class discussions or as short essay examination questions.

We want to acknowledge the careful readings given this edition by Dharma deSilva, Jeffrey Fadiman, and Gideon Falk. Their comments were helpful in revising the text. Further, Hanneke Jorg's comments led to the addition of focus cases. Collaborations with Richard Reeves-Ellington, Cynthia Smith, and William Yeack have contributed to the pragmatic/humanist stance taken in this book.

We'd also like to thank those people who responded to the questionnaire: William Stearns II, J. Robert Foster, J.M. Buxbaum, Baher A. Ghosheh, Animesh Ghoshal, and James Sood.

Vern Terpstra
The University of Michigan

Ken David
Michigan State University

Contents

List of Figures and Tables

The Basics of Culture

PROLOGUE: THE CHALLENGE OF INTERNATIONAL BUSINESS IN THE 1990s

International business people no longer brush aside culture as a vague, nonquantifiable variable that will take care of itself if proper business analyses have been accomplished. This section illustrates the point that culture makes a difference in international business relationships.

Cultural risk poses threats stemming from differences in values and codes of behavior between companies and regulators, among business organizations, and even within a large organization. Cultural miscommunication is costly.

Managing cultural risk means seizing opportunities by learning how to read and respond to the organizational culture of regulators, business associates, customers, or clients in order to build effective partnerships and strategic alliances.

Global and regional business integration during the 1990s will increase the opportunities and risks. Consider the following business situations involving differences in national, business, or organizational cultures.

- Projects within a company involve units from different nations.

    The Mersk shipping line of Denmark (in New York, Moller Lines) has an outstanding record of customer service in its multiple-country offices. To ensure quick, responsive service to customers while meeting company objectives, Mersk invests heavily in a two-year training program of corporate cultural as well as technical training. Mersk employees act confidently under pressure, even when faced with tricky situations and no time to confer with the Danish headquarters.

- Companies are planning for operations in Europe after 1992. Anyone doing business in a European Economic Community country in 1992 will face challenges because every firm will be an international firm. Even if you operate in only one national market, you will have more international competitors than before.

The European subsidiary of California-based Avery Company is anticipating the end of trade and tariff barriers within EC countries by changing their practical systems; they are currently reducing fourteen sales/distribution offices to five logistically linked distribution centers and separate sales offices. To meet the challenge of European integration, Avery is taking steps to ensure that they are perceived as a European firm with European interests.

- Companies have international ventures with a foreign firm. Many Third-World countries favor international joint ventures over wholly owned subsidiaries.

A Canadian company and an Indian company had successfully completed the first phase of a multimillion-dollar pipeline construction project. The operating directors had worked out plans for the second phase to their mutual satisfaction. When the CEOs of the respective companies met to confirm the plans, the entire project was jeopardized—not by personality clash, but by differences in priorities concerning time and delegation of responsibility. (Details are found in the focus case at the beginning of Chapter 1.)

- Consulting firms with long-term service relationships must reach out and understand their clients' organizational cultures.

A company with excellent training and skills in management-information system (MIS) consulting encounters trouble on projects because their consultants have had no training in reading and responding to the client's corporate culture and do not always understand the social impact of the technically superior MIS on the client organization. Pilot teams adopt participant-observation techniques to learn the client culture. Then they negotiate shared understandings with the client in areas necessary to accomplish project objectives.

- Mergers, acquisitions, and strategic alliances are attractive for various reasons but face cultural problems.

The term *culture clash* has appeared frequently in the popular press. Various potential mergers such as that of DuPont and Conoco are rated highly in terms of financial, technical, and marketing synergies, yet they face difficulties in the post-merger period because personnel do not know which rules to follow.

- Projects within a company involve units from different professional cultures.

In new car model projects, General Motors used to require that their Design Engineering, Production Engineering, and Marketing Departments shield information from one another to prevent leaks to the competition. Recently, they adopted a project team approach.

A German auto company allows interaction between Design and Production Engineering at certain phases of a new car model project. They have no system in place to handle the professional culture clashes between these units when, for example, Production protests that Design's styling and performance plans are not feasible for production.

Toyota organizes a core team of design, production, and marketing personnel to work on a new car model. At different phases of the project, different proportions of the representative departments comprise the team. Coordination problems are minimal.

In summary, whenever a company must manage intensive communications across organizational lines, managing cultural risk is a task crucial for superior performance. Because people in business organizations are triply socialized (in national, professional, and corporate cultures), there are degrees of cultural risk. Because cultural risk is rarely given sufficient emphasis, it is consistently undermanaged.

Forward-looking firms are preparing for international integration of activities by augmenting their communication networks and revising their strategic planning processes to include programs for effective cultural management.

CONTENT OF PART ONE

Chapter 1 will introduce the reader to the fundamentals of culture and the need for international managers to cope with the task of intercultural management. Chapter 2 will focus on language, the most basic cultural system, for language is the medium through which culture is learned and communicated.

CHAPTER ONE
Culture

This book focuses on the challenge of operating in a foreign cultural setting. The following episode illustrates the challenge of overcoming blinders imposed by your home country's cultural upbringing.

FOCUS CASE:
Value Conflicts in an International Joint Venture

En route to Delhi, Kenneth David met the president of a Canadian construction firm. The Canadian firm and a large Indian firm were engaged in a joint venture to build a pipeline. The Canadian's second in command had worked out operating details with his Indian counterpart. The Canadian chief executive's plan was to affirm the arrangements in a meeting with the chief executive of the Indian firm and to depart Delhi the next evening for Singapore.

The next day, the Canadian CEO called David because he had a problem. The Indian CEO was requesting three days to review the operating details. The Canadian second in command was furious and accused the Indian joint venture partners of lack of common decency and more.

Questioning of the participants revealed that there was nothing common in the two firms' priorities and interpretations of the situation. The Canadian side prioritized time and underplayed hierarchy. The Canadian CEO was quite willing to delegate negotiations to his second in command and basically did not care if the Indian CEO was fully informed of the minute details. The Indian CEO, on the other hand, wanted to be fully briefed on the details. Partly because he did not have confidence in his subordinate and partly because he wanted to display full knowledge of the situation to both the visiting Canadian and his subordinate during the formal meeting, the Indian CEO downplayed a time delay. Imposing a delay on a visiting chief executive was a small ritual intended to impress his Indian subordinate.

Among joint venture partners, neither side can impose its corporate culture on the partner as the headquarters of a multinational corporation can impose its culture on its foreign (wholly owned) subsidiaries. Something of a joint corporate culture can be constructed by negotiation, however. Communication in intercultural business relationships is a business task to be managed.

THE TASK

Transcending these limits is a formidable but essential task if operations in foreign countries are to succeed. Cultural briefing can never teach you everything you need to know. Proper training, however, can help you to be cosmopolitan—that is, to know how to learn what you need to know about a foreign cultural environment.

How do you begin to recognize the fact that you have cultural blinders? Have you ever traveled to a very different culture and felt that the natives were behaving strangely or even childishly? If you live for extended periods in foreign cultures, as have the authors, you may discover that the natives express the same view about you. There is a good reason for this mutual view. When one is a child, one experiments with many ways of behaving and thinking. All but one way of behaving and thinking is socialized out of you while you are growing up. In your adult life, all the rejected ways are felt to be childish and inappropriate.

Put another way, much of what you were brought up to know in your culture is prejudice when applied to another culture. Almost every perception and behavior is guided by the human invention we call culture. Each culture shapes perception and behavior by paying selective attention to some details of reality and ignoring others, by permitting some actions and forbidding others. Each culture's inventions, however, are felt to be natural by persons of that culture. And all other cultures' inventions are felt to be alien and unnatural, though sometimes desirable.

Americans are especially prone to disregard other cultures. The vast size of the country and the common language spoken in the United States make it possible for Americans to avoid real exposure to foreign ways of behaving and thinking. The ideology of the melting pot hides the fact that American culture is mainly a closed culture. Until the 1980s, the United States was a closed economy in which foreign trade was a small percentage of the gross national product.

During the last decade, global economic connections have increased markedly. American executives have become aware that their economy is open to foreign competitors who are gaining substantial market shares in some industries. European executives are looking forward to 1992, when most trade and tariff barriers will end for members of the European Economic Community. American and Japanese executives have begun to protest against Fortress Europe, the potential trade barrier of the Integrated European Community. European executives in turn protest the use of the United States as a staging area for the sale of Japanese goods to Europe. In recent years the People's Republic of China has been trading openly with Hong Kong, Japan, and Western countries. Further, despite politically motivated trade barriers of the past, the PRC has been covertly trading with the Republic of Korea and even Taiwan.

Around the world, market barriers are breaking down. Anyone operating in any of these areas must respond to the new economic patterns. It is time to break down the cultural barriers as well.

DEFINITION OF CULTURE

What is culture? The following definition is intended to bridge the gap between academic and business perspectives:

Culture is a learned, shared, compelling, interrelated set of symbols whose meanings provide a set of orientations for members of a society. These orientations, taken together, provide solutions to problems that all societies must solve if they are to remain viable.

Although some elements of this definition will be unfamiliar to managers, other elements, such as the problem-solving mode and the analogy of a society to a viable business (an ongoing concern), should bring the definition into the world view of managers. Let us consider the unfamiliar elements.

- *Culture is learned.* No matter where one wishes to draw the line at how much of human behavior is instinctual, humans, compared with animals, have far more of their behavior programmed by cultural learning than by biology.

- *Culture is shared.* Coordinated action among humans is possible only when understandings of reality are shared and can be communicated to others. When an individual has a substantially separate understanding of reality—as does the heroine of *I Never Promised You a Rose Garden*,[1] for example—that person has the problem of psychosis.

- *Culture is compelling.* Human social action does not require that everyone share an identical motivation before they act together. Human social action does require a measure of commitment that people should want to do what they have to do. The appearance of common motivation suffices to facilitate common action. If social codes for behavior are known and shared but not compelling for most of the people most of the time, that society has a problem coordinating behavior.

- *Cultural symbols and meanings are interrelated.* The interrelation is not a mechanical interrelation, as in the parts of a machine, but is an interrelation of contrasts, of differences that make a difference for persons in the society. An English speaker will not perceive a difference when the two sounds /pat/ and /phat/ arc heard. If the latter, with a breathy /h/ sound, is heard, the hearer may perceive that the speaker has a cold, but not that the speaker means something different. For a Hindi speaker, on the other hand, the two sounds bear different meanings. Humans learn by discerning contrasts. A child cannot understand the meaning of hot without understanding the meaning of cold.

   This interrelation of symbols and their meanings has consequences: a change in one element will change related elements. Peasants of Bangladesh used to define affluence and poverty by relative sizes of landholding measured in eighths of an acre. After seeing reruns of the Ozzie and Harriet television series, which displayed the material possessions of a middle-income American family of the 1950s, they redefined the meaning of the terms affluence and poverty. Unintended consequences occur when an outside agent, such as a business firm, incites cultural changes in a society.

Functions of Culture

What does culture do? Here we abridge the comprehensive functions of culture to a list that will suffice for our purposes. Every human culture must deal with the following problems if the society is to continue to have a social life that appears ordered to its members:

- Acquisition of food, clothing, and shelter.
- Provision of protection from enemies and natural disasters.
- Regulation of sexuality.
- Child raising and instruction in socially approved and useful behavior.
- Division of labor among humans.
- Sharing and exchanging the product of human work.
- Providing social controls against deviant behavior.
- Providing incentives to motivate persons to want to do what they have to do.
- Distributing power and legitimizing the wielding of power to allow setting of priorities, making decisions, and coordinating actions that obtain social goals.
- Providing a sense of priorities (values) and an overall sense of worth (religion) to social life.

The Four Operations of Culture

We can summarize the functions of culture by saying that culture is a set of understandings shared among persons who have been similarly socialized. These learned understandings define our social reality in four ways.

Culture Classifies Phenomena into Discontinuous Units

How are things classified?

Nature is perceived with culturally learned distinctions: Children classify large bushes and small trees as similar things until they learn differently. Some companies never classify difficult situations as "dilemmas" or "crises" but always refer to "challenges," "issues," or "opportunities."

Cultural symbols draw distinctions that make a difference for persons in society: A sportscaster asked a young, brash umpire what baseball was all about. "Baseball is balls and strikes, and I call them as I see them," was the reply. Not satisfied, he asked an old, wise umpire the same question. "Baseball? There are just pitches. And they ain't balls and strikes until I call them balls and strikes!"

These distinctions of pitches, balls, and strikes may not make a difference for many non-American readers. A counterexample (that might confuse Americans) could be drawn for European football. The young referee says, "Football is just yellow cards, red cards, and penalty kicks, and I call them as I see them." And the old, wise referee says, "Football is just fouls. And they're not yellow or red cards until I call them yellow or red."

Culture Codes the Classified Units

What are proper codes for behavior?

People learn not only to classify items, but also how to behave towards them. Once an object or relationship is culturally identified, rules for proper conduct (codes for conduct) toward that unit can be defined. There is a procedure for disagreeing with a superior at IBM; doing so at Ford is tantamount to resigning from the company.

Coding is both ideal and practical. Americans know they can be ticketed for driving more than 55 miles per hour on most interstate highways; many know that a speed of about 63 miles per hour is generally safe from prosecution.

Culture Specifies Priorities Among Codes for Conduct

What are priorities among codes for conduct?

Priorities are necessary because different social situations call for different actions. If two people are in a conference, it is impolite for one to push the other violently. But if someone is in the path of a runaway truck, pushing that person aside is appropriate; the code to save a life has priority over the code of politeness.

Priorities among codes are called *values*. An engineer flew out of town at short notice to repair a major customer's equipment. Because the work took a week, she found it necessary to buy some clothes. When the accounting department rejected her claim for these expenses, the CEO publicly overruled the accountants, thus demonstrating that the firm's code for customer service was more important than its normal code for expenses.

Culture Legitimizes and Justifies All Its Classifications, Codes, and Priorities

How are all these cultural understandings legitimized?

Humans are frequently skeptical of anything known to be invented or legislated by other humans. They often require some more-than-human basis to justify both the cultural operations we have described and actions based on those operations. Religiosity, whether in the form of a formal religion or a political ideology, answers this need. Some companies, such as Amway, have a quasi-religious legitimation for "the way things work around here." Such companies attempt to enlist the commitment of their staff. Other companies rely on coercive techniques, rather than legitimation, to enforce compliance to expected behavior.

Frontstage and Backstage Culture

Now we can precisely state the task for managers who aspire not only to overcome culture shock, but also to move towards competence in dealing with a foreign culture: *Your job is to get beyond the frontstage culture and approach the backstage culture of the country with which you are dealing.*

The distinction between frontstage and backstage refers to two commonsense perceptions. First, a theater audience certainly knows more about what takes place in the theater than the general public who have not been admitted to the theater. Second, much goes on behind the scenes that is known to the director, actors, and stage crew but is not revealed to the paying audience. Your job abroad is not only to get into the theater, but also to try to get backstage.

Frontstage Culture

Frontstage culture includes the standard, normal, proper ways of doing things that insiders are willing to share with outsiders. A newcomer to the society can acquire frontstage cultural knowledge relatively easily. This does not mean that you can learn frontstage culture from your travel agent. It means that insiders do not define this kind of knowledge as classified information to be kept from outsiders.

A good example of frontstage culture is the country-at-a-glance style of description that appears in texts on doing business abroad. In a typical Japan-at-a-glance entry, we find the following:

Sensitivities: The Japanese are highly status-conscious. Always show respect, give face, and preserve harmony. Loudness of any kind is offensive. Never single an individual out of a group, either for criticism or praise. Avoid any hint of excessive pride.

Forms of Address: People are addressed by their surname and the suffix *san,* as in Jones-san. Never use first names.

Courtesies: Japanese usually bow to each other, but handshaking is common in business. If you bow to a peer, bow as low and long as the Japanese. If you're visiting a Japanese-style home, remove your shoes before stepping inside. All etiquette is aimed toward creating *wa,* good feeling and harmony. The Japanese are formal but warm.

Business Do's: Travel with hundreds of business cards and use them whenever you must give your name; give them to everyone present. Connections and introductions are essential. Always allow time for the Japanese to get to know and trust you. Be prepared to give gifts in a number of situations. Do participate in evening entertainment—a time to communicate freely with your Japanese associates over *sake.*

Business Don'ts: Don't rush. Avoid conflict or any embarrassment that would cause loss of face. Don't always assume that "yes" means agreement or understanding.

Negotiations: Japanese typically negotiate in teams made up of experts in relevant fields. Interpreters are often necessary. Negotiations begin with gentle probing of fundamental issues such as the motives of the parties and the potential for long-term, mutually beneficial relationships. Negotiations will continue over a period of time with several meetings, or information will flow by correspondence. Expect some bargaining, but do not greatly inflate your proposal. Throughout, it is important to maintain a posture of integrity, courtesy, and interest. When problems arise, involve an intermediary.[2]

Backstage Culture

Backstage culture refers to knowledge that insiders define as standard ways of doing things that they are not willing to share with outsiders. There are various reasons for keeping some information restricted.

- Insiders may regard the activity as illegal, illicit, or just shameful.

    One culture's illegal, illicit, or shameful activity is another culture's normal practice. American businesspeople usually avoid revealing any information about bribery, even when they are dealing with managers. For example, some Middle Eastern managers consider "commission business" a normal operating procedure.

- Insiders may define the activity as private knowledge that in some way gives competitive advantage to those who know it.

    Foreigners trying to start business in Japan are usually frustrated by a nongovernmental, nontariff barrier: the distribution system. The Japanese distribution system has multiple links in its chain and far more restrictions to entry than do Western systems. What foreigners do not realize is that distribution systems are backstage knowledge within particular industries—even to the Japanese. A Japanese executive in one industry is typically quite uninformed about the tricks of the trade in other industries.

While the information cited from the Japan-at-a-glance entry is pertinent and accurate, it does not suggest the depth of behind-the-scenes information that exists. Here is one example of backstage information about Japanese negotiations.

    In the Japanese negotiating team, the prime speaker is usually not the person with final decision on the negotiations. Members of the Japanese team look covertly toward one member of the team who communicates decisions nonverbally. In some Japanese companies, when the team thinks that the foreign negotiating team has learned this ploy, they take it a step further. One team member is designated as a *decoy* nonverbal communicator and the rest of the team appears to look to the decoy for guidance.

Summary

In this section, we have discussed the following points:

- Culture is a learned, compelling set of symbols that is shared among persons who have been similarly socialized.

- These symbols have meanings that enable members of a society to classify, code, prioritize, and justify social reality. These four operations underlie the organization of this book (see page 18).

- There is a social distribution of information according to which insiders are willing to share frontstage culture with outsiders but try to conceal backstage culture from outsiders.

- The managerial task is to gain not only frontstage cultural knowledge but also sufficient backstage cultural knowledge to do the job.

CULTURAL RISK: THE BASIS OF PROBLEMS OF INTERCULTURAL COMMUNICATION

Now we shall see how this definition of culture applies to the cultural environment of international business. Lack of intercultural communication skills is a problem for firms from many nations. After surveying large American multinational corporations, Korzenny found that even these corporations, otherwise sophisticated in organizing their business tasks, have not systematically organized this activity. Rather, personnel departments impart general information (economic, political, historical) about the country to which an executive is being sent. Further cultural training consists of suggestions for getting along in daily life.[3] Only a few companies have established systems to collect and use information to facilitate intercultural communications and update future training programs. Firms that are convinced of the efficacy of a production learning curve (the reduction of production costs as experience is gained) have yet to face the challenge of harnessing experience in a cultural learning curve.

Relationships between firms from different cultures present challenging problems. Problems of cultural miscommunication stem from the fact that persons in any business firm are triply socialized: into their national culture, into their business culture, and into their corporate culture. Definitions are in order.

National Culture

Primary socialization is the learning of symbols and their meanings. Socialization thus aims to provide sufficient shared understanding among persons in a society to allow adequately predictable, coordinated social activity. This cultural socialization is not homogeneous in any society; knowledge is socially distributed by gender, ethnicity, region, social class, and religion.

The impact of this cultural training does not dispel over time. IBM engages in extensive selection and training procedures to inculcate a shared set of understandings among its managers and other employees. Yet even this process does not deprogram the original socialization of its personnel. A study of IBM personnel in subsidiaries in 50 countries found extensive differences in work-related values.[4]

National Cultural Risk

Even firms with extensive international business experience sometimes blunder in intercultural communications. For example, Evitol shampoo unexpectedly sold poorly in Latin countries; the reason was that the sound of "evitol" was similar to words meaning "dandruff contraceptive." Similarly, the makers of Fresca soda found they were selling "lesbian soda," and Ford discovered that their model named Pinto evoked not the image of a dashing small horse but that of "a small male appendage."[5]

Cultural risk is far more complicated than these international word-play blunders. The focus case described earlier in this chapter illustrates how cultural misunderstanding almost wrecked an ongoing international joint venture worth millions of dollars.

Business Culture

Secondary socialization is the learning of additional cultural knowledge relevant to a person's participation in the wider socioeconomic world.[6] Examples of secondary socialization are the learning of business culture, legal culture, or medical culture. One could argue that professional schools spend more time imparting the professional culture than teaching technical skills or knowledge.

Business culture stems from national culture. Wider cultural codes for conduct are further specified in business contexts.

> The Netherlands has a tradition of responsiveness to social needs. This social responsiveness was translated into business policy when KLM Royal Dutch Airlines revised its travel-benefits policy for families of employees. The old rule was that the immediate family could travel for a very low fare. Several years ago, many KLM stewards protested the rule. They found it unfair that brand new heterosexual spouses received the benefit, while long-term homosexual partners did not. KLM responded that any couple who formally registered as living together—a normal legal practice in the Netherlands—could receive the privilege. It further stipulated that no employee could register a new partner for the travel privilege within a year of the previous one. The implication of KLM's policy is that privilege is a function of stable relationships rather than of marital status or sexual preference. Such policy would be unthinkable in the apparently liberal United States.[7]

Business cultures comprise the effective rules of the game, the boundaries between competitive and unethical behavior, the codes for conduct in business dealings. Business cultures vary. As an example of differences in business culture priorities, French financial managers are more concerned with solvency, while American financial managers are more concerned with return on investment.[8]

Readers may be more familiar with the notion of business culture than they realize. Many comparisons have been drawn between Japanese and American management. For an example of differences in business culture (classifications, codes, and priorities), Japanese managers classify managers into groups; an effective code for conduct is harmony and cooperation within the working group; there is priority on the accomplishment of tasks by groups. By contrast, Americans classify managers as individuals; an effective code for conduct is that individuals are competing for power and position and may not necessarily cooperate in working on related tasks; there is priority on the accomplishment of each individual's job. These pictures are, in our view, general and monolithic because corporate cultures among Japanese corporations differ just as much as they do among American corporations.

Business culture is constrained by the wider culture in two senses. First, the codes of allowable behavior do not contradict the codes of allowable behavior in the wider culture; rather they select from the wider culture. For example, Kakar discusses two forms of paternalistic leadership in Indian society: benevolent leadership and autocratic leadership. After the colonial experience, Indian business culture selected only the autocratic style of management.[9] Second, different societies have very different entry barriers to the acquisition of business culture. Superior Graduate Management Aptitude Test scores can overcome this entry barrier in the United States, whereas family connection provides access to specialized business experience in many developing countries.

Business Cultural Risk

Business cultures collide. Kenneth David heard an American businessman bemoaning the incidence of corruption in India. His joint venture partner patiently explained to him the continuity of this form of gift giving with traditional exchanges with Brahmin priests. When the American remained unimpressed, the Indian added, "Here, we give gifts after a law has been passed and you call it corruption. In your country, you give gifts before a law has been passed and you call it lobbying!"

Another example of differences in business culture is the relative success of the management-by-objectives (MBO) technique in the moderately egalitarian United States, where the technique was invented. MBO fails to work in highly ranked French organizations, where bosses and subordinates are very uncomfortable negotiating the subordinates' future goals. It also does not work well in more egalitarian societies such as Sweden and Holland where such intervention is felt to be too autocratic.[10]

Corporate Culture

Just as business culture stays within the limits of the wider culture, corporate cultures are constrained by business culture. At each step there is a progressive specification of codes for allowable behavior. In societies where family firms predominate, corporate culture is acquired concurrently with business culture. In societies with formal business training, it may follow.

How shall we define corporate culture? The quickest definition is "the way things work around here"! To elaborate, management scholars have studied various elements and processes of corporate culture that can be classified under the four operations of culture we have already discussed:

   1. Cultural classifications: studies of special languages or jargons in companies.[11]

2. Pragmatic cultural codes for conduct imparted by various media of socialization: the nonrandom recruitment process in which candidates self-select companies as well as being selected by them;[12] the interpretation of corporate stories of heroes, successes, and failures;[13] and role modeling of appropriate behavior—that is, imitating behavior of successful managers with whom the manager interacts.[14]

3. Ideal codes for conduct and value priorities imparted in corporate rituals such as board meetings or occasions where superior performance is recognized and in qualitatively stated corporate objectives (e.g., "IBM means service!") as opposed to quantitatively stated objectives (e.g., "Increase market share by 4 percent this year!").[15]

Is the notion of corporate culture a viable concept? Schneider holds that the potential for shared corporate cultures stems from the nonrandomness of corporate recruitment. Astute job candidates map the territory before they seek employment with a particular company. Schneider focuses on the processes of attraction, training, and attrition in corporate socialization.[16] IBM and Tandem carefully screen job candidates in order to attract to the corporation persons who will live comfortably with the corporate codes for conduct and will appreciate the kinds of rewards given for outstanding performance. Ford tends to hire more broadly and let the competitive work ethic weed out culturally incompatible managers. Whether by attraction and training in the former cases, or by attrition in the latter case, the remaining members of the corporation are likely to share the corporate culture.

Corporate culture is not, however, homogeneous. Although a firm may have a dominant culture, many subcultures may coexist and interact.[17]

- Various subcultures within one organization may be divided along occupational, functional, product, or geographical lines.[18] Occupational subcultures have been widely noted in the literature. Lawrence and Lorsch discuss differences in time, goal, and interpersonal value orientations among persons in the sales, production, and research and development departments within a corporation. Pettigrew has written of the specialized vocabularies of occupational subcultures in corporations.[19] Deal and Kennedy describe occupational subcultures and the need for the "symbolic manager" to coordinate their disparate orientations.[20] Jennings counsels managers who are planning their route to the executive suite not to regret but to accept lateral transfers to business functions for which they were not originally trained. In this way they will acquire the orientations of the various functional departments and be more able to lead them.[21]

- There exist differences in culture from the top to the bottom of an organization. More specifically, three types of subcultures may be classified according to the content and commitment of the subculture in relation to the organization's dominant culture: (1) an *enhancing subculture* that displays a fierce adherence to the core values of the dominant culture; (2) an *orthogonal culture* that accepts the dominant culture's values as well as additional sets of values that do not conflict with the core values; (3) and a *counterculture* that challenges the core values of the dominant culture.[22]

Understanding the culture of any company involves identifying the various subcultures and understanding how they interplay to influence organizational behavior and relationships with other organizations.

Corporate Cultural Risk

Corporate cultures differ widely. A well-publicized risk of mergers and acquisitions is the potential cultural clash between companies that appear to match well in financial, technological, and other business criteria. Effective executives may be out of place in the new situation. After India expelled IBM, the Tata-Burroughs Company, a former competitor, hired many of the talented Indians who had been IBM executives. Most of them eventually left these jobs. The reason was that Burroughs corporate culture demands a more entrepreneurial executive, whereas IBM executives are more skilled at completing projects with conferences and extensive use of support systems within the company. Performance can be evaluated only in the context of corporate culture: "the way things work around here."

Summary

Our position differs from that of business scholars who conceptualize culture as external to the organization and organizational climate as interior to the organization.[23] In contrast with such arbitrary distinction of exterior and interior culture, Weick proposes that there are more continuities than differences between the wider culture and culture in the corporation.[24] Our position stresses continuity: Every person in a business organization is triply socialized in national, business, and corporate cultures.

This point is not just academic. Expatriate managers and partners in international joint ventures are managing organizations where different cultures meet. Their personnel do not leave their previously learned cultures and business cultures at the door. Social relationships with suppliers, customers or clients, and government officials are not exterior to the operations of the enterprise. Intercultural communication is a business task to be managed.

INTERNATIONAL BUSINESS AND INTERCULTURAL MANAGEMENT

Standard texts on international business are full of suggestions on how firms should adapt to meet the additional complexities and uncertainties of operating in the international environment. Suggestions are made for managing the business tasks that were previously known from domestic operations (production, finance, marketing, and so on).

But before the recent spate of writings on corporate culture, the management of intercultural understanding had never been defined as a business task in domestic operations. Standard international business texts do not emphasize the task of managing cultural risk.

Insufficient attention to intercultural communication has its consequences.

> . . .[D]espite market research and market opportunities, there is an abundance of international business blunders.[25]
>
> The post mortems performed on past marketing mistakes strongly suggest that most mistakes occur in the process of carrying out marketing plans rather than in basic thinking. In other words, it is the execution of marketing plans in terms of interpersonal communication, negotiations and mass communication where most mistakes occur. Therefore, the message is clear: the cross-cultural setting creates situations in which the marketer must decide whether he should extend or adjust his way of doing business in a foreign market.[26]

In companies with extensive international operations, there are no departments for intercultural management. Certain tasks are segregated in various functional departments. The personnel department is concerned with selection and training of managers for foreign assignments. The international marketing department gathers foreign marketing intelligence. Multinational firms are far more proficient at managing the more technical and quantifiable tasks such as accounting, finance, manufacturing, and logistics than they are at managing more culturally sensitive tasks such as personnel management and marketing. All business functions, but especially these latter areas, can be aided by intercultural management.

Noting that intercultural management is one small corner of the management literature,[27] Adler defines the field of intercultural management as

> . . .the study of the behavior of people in organizations located in different cultures and nations around the world. It focuses on the description and explanation of organizational behavior across countries and cultures, and perhaps most importantly, the interaction of peoples from different countries working within the same organization or the same work environment.[28]

Our definition of the scope of intercultural management is broader than Adler's. Problems of cultural miscommunication occur whenever persons are socialized differently—in culturally defined classifications, codes, priorities (values), and justifications of reality. In our view such miscommunication may well occur within a country, within a culture. For example, the acquisition of Conoco by DuPont was heralded as a good move because the companies were complementary in technical skills; cultural incompatibility between the two companies, however, has impaired the venture. Intercultural management should be concerned with domestic as well as international business relationships that are subject to risk of cultural miscommunication and should inquire into processes of managing such cultural risk.[29]

What are the policy implications for firms with extensive intercultural business relationships? Firms face the question of appropriate cultural policy just as they face the problem of appropriate technology and appropriate product policy in other contexts. A firm's corporate culture manages business relationships that are constrained by its country's societal and task environments. A corporate culture that is appropriate within the broader cultural frameworks of its own society (its business culture and national culture) will be alien if imposed in a foreign setting. In many situations, firms cannot impose their corporate culture on foreign business collaborators. Should they totally adapt? hold their own? seek to work out a compromise corporate culture with foreign business collaborators? build a portfolio of adaptive techniques from experience in the various societies in which they operate? There is no single answer. Cultural policy cannot be stated monolithically to apply to all business situations.[30] In the course of this book, we shall be concerned with the varying need for intercultural management. Different situations call for different cultural policies.

For general guidelines, we want to contrast prevailing practice with some steps toward effective multicultural management.

Prevailing practice can be labeled *apparent multicultural management*. Various large companies maintain centralized training centers for managers and executives from various countries. The advantages of this regime are that core company values can be transmitted along with technical expertise and that individuals can develop a useful network of foreign colleagues for future intercultural projects. On the other side, it is an illusion to think that a worldwide corporate culture exists. Studies by Hofstede and Laurent show that national cultural values persist despite intensive centralized training. Headquarters may be under the illusion that it can easily understand all the cultures in which it does business and fail to account for local cultural conditions that affect operations abroad.

By contrast, here are several steps that have proven effective in creating a *geocentric intercultural management regime:*

- Centralized training is augmented by periodic training courses located in foreign sites.

- The entire family of the executive is prepared for a foreign assignment.

- Executives are systematically debriefed (before reassignment) to capture details of the business culture where they were stationed.

- Participants in intercultural projects are also debriefed.

- A corporate memory is established to record the results of expatriate and intercultural project debriefings.

The overall advantage of this set of practices is analogous to the practice of multinational sourcing of materials or components at least cost. These practices yield the capability to acquire effective management practices from various sources as opposed to policies derived almost exclusively from the business culture of the country where corporate headquarters is located.

Business people tend to regard culture as one of the soft facts of life that have low priority in decision making. It is hoped that this introductory chapter has begun to revise that attitude.

THE FOUR OPERATIONS OF CULTURE AND THE ORGANIZATION OF THIS TEXT

The four operations of culture discussed in this chapter—classification, codification, prioritization, and justification—underlie the organization of this book. Seven major components of the cultural environment of international business are considered in this text and arranged in line with this framework. Chapter 2 deals with language, the vehicle through which the four operations are communicated. As language is the minimal requirement for the cultural ordering of reality, it is included in Part I, The Basics of Culture.

Part II, Culture and the Shaping of Human Motivation, groups three related topics. Chapter 3 deals with education, the process by which the four operations are learned. Chapter 4 deals with religion, the cultural system that justifies the codes for conduct each culture has invented. Religion emotionally motivates these codes for individuals in society. Chapter 5 deals with values, the cultural operation of priorities among codes for conduct.

Part III, The Social Organization of Human Behavior, brings together a series of topics, each concerned with one aspect of either environmental or social relationships. Each topic involves the classifying and coding of human behavior. Chapter 6 deals with technology, the cultural system that encodes relationships between humans and their natural environment. Chapter 7 deals with five aspects of human social relationships: kinship, group behavior, systems of rank, unions, and social change. Chapter 8 completes the survey of human relationships with a look at national and international politics.

The book is designed to ease the task of transcending cultural barriers and to assist the reader in gaining a better understanding of the cultural environment of international business. This introductory chapter has described culture and begun the discussion of the business task we call intercultural management. Each of the subsequent chapters has a similar format for presentation. Each chapter

- identifies a component of the cultural environment;
- notes, in broad strokes, international differences in that component; and
- discusses the component's implications for international business management.

QUESTIONS

1. Identify the elements in the environment of a firm. How do these influence the firm's operations?

2. In our behavior, we do not do "what comes naturally," rather we do "what comes culturally." Discuss.

3. Distinguish between culture, business culture, and corporate culture. How are these learned in industrial countries? in developing countries?

4. Why are U.S. firms often less skilled in cross-cultural dealings than are European firms?

5. Why might firms in different industries have different business subcultures?

6. Find and discuss examples of firms in the same industry or service area that have different corporate cultures. Find examples of acquisitions or mergers that were impaired by cultural incompatibility.

7. How can a firm develop an appropriate cultural policy?

ENDNOTES

1. Hannah Green's 1964 book recounts the psychiatric treatment of an adolescent girl who built a personal pantheon of gods, some pleasant and others terrifying, that represented real figures in her life.
2. Lennie Copeland and Lewis Griggs, *Going International* (New York: Random House, 1985), p. 240.
3. Betty Ann Korzenny, "Cross-Cultural Issues in the Process of Sending U.S. Employees of Multinational Corporations for Overseas Service." (Paper presented at the annual meetings of the Speech Communications Association, San Antonio, TX, 1979.)
4. Geert Hofstede, *Culture's Consequences: International Differences in Work-Related Values* (London: Sage, 1980).
5. David A. Ricks, *Big Business Blunders: Mistakes in Multinational Marketing* (Homewood, IL: Dow Jones-Irwin, 1983).
6. Lucien W. Pye, *Politics, Personality, and Nation Building: Burma's Search for Identity* (New Haven: Yale University Press, 1962), pp. 52–53.
7. Kenneth David, "Organizational Process for Intercultural Management." (Paper presented at the Strategic Management Association meetings, San Francisco, CA (October 1989.)
8. David K. Eiteman and Arthur I. Stonehill, *Multinational Business Finance*, 3d ed. (Reading, MA: Addison-Wesley, 1982), p. 6.
9. Sudhir Kakar, "Authority Patterns and Subordinate Behavior in Indian Organizations," *Administrative Science Quarterly* 16 (1971): 298–307; "The Theme of Authority in Social Relations in India," *Journal of Social Psychology* 84, no. I (June 1971): 93–110.
10. Geert Hofstede, "Do American Theories Apply Abroad," *Organizational Dynamics* 10, no. 1 (Summer 1981): 63–80.
11. Andrew M. Pettigrew, "Strategic Aspects of Management of Specialist Activity," *Personnel Review* 4 (1975): 5–13; Murray Edelman, *Political Language* (New York: Academic Press, 1977); Louis Pondy, "Leadership Is a Language Game," in M. McCall and M. Lombardo, eds., *Leadership: Where Else Can We Go?* (Durham, NC: Duke University Press, 1978); Paul Hirsch and J. Andrews, "Ambushes, Shootouts, and Knights of the Round Table: The Language of Corporate Takeovers," in L. Pondy, P. Frost, G. Morgan, and T. Dandridge, eds., *Organizational Symbolism* (Greenwich, CT: JAI Press, 1983); R. Evered, "The Language of Organizations: The Case of the Navy," in Pondy, et al., op. cit.
12. Benjamin Schneider, "Organizational Climates: An Essay," *Personnel Psychology* 28, no. 4 (Winter 1975): 447–479.
13. Burton Clark, *The Distinctive College: Antioch, Reed, and Swarthmore* (Chicago: Aldine, 1970); Alan Wilkins, "Organizational Stories as an Expression of Management Philosophy: Implications for Social Control in Organizations" (Doctoral diss., Stanford University, 1978); Alan Wilkins and Joanne Martin, "Organizational Legends" (Research Paper no. 521, Graduate School of Business, Stanford University, 1979); Joanne Martin, "Stories and Scripts in Organizational Settings," in A. Hasdorf and A. Isen, *Cognitive Social Psychology* (New York: Elsevier, 1982); Terrence E. Deal

and Allan A. Kennedy, *Corporate Cultures* (Reading, MA: Addison-Wesley, 1982); Thomas Peters and Robert H. Waterman, Jr., *In Search of Excellence* (New York: Harper & Row, 1982).

14. Joanne Martin and Caren Siehl, "Organizational Culture and Counter-Culture: General Motors and Delorean" (Research Paper no. 633, Graduate School of Business, Stanford University, 1981).

15. Deal and Kennedy, op. cit.; Peters and Waterman, op. cit.; Michael Moch and Anne S. Huff, "Chewing Ass Out: The Enactment of Power Relationships Through Language and Ritual" (Presentation to the Academy of Management meetings, Detroit, 1981); Robert P. Gephart, "Status Degradation and Organizational Succession: An Ethnomethodological Approach," *Administrative Science Quarterly* 23, no. 4 (November 1978): 553–581; H. Trice and J. Beyer, "Studying Organizational Cultures Through Rites and Ceremonials," *Academy of Management Review* 9 (1984): 653–659.

16. Benjamin Schneider, "Organizational Climates: An Essay," *Personnel Psychology* 28, no. 4 (Winter 1975): 447–479.

17. Kathleen L. Gregory, "Native-View Paradigms: Multiple Cultures and Culture Conflicts in Organizations," *Administrative Science Quarterly* 28 (1983): 359–376; Caren Siehl, Cultural Sleight-of-Hand: The Illusion of Consistency (Doctoral diss., Stanford University, 1984); Meryl R. Louis, "Sourcing Workplace Cultures: Why, When, and How," in Ralph H. Kilman et al., eds., *Gaining Control of the Corporate Culture* (London: Jossey-Bass, 1986); A. Nahavandi and A. Malekzadeh, "Acculturation in Mergers and Acquisitions," *Academy of Management Review* 13, no.4 (1988): 79–90.

18. Vijay Sathe, *Culture and Related Corporate Realities* (Homewood, IL: Irwin, 1985).

29. Andrew M. Pettigrew, "Strategic Aspects of Management of Specialist Activity," *Personnel Review* 4 (1975): 5–13.

20. Deal and Kennedy, op. cit.

21. Eugene E. Jennings, *Routes to the Executive Suite* (New York: McGraw-Hill, 1971), pp. 86–87.

22. Tim R. V. Davis, "Managing Cultures at the Bottom," in Kilman et al., op. cit.; Joanne Martin and Caren Siehl, "Organizational Culture and Counterculture: An Uneasy Symbiosis" *Organizational Dynamics* (Autumn 1983): 52–64; Sathe, op. cit.

23. Anant Negandhi, "Cross-Cultural Management Studies: Too Many Conclusions, Not Enough Conceptualization," *Management International Review* 14, no. 6 (1974/76); 59–65; Schneider, op. cit.; Jose De la Torre and Brian Toyne, "Cross-National Managerial Interaction: A Conceptual Model," *Academy of Management Review* 3, no. 3 (July 1978): 462–475.

24. Karl Weick, *The Social Psychology of Organizing,* 2d ed. (Reading, MA: Addison-Wesley, 1979).

25. D. Ricks, M. Fu, and J. Arpan, *International Business Blunders* (Cincinnati: Grid, Inc., 1974).

16. Jagdish N. Sheth, "Cross-Cultural Influences on Buyer-Seller Interaction/Negotiation Process," *Asian Pacific Journal of Management* 1, no. 1 (September 1983): 46–55.

27. A survey of 11,219 articles in 24 major U.S. management journals shows that cross-cultural management studies (defined as organizational behavior articles that are international and that include culture as a variable) constituted only 3.6 percent of all articles published in these journals: 1.9 percent were unicultural studies (study of management in any single country other than the United States); 1.4 percent were comparative (comparison of organizations in two or more countries); and only .9 percent were intercultural (focus on interaction between organizational members from two or more countries or cultures). See Nancy Adler, "Cross-Cultural Management Research: The Ostrich and the Trend," *Academy of Management Review* 8, no. 2 (April 1983).

28. Nancy Adler, "Preface," *International Studies of Management and Organization* 13, no. 4 (Winter 1982/83): 3–6.

29. Kenneth David, "Managing Cultural Problems," in Thomas L. Brewer, Kenneth David, and Linda Lim, *Investing in Developing Nations: A Guide for Executives* (New York: Praeger, and Washington, DC: Overseas Private Investment Corporation, 1986), pp. 51–82.

30. Ibid.

CHAPTER TWO
Language

A language is, in a sense, a philosophy.

Clyde Kluckhohn

Britain and America are two nations separated by a common language.

George Bernard Shaw

WHY BE CONCERNED WITH LANGUAGE?

International executives tell many horror stories about lost or reduced sales following the translation of brand names or messages into other languages. As perceived by the local population, these words had unintended meanings that ranged from the absurd to the obscene. Figure 2-1 contains some examples.

FIGURE 2-1

INTERNATIONAL BUSINESS WORD-PLAY MISTAKES[1]

- A restaurant in the remote Gaspé peninsula of Quebec province, where archaic French is spoken, translated its "Creme Glacé Parfait" dessert as "Ice Cream (Perfect)." But when Saatchi & Saatchi prepared to launch a new shampoo named "Pert" in Canada, they discovered they would be selling "Lost" shampoo. They adopted the brand name "Pret," which means "Ready."
- Tomato paste becomes tomato *glue* when translated into Arabic.
- Herculan carpeting becomes "the carpeting with the big derriere" when translated into Spanish.
- In the 1920s, Coca-Cola chose a set of Chinese characters that *sounded* like Coke. Those characters also meant "bite the wax tadpole." The current characters mean "happiness in the mouth." Coca-Cola's worldwide brand message, "Coke Adds Life," was received as "Coke brings you back from the dead."
- Ford had difficulties with Spanish perceptions of three models: Its Fiera truck was perceived as an "ugly old woman," its Caliente passenger car was translated as "streetwalker" in Mexican slang, and its sporty little Pinto was interpreted as "a small male appendage."

A loss in sales, of course, is a trivial problem compared with a complete disruption of civil order and business operations in a country. As seen in the following

We acknowledge the aid of Dr. Carol Scotton, Professor of Sociolinguistics, Michigan State University, for suggestions made for this chapter.

focus cases, such conflicts have been crystallized in the idiom of lang uage in developing nations; similar difficulties exist to a lesser extent in developed nations.

FOCUS CASES:
Language Conflicts

SRI LANKA

Linguistic identifications are often a distinctive feature that separates ethnic groups. Geertz studied the primordial sentiments that became politically mobilized in new nations after their independence. Ethnicity, race, history, territory, religion, and language are primordial identifications in the sense that people feel that they are born to them. All these identifications have been used as rallying cries to mobilize conflicts between groups.[2]

What may surprise Westerners is the fact that conflicts they would describe as ethnic conflicts are represented by the people as language conflicts. In 1956, protesting to their previous colonial rulers against continued economic dependency, the Sinhalese-speaking people of Sri Lanka agitated to remove English as their country's official language. Later, they mobilized against the economic power of the smaller but prosperous Tamil-speaking sector of the population.

Because the Sinhalese speakers are predominantly Buddhist, of the Aryan race, and residents of the southern region in Sri Lanka, while the Tamil speakers are predominantly Hindu, of the Dravidian race, and residents of the northern and eastern regions of the country, any of these primordial sentiments could have been mobilized for political action. The conflict was cast in the idiom of language. "Language" riots occurred when the Sinhalese tried to impose Sinhalese as the national language. The entire conflict is referred to in both Sinhalese and Tamil newspapers as a "language" conflict.

BELGIUM

Belgium is a small country that is not known for civil violence between ethnic groups. The pervasive division between the French-speaking Walloons and the Flemish speakers is profound.

French influence is strong in the south of Belgium. Versailles-like architecture and gardens of the small castle of Annevoie are no coincidence: It was built by aristocrats fleeing the French revolution. Dutch influence is strong in the north; all of Belgium was once a section of Holland.

Currently, as a Belgian native puts it, there is almost entire cultural autonomy between the two sections. Rural social structure is very close-knit—you know everything about your neighbors—but local knowledge stops abruptly at the language line. Political separatism is not far off. Local, district, and regional administrative divisions are either Walloon or Flemish. A mayor was recently unseated for trying to impose the use of French in a Flemish-speaking city. Major political parties are affiliated with major labor unions. But each party and each union is subdivided into Walloon and Flemish units.

WHAT IS LANGUAGE?

Language is the feature of human beings that most sets them off from other forms of life. Although many animals communicate (the nectar dance of a bee, the threatening growl of a dog, the warning cry of a deer), these communications are limited to happenings in the present and to positive statements. There is no way that a dog can tell you that he is not friendly now, but that he will be friendly next week. Human language, by contrast, communicates information about past, present, and future events. Without the information storage and communication functions of language, complex technology and complex forms of human organization would not be possible.

Language and the Definition of Social Life

Language is more than an abstract conveyor of information.[3] For persons in a culture, language defines social life as they know it. Human language is the primary medium of cultural socialization, the means by which cultural understandings are communicated from one generation to the next. Language is the repository of the four cultural operations—classifying, coding, prioritizing, and justifying reality— that render organized social life possible. It is a guide for classifying reality into perceptual units that make a difference for people in the culture. Inuits (Eskimos), for example, classify snow into many more units than do Americans. These distinctions are relevant information for them though not for us. Language is a guide for coding behavior in the sense of interpreting human behavior and communicating shared expectations about it. It expresses social priorities and can be very emotionally charged. Witness the feminist protest against the use of the pronoun *he* to signify both *he* and *she*. In other words, every language is a special way of looking at the world and interpreting experience.

> What a Russian says to an American doesn't really get across just from shuffling words—much is twisted or blunted or lost unless the American knows something about Russian life, a good deal more than the sheer linguistic skill needed for a formally correct translation. The American must indeed have gained some entrance to that foreign world of values and significances which are pointed up by the emphases of the Russian vocabulary, crystallized in the forms of Russian grammar, implicit in the little distinctions of meaning in the Russian language.[4]

Put more generally, a language is not a universal means of communication. Rather, it is a means of communication within a particular culture. Whorf even suggests that each language signifies and perpetuates a particular world view—that is, a general frame of reference that molds the thought of its users: "The structure of the language one habitually uses influences the manner in which one can understand his environment. The picture of the universe shifts from tongue to tongue."[5]

The vocabulary of each language reflects the primary emphases and technology of the culture. The Arabic language contains more than 6,000 different words for camel, its parts, and its equipment.[6] The English language is more limited than the Inuit languages in describing snow and more limited than the Arabic language in describing camels, yet English is relatively rich in vocabulary dealing with automotive transport, industry, and commerce. Figure 2-2 illustrates differences in an elementary form of technology, the designation of colors in a spectrum. The diagram is a rough indication of how colors of the spectrum are divided by speakers of English, Shona (a language of Zimbabwe), and Bassa (a language of Liberia).[7]

FIGURE 2-2

COLOR SPECTRA: ENGLISH, SHONA, AND BASSA LANGUAGES

English

Purple	Blue	Green	Yellow	Orange	Red

Shona

Cips^{W}uka	Citema	Cicena	Cip^{W}uka

Bassa

Hui	Ziza

INTERNATIONAL DIFFERENCES IN LANGUAGE

There are approximately 3,000 different languages in the world. Estimates that recognize differences in dialects range as high as 10,000. Because each language and even each dialect reflects cultural differences, the latter figure may be taken as a rough estimate of the number of different cultures in the world. Since the number of nations is fewer than 200, some nations include many different cultures and dialects within their political boundaries. India, with an estimated 3,000 dialects, is the most extreme example.

The National Language

It is not always true that nations have different national languages. First, 23 nations have two or more official national languages. Switzerland and Singapore have four official languages. Second, there are groups of countries that employ the same official language. Due to the conquests of Islam in the seventh to ninth centuries, about a dozen countries share Arabic as a national language. As a result of imperial and colonial conquests from the fifteenth through the nineteenth centuries, English, French, and Spanish are each the national language in at least 20 countries. Russia's dominance of Eastern European countries has led to a growing use of the Russian language. The extension of a language over several national territories indicates some degree of cultural carry-over, not only in language, but also in legal and educational systems and other dimensions of culture.

A word of caution is in order. Even though nations have a common official language in the sense of sharing a written language and speaking a language that is mutually understood, these nations do not have the same culture.

> Nothing more clearly distinguishes one culture from another than its language. We sometimes confuse writing systems with the spoken language of the people, otherwise we could say that the infallible sign of a separate culture is a separate language and the inevitable result of a separate language is a separate culture. For example, England, the United States, and Ireland all use English today as a literary written language, but they speak British, American and the "brogue" (when not Gaelic). They are, in fact, three separate, though related cultures. It is the spoken, not the written language that is basic.[8]

Spoken languages differ in pronunciation, vocabulary, and usage. While an American would say that he put some gas in his truck, drove to his girlfriend's apartment, took the elevator to her floor, and then rang the doorbell, an Englishman would say that he put some petrol in his lorry, drove to his girlfriend's flat, took the lift to her floor, and then knocked her up. Americans are surprised when a ticket taker in a British bus scowls at them if they do not say "thank you" on receiving their change. This is what Shaw meant when he said that Britain and America are two nations separated by a common language.[9]

There is a further difference among countries with the same official national language. In many countries that were formerly colonies, the majority of the population does not speak the official language. This is the case in India and the former British and French colonies in Africa.

Language Diversity Within Nations

Nations also differ in the number of languages used within their boundaries. While there are only about 100 official languages for all the world's nations, at least 3,000 languages are spoken in the world. Defining a native speaker as a person who has learned the language in childhood, well under half the nations are linguistically homogeneous in the sense that 85 percent or more of the population speaks the same native tongue.[10]

The degree of linguistic heterogeneity varies greatly among countries. In nations such as Japan, Sweden, and Saudi Arabia, nearly all the citizens speak the native tongue. Some might place the United States in this category, but data from the 1970 census indicated that of a population of just over 200 million people, 33 million had a mother tongue other than English: Spanish, 7.8 million; German, 6 million; Italian, 4 million; Polish and French, 2.5 million each; Yiddish, 2 million; Russian, 1.5 million; and so on.[11]

Scotton has clarified the various forms of multilingualism. Every multilingual community, by definition, is marked by unevenness in verbal repertoire. This takes different forms.

> First, not everyone knows the same language varieties and not everyone knows them to the same degree. The family a person is born into, where he lives, religion, social contacts—these and other factors all determine which of the language varieties present in a multilingual community a particular person may know. For example, a Canadian with English-speaking parents who grows up in Quebec is much more likely to know French than his English-speaking counterpart in Edmonton or even Toronto.
>
> Second, language varieties are unevenly used in any multilingual community even if they are widely known. For example, in the Philippines, even those who know English probably use Tagolog in a wide variety of situations.
>
> Third, some varieties are used mainly in certain situations or by certain social groups. For example, a Spanish-speaking saleswoman in a New York City department store expects to use English as her main work language even though she will use Spanish almost exclusively at home.[12]

Colonialism and Linguistic Diversity

Two generalizations have been made concerning linguistically diverse nations. First, linguistic diversity usually indicates cultural and political fragmentation within a nation. Second, over 80 percent of the linguistically heterogeneous nations are underdeveloped nations. What shall we make of these generalizations?

Concerning underdevelopment, we shall discuss in Chapter 8 the asymmetrical trade relations between colonial powers and colonized areas: the development of underdevelopment during the colonial period. A parallel process is the development of linguistic diversity during the colonial period. Put in an historical frame, European powers drew boundaries around regions that included diverse cultures and languages at the time of colonization. The colonial process created linguistically heterogeneous regions that later became nations. And after independence, these nations were called upon to fabricate a national integration and achieve economic progress. Certainly economic progress and political integration are not aided by linguistic diversity.

Language Hierarchy

In highly diverse situations, *lingua francas* have developed to reduce confusion, misunderstandings, and hostilities. A lingua franca may be a minimal language, as is the case of the sign language developed by native Americans. Various versions of pidgin English exist in different parts of the world.

In cases of linguistic diversity, there arises a pecking order, or hierarchy, of languages with one of the languages serving as a common language. The language situation in Zaire (formerly Congo) illustrates this point.

Zaire has over 100 language groups. Each group's language not only distinguishes it, but also separates it from the others. When economic or other exchanges occurred, a common language became necessary. The language of a dominant group was often used. Three indigenous lingua francas developed. Further, in the eastern part of the country, Swahili—the language of Zanzibar— became a fourth lingua franca when it was brought in by Arab slave traders. Thus Zaire has four lingua francas, each one linking a portion of the tribal groups.

In most linguistically diverse nations of Africa and Asia, there is a second stage in the language hierarchy. Most of these nations were formerly colonial territories of a European power.

Zaire was a Belgian colony for about 60 years. The Belgians found it easier to deal through four lingua francas than through over 100 languages. These lingua francas became the languages of education and of the lower levels of government. Each covered part of the colonial territory. One of them, Lingala, became the language of the army, unifying recruits who grew up with many different native languages. In this case the colonial power reinforced the role of the previous lingua francas.

The third stage of the linguistic hierarchy was the home country language of the colonial power.

In Zaire, French became the official national language, the language of the upper levels of government. Initially, few natives spoke this language. Eventually, many learned it, as it became the important and prestigious language—the language of higher education, economic advancement, and government employment.

A similar hierarchy prevails in most former French and British colonies.

For example, there are three regional lingua francas in Nigeria: Hausa in northern Nigeria, Yoruba in southwestern Nigeria, and Ibo in Biafra (southeastern Nigeria). Although English is the official language, it is by no means widely known. English is acquired almost exclusively in school and its use is a status symbol.[13]

The international manager should learn not only which major languages are spoken in the country and the percentage of the population speaking each language, but also more specific information on the purposes of each language: which language is spoken by whom on what occasions. An international manager must exercise care in these situations.

In Tanzania, Swahili is the official language. It is better to communicate with managers and workers in Swahili and reserve English for communications with government officials. In Kenya, by contrast, English is the official language, while Swahili is the informal language. English should be used both with government officials and with managers. The latter will feel offended if addressed in Swahili. Kikuyu is the language of the dominant ethnic group. As such, it is not a neutral lingua franca for interethnic communications.[14]

POLICY IMPLICATIONS FOR COUNTRIES: LANGUAGE AND THE POLITICAL ECONOMY

The linguistic situation we have been describing has significant implications for the political economy of individual nations. The term *nation* denotes political sovereignty—the right to rule. The term *country* denotes a morally and culturally unified community. Language is one of the strongest forces to unify or separate communities. And we have already noted that a majority of nations have a diversity of languages. See Figure 2-3 for lists of countries falling into the categories of linguistically homogeneous and heterogeneous nation-states.

Linguistically Homogeneous States

There are three areas of potential language problems for linguistically homogeneous nations: facility of the language for international communication; capacity of the language for developing the economy; and, related to the first two points, the choice of language for training and study.

A Language for International Communication

There is a range of national solutions to the first potential problem, international communication. For English- and French-speaking nations there is no problem, as these are the leading international languages both of diplomacy and of commerce. To a lesser degree, Spanish also serves as a major international language.

The problem is greatest for the many small countries whose language has little or no use in international relations. Examples are the Netherlands, Sweden, Greece, and Korea. The Arab states could be included, as Arabic is internationally useful only in dealing with other Arab states. Among such nations, the problem is somewhat reduced if the nation has a highly desired resource (as for OPEC nations) or is a highly desirable market (as for mainland China), for then prospective partners or suppliers will make some attempt to learn the language. The problem can be significant even for larger and more economically powerful states such as Japan. In these nations there is pressure to learn foreign languages in order to facilitate participation in the world economy.

A Language for Development

The second potential problem, the capability of the language to aid development of the economy, applies with greatest force to the less-developed countries. Although

FIGURE 2-3

LINGUISTICALLY HOMOGENEOUS AND HETEROGENEOUS NATIONS

Linguistically Homogeneous Nations

Albania	El Salvador	Jordan	Portugal
Argentina	France	Korea, North	Rwanda
Australia	Germany, East	Korea, Republic of	Saudi Arabia
Austria	German,	Lebanon	Somalia
Brazil	Republic of	Libya	Sweden
Burundi	Greece	Malagasy Republic	Tunisia
Chile	Haiti	Mexico	Turkey
Colombia	Honduras	Mongolia	United Kingdom
Costa Rica	Hungary	Netherlands	Uruguay
Cuba	Iceland	New Zealand	Venezuela
Denmark	Ireland	Nicaragua	Yemen
Dominican	Italy	Norway	
Republic	Jamaica	Paraguay	
Egypt	Japan	Poland	

Linguistically Heterogeneous Nations

Afghanistan	Ecuador	Mali	Sudan
Algeria	Ethiopia	Mauritania	Switzerland
Belgium	Finland	Morocco	Syria
Bolivia	Gabon	Nepal	Tanzania
Bulgaria	Ghana	Niger	Thailand
Burma	Guatemala	Nigeria	Togo
Cambodia	Guinea	Pakistan	Trinidad
Cameroon	India	Panama	Uganda
Canada	Indonesia	Peru	United States
Central African	Iran	Philippines	U.S.S.R.
Republic	Iraq	Romania	Upper Volta
Chad	Israel	Senegal	Vietnam
Congo	Ivory Coast	Sierra Leone	Yugoslavia
Cyprus	Laos	South Africa	Zaire
Czechoslovakia	Liberia	Spain	
Dahomey	Malaysia	Sri Lanka	

Source: Arthur S. Banks and Robert B. Textor, *A Cross-Polity Survey* (Cambridge, MA: M.I.T. Press, 1963), 72–75; and World Bank Atlas (1983).

many less-developed countries are linguistically heterogeneous, others are not: Burundi, Jordan, Saudi Arabia, Somalia, Tunisia, and Yemen. A language, as we noted earlier, reflects the predominant technology and other features of the level of economic development. To the extent that economic development requires changing the culture, the national language in some of these nations is not a particularly happy medium to facilitate development. Many national languages lack the necessary technical vocabulary, and few technical and professional books and journals are printed in them. Continual translation of foreign materials is possible, but it delays the dissemination of information. Some other language may have to serve as a lingua franca between the existing culture and the professional and commercial cultures being sought.

A Language for Training

This brings us to the third language problem or decision facing the less-developed linguistically homogeneous states: the choice of a second language for instruction. The choice of a second language for formal instruction is usually made at the national level. The government decides which languages shall be offered. For a while after independence, some new nations chose to avoid the language of the former colonial power as a matter of national pride. Later, the problem seemed of less consequence. French or English, the language of the former colonial power, has been chosen in various nations. The Malagasy Republic, Rwanda, and Tunisia, for example, all chose French. Other nations have a choice imposed on them. Eastern European nations, for example, used to require the study of Russian, but may not now continue to do so.

Linguistically Heterogeneous Nations

Perhaps the most dramatic indicator of the relationship among previous patterns of colonial domination, linguistic heterogeneity, and the level of development of the national economy is the fact that the great majority of the more than 60 linguistically heterogeneous nations are less developed. Notable exceptions are Belgium, Canada, Czechoslovakia, Finland, Singapore, Switzerland, the United States, and the USSR. Because coordinated, effective social activity requires predictability and shared expectations concerning behavior, language diversity is a hindrance. Picture a committee meeting that periodically splits into small caucus groups, each speaking its own language. It is not only communication, but also the sense of teamwork that suffers. People are alienated when others choose to speak a language they do not understand.

Political life in linguistically heterogeneous nations is influenced in the direction of pluralism and fragmentation. Political scientists often use the linguistic situation as a shorthand indicator for the political integration and stability of a society. Language differences reflect not only different cultures and life-styles, but also different loyalties. While language is the communication device that can promote community, language differences can perpetuate the divisions in a society. The unity of linguistically heterogeneous nations can be fragile.

> Other things assumed equal, the stage of rapid social mobilization can be expected, therefore, to promote the consolidation of states whose peoples already share the same language, culture, and major social institutions; while the same process may tend to strain or destroy the unity of states whose population is already divided into several groups with different languages or cultures or basic ways of life.[15]

This problem is not restricted to less-developed nations. Some advanced nations, such as Switzerland, work hard to neutralize linguistic diversity. In others, such as Canada and Belgium, language is a national political problem.

India is the most widely studied example of linguistic diversity and its associated problems. It is worth brief consideration as a case study. Fifteen major languages are listed in the Eighth Schedule of the Indian Constitution. These are identified in Table 2-1.

TABLE 2-1

MAJOR LANGUAGES IN INDIA (1983 DATA)

	Percent	*Population (thousands)*
Indo-European Language Family		
1. Hindi	28.1	219,920
2. Bengali	8.1	63,690
3. Marathi	7.6	59,690
4. Urdu	5.2	40,910
5. Gujarati	4.7	36,700
6. Oriya	3.6	28,220
7. Bhojpuri	2.6	20,510
8. Punjabi	2.5	19,890
9. Assamese	1.6	12,820
Dravidian Language Family		
1. Telugu	8.2	63,960
2. Tamil	6.9	53,780
3. Malayalam	4.0	31,860
4. Kannada	3.9	30,860
Others	12.5	96,500
TOTAL	100.0	783,044

Source: Adapted from the Index to the *Encyclopaedia Britannica* (1988), 619, 759.

Identifying these major language groups does not imply linguistic homogeneity within any of the language regions.

There is likely to be a considerable amount of dialectical diversity within each language over the region where it prevails. Generally, three strata among the various speech varieties in a given region may be distinguished. Dialects are used at the village level. Then there are subregional dialects, having a wider area of intelligibility. Third a standard language prevails over the local and subregional dialects.[16]

Despite the three strata identified, there are relatively few barriers to communication within each of the major language regions of India. This does not, however, lessen the enormity of the more serious problem of communication among the major language groups themselves.

There are still some one dozen major languages involved. Further, these languages have speakers running into many millions who, very importantly are concentrated in compact regions and, even more importantly, are organized politically into constituent states of a federation. Again, these languages have many centuries of history behind them, and their own individual scripts. Each has its own special literary heritage, which is a matter of intense pride and loyalty among its speakers.[17]

The Indian situation highlights the problems of linguistic diversity.

Diversity and Language Planning

Recognizing the barriers to unity caused by language diversity, many of the formerly colonized states undertook plans to facilitate communication within the nation. They faced the same questions as linguistically homogeneous states: Which language for international communications? Which language for development? Which language for formal instruction? Their planning was complicated, however, by the diversity of languages already in use. In addition to the number of languages there was usually the problem of hierarchy among them: local group-specific languages, language of the dominant group, regional language or lingua franca, and the official language, often that of the previous colonial power.

Language planners should consider several features of the multilingual situation before formulating a language policy. First, they should ask how dissimilar are the varieties of language spoken in the community. Speakers of the minority language often claim they are at a great disadvantage in learning an official language because their own language is so different. In some cases, however, minorities have demonstrated a strong capability to learn a rather different language. The Berber peoples of North Africa are known as quick learners of Arabic. In Uganda, speakers of Ateso, a Nilotic language of Africa, learn Bantu languages quite readily.[18]

Second, language planners can consider making a language the national language when it is numerically superior in terms of speakers and has standard spelling.

In the country of Burundi in Eastern Africa, the Kirundi language is spoken by almost all the citizens. Because no agreement has been reached for Kirundi, French continues there as the official language for all administrative and educational purposes. By contrast, both Swahili and Hausa were standardized with a spelling rather early by African standards; both spread widely as lingua francas. Even if a language is not superior numerically, it may be chosen because of its associated political or cultural attributes. Even though the Galla language has a slightly larger number of first-language speakers in Ethiopia, Amharic was chosen because it became the court language in Ethiopia in the thirteenth century.[19]

Third, when no one indigenous language dominates a nation according to the criteria we have noted, an outside language usually becomes the official national language of government and of education. The outside language has the advantage of neutrality. It will not fuel interethnic rivalries.

The alternatives available to language planners were basically a strategy of uniformity or a strategy of diversity. The colonial powers regularly followed a policy of working toward uniformity. In their administrations the lingua franca gained at the expense of the tribal or ethnic languages. The use of the colonial language was officially promoted throughout the land. Israel has followed a uniformity strategy by using classical Hebrew to unify immigrants from many countries. Immigrants are required to begin a standardized language course as soon as they arrive. This course gives a workable knowledge of Hebrew within six weeks.

Linguistic Independence?

Most of the newer states in Africa and Asia are in a different situation from that of Israel or the colonial powers. As a practical matter, one of their major decisions was what to do with the foreign official language inherited from the colonial power. There are several rather strong arguments against retaining the colonizer's language as the official language of the nation.

1. One argument is the question of national identity. Nations employ many symbols to express their independence and uniqueness: a flag, a national anthem, and national holidays. Language is often considered one of these primary national symbols. Use of the colonizer's language does not fill that role very well. Gandhi asserted that to "get rid of the infatuation for English is one of the essentials of freedom."

2. Another argument against retaining the colonizer's language has to do with the antidemocratic role it played in imperial days. Under colonial rule, competence in the foreign language was the defining characteristic of the elite. In effect, the foreign language created two nations—a small ruling class and the mass of the people. Should the elite in the independent nation continue to be defined by the imperialist's language? Should a foreign language be an instrument of power?

3. A related problem is the communication gap that exists between the government and the people when the government officials use a foreign language. Many feel that this communication barrier is a cause of the failure of development programs.

4. Educators (and UNESCO) agree that schooling, especially in the early years, is best received in the mother tongue.

5. The removal of the foreign language is necessary for the autonomy and health of the nation's cultural life. Gandhi referred to English as "a cultural usurper." How can a foreign language serve as a congenial medium for the encouragement of the national culture?[20]

Or Linguistic Interdependence?

The preceding five points constitute a powerful force against retaining the colonizer's language. After reading them, one might be surprised to look at these nations 20 to 40 years after independence and observe that the colonizer's language continues to play a major role. With the exception of South Africa and Tanzania, all the sub-Saharan African nations retained French or English as the national language. Several equally powerful forces work for retaining the colonizer's language.

1. One force is sheer inertia. Since the colonial language has usually been around for a century or more, it is not easy to remove.

2. Another force is the preoccupation of the new governments with a host of other post-independence problems of seemingly greater importance and urgency than the language question.

3. Still another force for retaining the colonial language is that often there are no local languages adequately developed in terminology for the purposes of a centralized bureaucratic administration and higher education.

4. A fourth force for retention is that many vested interests are associated with the use of the foreign language. The educated elite and the bureaucracy, though a relatively small percentage of the population, gained their influential positions in part through competence in the foreign language. They fight to maintain their advantage and the position it gives them, but sometimes this strategy backfires. The Ibos of Nigeria and the Tamils of Sri Lanka each had a higher percentage of governmental and professional positions than their percentage of the population. In each case, other language groups fought to change these situations.

5. A fifth force is the difficulty of finding a local language to replace the foreign one. Choosing any of the national languages instantly creates new problems. It incurs the wrath not only of the displaced elite, but also of all other language groups. It creates a new linguistic elite. Only one-fourth of the Indian population speak Hindi. When Hindi was declared an official language, language riots occurred. The foreign language at least has the virtue of being neutral.

6. A final argument for the foreign language is that it is usually a modern language, capable of meeting the requirements of modern industry, commerce, and technology that the new state wishes to acquire. Tunisia, an Arabic-speaking nation, chose to retain French for higher education as well as for extensive use in commerce and administration.

Summary

In this section, we have noted that language has important political and economic impacts. Major difficulties arise in those nations with language (and cultural) diversity. The needs of economic integration and development, political unification, and international communication all push the newer nations to adopt a single language—

usually of European origin. Working against the European language are national pride, the desire for cultural independence, and other practical problems.

We move now from an area in which the international manager can offer only sympathy to an area where one must get involved in decisions, that is, the relation of the linguistic situation to international business.

POLICY IMPLICATIONS FOR THE MULTINATIONAL FIRM: LANGUAGES AND INTERNATIONAL BUSINESS

The multiplicity of languages and the parallel diversity of cultures in the world economy have a constraining influence on the operations of international business. To a large degree, international business depends on communication. Languages are the principal means of communication. Every time a language and cultural barrier must be crossed, there is a potential communication problem. Even functional departments within a corporation develop their own distinctive lingos and sometimes have trouble communicating with one another.

Top management in a large international consulting company knew that interdepartmental trouble was brewing when they learned that two major divisions used sarcastic labels for one another: Accountants in the audit division referred to computer experts in the management information consulting division as "wireheads"; the reciprocal term for the accountants was "bean counters." (Kenneth David, field research)

This type of problem is magnified considerably when organizations differ in culture, professional culture, and corporate culture.

A variety of intercultural communication situations face the multinational firm. Expatriate managers must communicate with indigenous managers. The firm must communicate with its employees, suppliers, customers, distributors, and host government officials. Headquarters must communicate with its foreign subsidiaries. In Chapter 7, we will more closely examine the varying need for an international firm to be nationally responsive in these relationships. Here, our focus will remain on the linguistic aspects of these relationships from the viewpoint of an international owner or manager operating outside the home country.

Communication with Employees

Among its employees, a firm's production workers usually have the least education and most limited language capability. To require these workers to learn the language of the firm's foreign owners is rarely feasible. This means that all communication between management and these workers must be in the workers' language. Such communication most commonly takes place via the bilingual national managers, who speak both the national language and the language of the foreign owners.

The situation is complicated, however, when the work force speaks more than one language. In an African nation where workers from several tribes may be employed in the same factory, a lingua franca may be used. This results in some static in the communication, however, as the lingua franca is a second language for most of the tribes. They do not understand as well in the lingua franca as in their mother tongue. In Belgium, where there is great hostility between the French- and Flemish-speaking segments of the population, both languages are used.

Germany provides an even more complex example. Many German plants employ workers from as many as four foreign countries. This may necessitate separation of the work force along linguistic lines. Some bilingual production workers—for example, German-speaking Turks—are paid extra to interpret between the German supervisors and their national colleagues. Even then, many signs in a plant appear in several languages. At the Ford plant in Cologne, for example, almost half the work force, and almost all of the assembly line, is not German. The codetermination meetings with workers required by German law are held in three languages: German, Spanish, and Turkish. At the same plant, meetings with top management are held in English, especially if an American vice-president is present.

Firms often institute employee training programs to improve productivity, reduce accidents and waste, and so forth. Language differences complicate such training programs in various ways. One problem is that training materials are sometimes drawn from other parts of the firm's operations, usually in the home country. Getting translations that convey the same meaning in the host country language(s) not only involves expense, but usually results in some static in communication.

Less-developed countries can run into other problems. Because language reflects the technology of the culture, it may be almost impossible to find host-culture language equivalents for the industrial, commercial, or technological terms the firm wishes to introduce. For example, it may not be possible to train computer operators or programmers in an African language. This may necessitate worker instruction in English or French to achieve the desired result—at further cost in time and money. A company may hesitate to engage in such language programs for yet another reason: Workers with the valuable language skill may seek employment with another firm.

Communication with Suppliers

Communication with suppliers is less of a problem because it is in the supplier's interest to ease the barrier by learning the language of the customer. Nevertheless, many small national suppliers will speak only the local language and must deal with those in the firm who also speak it. A foreign firm may have to deal with such suppliers in order to comply with local content laws imposed by the host-country government. Larger suppliers, especially such institutions as banks and advertising agencies, are likely to be able to communicate in the language of the expatriate manager, at least in English or in French.

One communication problem in international business relates to the many people in foreign countries who are not directly employed by a company, yet serve the company or deal with its customers. These include local independent dealers and repair shops. Trying to solve this problem by facilitating understanding of its parts, service, and repair manuals throughout the world without having to translate them, Caterpillar

Tractor developed a unique system of printed communication called Caterpillar Fundamental English (CFE).

CFE is a printed one-way communication that does not require (or teach) pronunciation or writing of any of the words. It is a condensed, simplified, and specialized form of English designed to speed instruction of service personnel who work with Caterpillar machines. They would otherwise require manuals translated into a number of languages. Through a 30-lesson course, the students acquire a visual understanding of the 800-word vocabulary, although they may not be able to say the words.

In this stripped-down language, all words not necessary to service Caterpillar products are omitted. There are 70 verbs, 450 nouns, 100 prepositions, and 180 adjectives, adverbs, and pronouns.

The student CFE kit contains the 30-lesson instruction manual. This includes photos and drawings of Caterpillar parts and a pocket reference in which the student writes a native-language translation of CFE words. In addition, for the instructor, there are a dictionary, an instructor's manual, and a writer's guide to enable teaching the vocabulary.

Students need only a knowledge of Caterpillar products and literacy in their own language. Instructors must know English and the student's language. Thousands of CFE employees have taken the course.[21]

Communication with Customers

Speaking the customer's language, literally and figuratively, is a cardinal rule of marketing. Effective communication and successful persuasion virtually dictate using the native language of the customer. Especially when a First-World company is selling to a Third-World country, communicating in the native language is important because the company can be held responsible for the customer's use of the product. When the Nestlé company did not communicate to Third-World customers how their milk powder was to be used, world opinion held Nestlé liable for the product's misuse, which resulted in the undernourishment and even death of many small children.

Accurate and persuasive communication can be even more difficult in a multilingual society. It may require numerous expensive and difficult translations of print advertising, packages, and labels, and the recruitment of a sales force capable of reaching all the important linguistic segments of the market. Alternatively, it may mean omission of several language groups and the use of less-direct distribution channels, leaving the communication task with the intermediaries. In any case, successful marketing will require local language communication. The necessary linguistic skills must either exist within the firm or be found and hired outside.

Communication with Government

Twenty years ago, a fair statement was that protocol and national pride usually dictate that communications with government be in the national official language. In the 70 nations where English, Spanish, or French is one of the official languages, it presumably would not be difficult for the expatriate manager to have or acquire some of the necessary language skill. Over the past 20 years, many countries such as the Arab nations have begun teaching English as a second language; government officials are likely to have a reasonable knowledge of English.

The question is whether the foreign business person and the official share enough verbal and nonverbal understandings to reach mutually beneficial agreements. Especially in countries where nonverbal signals are crucial to communications, it can be difficult indeed. In such places it becomes critical to employ nationals either at a high level within the company or as legal counsel. A comment published a number of years ago is still quite applicable:

> Only a handful of gaijin (foreign) managers speak fluent Japanese, and even they sometimes find themselves at a disadvantage. The result is that most American managers rely heavily on interpreters, communicate little with most of their employees, and suffer from indifferent relations with many customers and government officials.[22]

Parent-Subsidiary Communications

A prime policy question in organizing relations between corporate headquarters and foreign subsidiaries is the trade-off between (1) control and coordination of all foreign activities and (2) responsiveness to conditions in each particular country.

In the days of the East India Company, parent-subsidiary communications were not a problem. Because the fastest means of communication between them was an ocean voyage lasting several months each way, the subsidiary was pretty autonomous. Today's technology allows corporate headquarters to keep in constant touch with all world markets. The headquarters' control process involves continuous communication, both oral and written, with all of its foreign operations. Most of these will be in countries with languages different from that of the headquarters country, but all communication with headquarters will be in "company language"—usually the language of the home country.

Within a subsidiary there will often be several people sending and receiving messages from headquarters: the general managers as well as finance, marketing, and technical staff. If an American company places Americans in these positions, it will probably minimize communication difficulties between parent and subsidiary. At the same time, it will increase the communication problems with government, employees, and others within the host country. Placing local nationals in the same positions simply reverses the communication problem. This illustrates how the staffing of the local subsidiary becomes tied in with the language and communication barriers in the firm.

Dealing with the Language Problem

Because of the costs associated with communication problems arising from language and cultural barriers, most firms find it necessary to make some efforts at solving the problems. Here we shall note briefly some of the techniques that are available.

Translations

Translations are an inevitable part of international operations. They are also an extra expense, whether done by special translators or by company managers incidental to their primary tasks. The firm may hire skilled translators for its foreign operations. It is unlikely that its managers have either the time or the expertise to be translators, except informally. Company translators can best deal with the firm's written communications with its various contacts. They are of less help in oral communication.

Although translations are inevitable in international business, they almost never result in the same quality of communication obtained when both parties speak the same language. Sometimes great misunderstandings can arise through translation. Everyone experienced in international relations has a collection of humorous anecdotes about translation errors or unexpected word plays (recall Figure 2-1). Aware of such blunders, the merged company of Sperry and Burroughs devoted much effort to select an appropriate new name. Their final choice, Unisys, has neutral connotations in all major languages.

Company practice by American subsidiaries in South-East Asia illustrates some of the linguistic hurdles we are discussing. Preparation of a report in an Indonesian affiliate and the linguistic ladder that document must follow can become a kaleidoscope of translation, retranslation, Indonesian-English restatements, rewriting, and frustration. Here is one example of the path a report takes:

1. Staff conference in Indonesian, laying out specifics.
2. Initial draft in Indonesian by staff member.
3. Concurrence on Indonesian draft.
4. Translation into English.
5. Middle manager reads Indonesian and English drafts—attempts improvements in English.
6. Subsidiary vice-president attempts improvement in English.
7. Report goes to general director, then to the United States.

To avoid blunders, even a small company can have someone on staff to do reverse translations: translate the document, check the communication by translating it back to the original language, and then transmit the approved document to the recipient.

Delegating the Communications Job

A firm can delegate some communications tasks to outsiders. Instead of hiring its own sales force, for example, the firm may use a national distributor who will handle all communications with the distribution channel. Similarly, the firm could rely on its advertising agency for all other communications with its markets. In dealing with suppliers, the firm can perhaps force them to use the company language. In dealing with the government, the firm can retain a national as legal counsel or place a prominent national on its local board of directors. In these ways a firm can delegate some of the communications tasks in international operations.

Some caution is necessary here, because the more a firm delegates, the further removed it is from its audiences and the less control it has over its business. In other words, although there are costs in handling the language problem directly, in many cases they can be offset by the value of the experience gained.

Language Training Programs

Just as firms have a variety of training programs to improve productivity, so they may find language classes for workers a good investment in foreign operations.

> General Foam Division of Tenneco employed largely Spanish-speaking workers and English-speaking supervisors with tower-of-Babel results. The resulting shaky communications brought high turnover, high accident rates, unsatisfactory quality control, and constant tension.
>
> The firm did not resign itself to these problems, but experimented with teaching its employees English and its supervisors Spanish. The classes focused not on literary aspect but on shop-floor necessities, the language of the work environment. The classes were considered a success. Worker motivation was high because the classes were held on company time and the content was tailored to job requirements and advancement. The firm's reward was evident also. According to the manager: "We saw results immediately. Everyone relaxed. We had fewer accidents. We even had fewer grievances. Production moved along better and we expect employee turnover to go down."[23]

Although the point is simple (language barriers cause problems, language classes help to overcome them), this illustration is instructive because it did not happen abroad, but within the United States. The firm employed Puerto Ricans in its New Jersey plants. Intercultural issues need not be international. In Sweden, language training has been mandatory for many years. Foreign workers must receive 240 hours of language instruction on company time.[24]

Bilingual Managers

Perhaps the most critical communication link in international operations is the one that ties the subsidiary to the parent. The language barrier is greatest in parent-subsidiary communications because it is here that the translation is made from the company language to that of the host country. To enable regular and fluent communication, a certain number of bilingual managers are needed in the subsidiary. National managerial personnel who wish to rise to top positions in the subsidiary must learn the company language.

Should expatriate managers also be bilingual? While there is unanimous agreement about the desirability of the international managers knowing the language of the host country, there is some disagreement about its necessity. Attaining fluency in a foreign language is a time-consuming and expensive investment. The manager must, in effect, do a kind of investment analysis in deciding how much foreign language study is appropriate for a given company and career and which foreign language to learn.

One useful example here is the practice of one of the world's larger international operations, the U.S. Department of State. Foreign service officers usually undergo rather extensive language training in preparation for overseas assignments. Where language is important for the work the officer will be doing, there is a six-month language training period in Washington, with additional training available at the foreign post. For very difficult languages, such as Japanese or Arabic, the training may extend as long as two years. The State Department feels this kind of investment is not only worthwhile but necessary for the success of its operations.

International companies tend to have far more limited language programs than those of the State Department. A common approach for firms is to give the manager with an overseas assignment a month's total-immersion course à la Berlitz. It is estimated that over 8,000 managers learn the Berlitz way every year. Of course, total immersion is rough, for it is just that: thirteen hours a day, five days a week. However, this usually provides sufficient foundation for a manager to get by passably on arrival and improve fluency during the time abroad. Some companies judge the performance of overseas employees partially by their progress in the language.

Although firms usually make some investment to minimize the language barrier for their expatriate managers, an important variable in their decision is the length of the overseas assignment. Any short visit of a few weeks, or even a few months, does not warrant much language training. The situation would be different if the same manager were to make annual visits to the same language area, because then the investment could be spread out over a longer period. Foreign assignments of over a year—and three years is common—make the investment in language training more worthwhile. Incidentally, three years at one post is also typical for foreign service officers in the State Department. It should be noted that the investment in language study is twofold: the executive's time for the program plus the cost of the training, which alone can add up to several thousand dollars (or a multiple of that if spouse and children are included).

Another potential variable in the decision on language training may be the language capability of the manager. Current company practice relies on the assumption that anyone of average intelligence can learn a foreign language with some effort. Lately, however, some doubts have emerged. A one-hour Modern Language Aptitude Test appears to predict with considerable accuracy a person's chances of linguistic success.

> In one experiment, the test was given to 691 U.S. Foreign Service Officers—all college graduates, and all presumably as highly motivated to learn a foreign language as the typical executive. The results indicated that 21 percent could expect to make good progress with a new language, while 27 percent were essentially unable to benefit from instruction. These rather startling forecasts were closely borne out by the group's subsequent experience with intensive language courses. Even after 430 hours of instruction in French, two out of five officers were unable to do much more than discuss the time of day or order a simple meal.[25]

Another factor is a career decision made by the potential trainee. In some companies, managers who do gain proficiency in a language may actually hinder their career development. They may be rewarded with posts where direct communication with local nationals is critical, but these positions may not be those linked with continued advancement in the firm. Thus what appears initially as a promotion may in a longer perspective turn out to be tantamount to reclassification from a regular executive career path to that of a technical or limited functional specialist.

To conclude our discussion on bilingual managers, we offer a few general thoughts. First, bilingual managers—both host-country and expatriate—are the most critical element in facilitating communications in international business. Second, because this is true, multinational firms need to encourage and facilitate language training for managers from both the home and the host country. This will not only improve communication but also promote the internationalization of management necessary in the multinational firm. Firms can encourage expatriates to learn the foreign language by giving release time, paying for the instruction, and rewarding language proficiency as a promotion criterion rather than as a handicap to further international mobility.

QUESTIONS

1. From what sources can you learn about the linguistic situation in particular foreign countries?

2. Guinea, West Africa (a former French colony), has a population of about four million divided into seven major tribes. Early in the 1970s, Sekou Touré, the leader of the country, ordered a campaign to reduce the high illiteracy rate among Guineans. Bypassing French, an official language of Guinea, Touré ordered that the literacy campaign be conducted simultaneously in each one of the seven major tribal languages. What benefits and problems do you see associated with this approach?

3. Femme Fatale, an American manufacturer, exports high-fashion lingerie to forty countries on five continents. What kinds of language problems might Femme Fatale encounter? How might they try to resolve them?

4. Papua, New Guinea, celebrated its independence from Australia on December 1, 1973. Its approximately 2.8 million people occupy a land area slightly larger than the state of California. The population is divided into 702 tribes and speaks about that many languages. What language policy would you recommend for this nation? What official language(s)? What language(s) for education? for diplomacy?

5. Find a foreign-language periodical with advertising. Translate a few of the ads into English. Discuss some of the problems of translating advertising into another language.

6. Identify 20 countries where French is a national language.

7. Quebec legislation has made French the official language of the province (but allowing English to accompany French). One section of the law provides fines

up to $5,000 for failure to use French on product labels, warranties, menus, and wine lists. It requires businesses seeking government contracts to be certified for competence in French. What does this law mean

a. for a British firm exporting toiletries to Canada?
b. for an American consulting firm with a regional office located in Montreal?

8. A U.S. typewriter manufacturer formerly had two keyboard models available for sale in India. To meet the growing market, the firm is going to expand the number of keyboard models to cover more Indian languages. How should the firm decide how many keyboard models to offer in India?

9. What would be the language needs or problems of an American manager of an American marketing subsidiary in Japan? of a Japanese manager of a Japanese marketing subsidiary in the United States? Would there be any difference in your answer if the country were India instead of Japan?

10. The following quotation is from a call for papers for a Paris meeting of the European Academy of Marketing (based in Brussels). The letter is in English.

All topics related to Marketing are welcome. You can submit your papers in English, French, or German. Nevertheless, because there will be no simultaneous translation, all papers must be presented in English.

What conclusions or implications would you draw from this notice about the linguistic situation? Why is English the dominant language for the study of marketing? Is this linguistic dominance neutral for the French or German scholars?

11. Three months ago, you arrived in Kenya as managing director of a British-owned tea-processing plant. Everyone on your administrative staff is a native Kenyan. As your predecessor told you, they are all bilingual, and you have little trouble understanding their lilting, musical, but precise English. You have introduced some upgraded technology in your plant. After some initial hesitation, the work force became accustomed to it. Last week, you were able to fulfill your company's agreement with the government and transfer the outmoded machinery to the association of small Kenyan tea-processing companies.

Thus, when you receive a letter on official government stationery, you open it with expectation of thanks for acting as a good corporate citizen. To your dismay, you read that the Kenyan Commission on Labor Practices has ordered you to cease operations immediately and stay closed until you rectify the gross imbalance in hiring practices. You call an emergency meeting of your administrative staff. There is an embarrassed silence after you outline the situation. Finally, your chief of operations informs you that your predecessor was not aware that he had hired a person of the Luo tribe as personnel manager. Subsequently, only Luo persons were hired.

Your operations chief tells you that the Commission, dominated like the rest of the government by persons from the Kikuyu tribe, would have objected sooner if they had known about the situation. Until recently, the relevant officer had accepted an adequate payment for his silence. The new officer, unfortunately, was not willing to accept a payment.

What do you do now? What does your superior in London do?

ENDNOTES

1. J. S. Arpan, D. A. Ricks, and D. J. Patton, "The Meaning of Miscue Made by Multinationals," *Management International Review* 4, no. 5 (1974): 3–16; F. A. Bowen, "Ad Bloopers Abroad—Amusing and Sometimes Costly," *F. A. Bowen Reports* (Janesville, WI: Bowen, 1982); David A. Ricks, *Big Business Blunders: Mistakes in Multinational Marketing* (Homewood, IL: Dow Jones-Irwin, 1983).
2. Clifford Geertz, "The Integrative Revolution: Primordial Sentiments and Civil Politics in the New States," in Clifford Geertz (ed.), *Old Societies and New States: The Quest for Modernity in Asia and Africa* (New York: Free Press, 1963).
3. In this chapter we discuss only verbal communication. For a good discussion of nonverbal communication, see Edward T. Hall, *The Silent Language* (New York, Doubleday, 1959).
4. Clyde Kluckhohn, *Mirror for Man, The Relation of Anthropology to Modern Life* (New York: McGraw-Hill, 1949), 125.
5. Benjamin Lee Whorf, *Language, Thought, and Reality* (New York: Wiley, 1956), 13.
6. Ibid., 116.
7. Henry A. Gleason, *An Introduction to Descriptive Linguistics* (New York: Holt, 1955), 42.
8. Conrad Arensberg and Arthur Niehoff, *Introducing Social Change, A Manual for Americans Overseas* (Chicago: Aldine, 1964), 30.
9. For an amusing and informative analysis of the differences between the King's English and the American language, see Mario Pei, *The Story of Language,* rev. ed. (Philadelphia: Lippincott, 1965), 300–315.
10. Arthur S. Banks and Robert B. Textor, *A Cross-Polity Survey* (Cambridge, MA: M.I.T. Press, 1963), 72–75.
11. *Commerce Today* (May 28, 1973): 17.
12. Carol Scotton, "Language Policies, National Development, and Communication" (Revision of paper prepared for Seminar on Development, Stanford University Institute of Mass Communications, June 1974).
13. Carol Scotton, "The Role of Norms and Other Factors in Language Choice in Work Situations in Three African Cities (Lagos, Kampala, Nairobi)," in Rolf Kjolseth and Albert Verdoodt, eds., *Language in Sociology,* (Louvain, Belgium: Editions Peeters, 1976), 201–232.
14. Ibid.
15. Karl W. Deutsch, *Nationalism and Social Communication* (Cambridge, MA: M.I.T. Press, 1953), 589.
16. Baldev Raj Nayar, *National Communication and Language Policy in India* (New York: Praeger, 1969), 25.
17. Ibid., 27.
18. Carol Scotton, "Neighbors and Lexical Borrowing: A Study of Two Ateso Dialects," *Language* 49, no. 4 (1983): 871–889.
19. Scotton, "Language Policies, National Development, and Communication": 5.
20. Adapted from Nayar, 12–17.
21. Adapted from *Business International* (April 6, 1973): 107.
22. *Business Week* (November 18, 1972): 41.
23. Adapted from *Business Week* (February 28, 1970): 104.
24. *Business Week* (March 31, 1973): 95.
25. *Fortune* (March 1971), 42.

PART II

Culture and the Shaping of Human Motivation

The following three chapters are grouped together because they all address the role of culture in chaping individual's thoughts and emotions. The thoughts and feelings of every person in the world are *unique in some ways* (for each person has some totally isiosyncratic thoughts and fantasies). They are *similar to all humans in others ways* (concerning the basics of survival). Finally, as a result of cultural conditioning, they are *similar to a limited set of persons in still other ways*. These thoughts and feelings share d as a result of cultural training are a source of cultural diversity that is part of the environment of international business.

Education, values, and religion are three aspects of what can be defined broadly as the cultural shaping of motivation. All human societies must devise means to instruct persons in how they are to participate in social activities, means to motivate persons to do what they are supposed to do, and means to alleviate emotional and mental difficulties stemming from social dilemmas or other unfortunate events. Without t hese emotional and meantal guidelines and aids, social life would be chaotic.

The basic problem for the cultural shaping of motivation can be understood in terms of the development of an individual in society. Jean Piaget, the developmental psychologist, states that children begin life by relating to others in an *ecogentric* fastion: my needs are all that exist. in early life a child is not mentally capable of understanding the perspectives of others. In the course of being culturally instructed, or socialized, the child becomes *decentered*. In contrast to the earlier stage, the child lea rns t hat he or she is not all that counts.

- The child begins to recognize the existence of others' perspectives.
- The child learns that social rultes exist to coordinate the perspectives and expectations of people into predictable patterns of social interation.

Education, then, has emotional as well as mental impacts. The process of learning how to behave in society does not necessarily provide motivation to follow the rules. Indeed, the individual is often doing what is not personally desired. This is alienation. Decentering may provide knowledge but not motivation to do what you are supposed to do.

Values are emotionally charged priorities for social life that help individuals choose to act properly in ambiguous or ambivalent situations. Values are typically based on religious notions. Values are related to religiosity in that they are concerned with reducing alienation—that is, realigning the emotions of an individual with the external social rules for behavior.

Religion refers to a more-than-human, extra-empirical frame of reference. It is a worldwide means of overcoming the very human tendencies toward skepticism and alienation from the social order.

To recapitulate: Education, values, and religion are three aspects of the question of individual motivation to perform socially useful behavior. Education is the imparting of rules for behavior. Values are predispositions and priorities among rules for behavior. Values are essential because humans are often faced with ambiguous or ambivalent social situations. As emotionally charged priorities, values help people not only to act properly, but also to act with commitment. Because it is based on a powerful though unverifiable order of reality, religion justifies the emotional commitments and social rules of society.

CHAPTER THREE
Education

WHY BE CONCERNED WITH EDUCATION?

Earlier we noted that gaining access to backstage culture—the subtle, insider's view of how things work around here—is an important task for managing international operations. Stating a task is not very helpful unless you get some idea of how to do it. Let us reverse the situation and ask what foreigners should do to gain inside knowledge of you and your organization. One technique they might find helpful is getting a general profile of your upbringing: the series of training experiences that got you where you are. A focus case illustrates this point.

FOCUS CASE:
Cultural Training in Japan

The following five sections provide a brief survey of the series of cultural trainings commonly practiced today in Japan. They illustrate the point we made in Chapter 1: Codes for behavior are progressively specified in national, business, and corporate culture.

EARLY TRAINING: CHILDHOOD GAMES

Children in many societies play some variation of a game in which they move towards a goal, physically moving and stopping according to some external command. Players are penalized if they are caught moving during the time they should be still.

In the United States, this game is called *Red Light, Green Light.* The one who gives commands is called "It." When the game is announced, everyone quickly calls, "Not It!" The last child to say the phrase is obviously It. It turns its back and yells "Green Light!" The others run toward It. When It yells "Red Light," they must stop. Anyone caught moving is It's prisoner. A chain of prisoners forms, holding hands with It. The winner is the first child to free the prisoners by touching the hands of It and the first prisoner. This game has clear winners and losers.

In Japan, a similar game is played with a Demon giving the commands. The Demon turns its back and recites a set of ten syllables, during which time the other children advance. Recitation finished, the Demon turns and catches prisoners. A prisoner chain forms. The distinctive difference is the event of freeing prisoners. When the Demon feels its hand touched, it immediately turns and commands the other to stop. Then the Demon is allowed to take up to three steps. The first child touched becomes the next Demon. If you picture the motions, the most likely child to be touched is the liberator. This game has an element of self-sacrifice to complement competition.

In which culture are grown-up workers more likely to accept the combination of competition and collaboration needed for quality circles?

CONTINUING TRAINING: JAPANESE MANGA[1]

Manga is the Japanese term for cartoons, comic strips, and animated films. Manga differ from Western comic books. They are intended for all ages. Although manga are forms of escapist entertainment to deal with a highly pressured world, they have the more serious purpose of transmitting general knowledge and general societal values.

Manga are widespread. Out of 5 billion publications sold in 1984, 27 percent were comic books. An average manga contains 350 pages, with 15 serial stories and only 10 to 20 pages of advertisements.

Some manga are escapist. Three main genres are erotically oriented strips, strips devoted to various games of chance such as Mah-jongg (tiles played much like a pack of cards) or Pachinko (a vertical pinball machine), and "salary man" strips that parody working life. Escapist literature is not surprising in a very crowded, highly demanding social structure that includes a work environment demanding much patience and cooperation though little initiative.

"Study comics" (*benkyo manga*) are textbooks. In a country where education beyond the high school level is severely limiting, these comics reach the general public with information on technical, political, economic, and social policies in an appealing format. They use story frames with well-depicted characters and footnotes to bring complex issues, facts, and figures into focus by personalizing and dramatizing them.

In order to promote acceptable social behavior, genres are specifically targeted by age and gender: *shonen manga* for boys, *shojo manga* for girls, *seinenshi* for young men (18–25 years) and *gigika* for adults in general. Themes of the comics written for each group promote certain values.

For boys, the comics deal with action and adventure; they value teamwork, spirit, courage, earnestness, perseverance, and heroism. Sports heroes and samurai warriors communicate these values. The warrior participates in great adventures and he is noble, strong, and brave. He always works well within a group, just as the Japanese are expected to sublimate their own personal aims for the benefit of a whole. These elements can be seen in the normal working day habits of responsiveness to fellow workers, superiors, and the company product. Later in life these values are reinforced in "production comics" (*zosan manga*), which feature stories about successful, motivated workers who are compatible with others on the job but are humble and amusing when away from work. A female counterpart is "Innovative Housewife," a comic that emphasizes conservation during hard times.

Shojo manga, which are aimed for girls, use different colors (pastels instead of bright primaries) and a different page arrangement (pictures flowing around and over one another instead of frames and strips) to portray a passive, dreamy world in which the chief values are truth, beauty, and love.

PROFESSIONAL TRAINING AND RECRUITMENT

There are advantages to being small and homogeneous. Japan selects students for its finer universities with a nationwide, extremely difficult set of examinations. Japan also coordinates the process of matching college students with employers. Universities have data banks on companies and hold information seminars (once during the third year, four times during the senior year) for their students. Students often use the summer break before their last year as a period for research on companies.

In October of the senior year comes the crucial nationwide hiring season. Companies hold public information sessions that are attended by thousands of students; students submit their professional resumés to the companies at this time. Interviews start in the third week of October. Most major companies conduct two or three interviews. Results are announced at the end of November. Major companies hire groups of people at this time; this age cohort is a major feature of company organization (see page 54). A candidate who does not get selected by his or her preferred company and wants to continue the attempt has to wait for the following year.

After graduation in March, candidates take company examinations in April. These exams are partly a ritual of passage; successful candidates celebrate as a group and begin the orientation period.

New recruits receive several weeks of basic training; they learn the company's history, mode of operation, and correct business etiquette. Training continues during the career. Long-term staff development is carried out at in-company language and technical training facilities or by sending employees to external courses. (In the next section, we will examine the details of one particular in-company training program). Another form of in-house staff development is provided by regular rotation of jobs; this gives employees experience in various aspects of the business before they are promoted and obliged to participate in decision making that affects the various units.

CORPORATE TRAINING

Thomas Rohlen, an anthropologist, participated in a three-month training program conducted by a bank located in a major Japanese city. The bank had about 3,000 employees. Its training program was administered routinely to all new employees and given often as mid-career training. About two-thirds of the program was devoted to technical and managerial skills; the remaining third emphasized what Rohlen terms *spiritual education.*[2]

The Concept of Spiritualism

The training program emphasized spiritualism, a set of Japanese ideas about human psychology and character development drawn from the Zen, Confucian, and Samurai traditions. Its main tenets were (1) social cooperation and responsibility, (2) an acceptance of reality, and (3) perseverance.

Spiritualism is a definite philosophy of socialization and human development. It uses native concepts of psychology (as distinct from ideas developed since Freud) and functions outside the normal school system. Employee and manager performance evaluation is based both on business goals and on adherence to these concepts of spiritualism.

Goals of the Training Program

The goal of any training program is to motivate employees to work in the best interests of the firm. This program was no exception. It focused on loyal role fulfillment, teaching that "the moral man is the man who works hard for his own company."[3] It attempted to inculcate pride in and respect for the work. The aim was not brainwashing; rather, it was intended that trainees should become familiar with the viewpoint of the bank, its competitive circumstances, and its intention to contribute to the social good.

Methods Used in the Training Program

The emphasis throughout was on learning through experience. Five major training events are reported here.

Zen Meditation. The trainees visited a famous Zen temple, spending some days there. The major purpose was to expose them to the way Zen monks embrace a very austere regime with equanimity. The trainees were taught Zen meditation as a means of reducing anxiety. They were taught to breathe slowly, concentrate, and thus survive physical discomfort and work efficiently. The monks impressed on them that one must find answers to one's problems within oneself, that self-improvement involves being less selfish and being of use to others, and that one should aim for working with others in harmony and value cooperation and sharing.

Military Training. Trainees visited a military base. In order to develop order within the group, they participated in military drills. To instill spirit and determination, they heard a lecture on mission in life. This lecture made reference to the kamikaze pilots (suicide squads) of World War II. Trainees learned that although kamikaze volunteers knew that Japan would lose the war and their actions meant certain death, scores stepped forward for these jobs. The spiritual strength of these martyrs was emphasized: their willingness to serve the country rather than pursue individual pleasure. The age similarity between the war heroes and the trainees proved to be a striking point.

Rotoo. Rotoo consisted of working without pay for strangers, a particularly hard thing to do in Japan where strangers ignore one another. The trainees often met with rude refusal. Hence, when someone accepted the offer of work, a trainee felt a sense of relief not to have to go begging of strangers any more; in comparison, almost any sort of work seemed delightful. This exercise probably helped clarify the meaning of work, that the enjoyment of work depended on the person's attitude toward it. Also, it shook the trainees out of social lethargy by requiring them to ask acceptance of strangers without social crutches such as rank or family. It forced one to ask, "Who am I?" Ultimately, rotoo proved that all work can be satisfying. From the bank's point of view, this was a particularly important lesson, because the bank must often assign dull and repetitive tasks to its employees.

A Weekend Among Farmers. Trainees spent some time in an agricultural community, helping farmers. This exercise was designed to heighten their appreciation of social interdependence and social service as well as their awareness of the self-reliant nature of farm people and the ingenuity fostered by simple rural living. The chairman of the bank would have liked all the trainees to spend a year farming, as he considered the long arduous cycle of agriculture to be the best education in the importance of persistence, receiving its due reward in the end. This weekend was a substitute of sorts for that impractical goal.

An Endurance Walk. This was the final, perhaps capstone, event of training. All trainees were required to walk twenty-five miles; nine miles as a group, nine miles in smaller squads, and the last seven miles alone, in silence. Competition was not the point; all they had to do was finish the course. But competition among the squads arose anyway—the slower walkers were hurried along and faster ones held back. This resulted in a grueling pace for the second nine miles and left the trainees in poor shape for the last seven, to be walked alone. Of the last seven miles, Rohlen reminisces: "I could see that I was spiritually weak, easily tempted and inclined to quit."[4]

Analysis of the Program

Overall, the training program stressed (1) the importance of teamwork, (2) the close relationship between physical condition and mental well-being, and (3) the importance of dogged persistence in accomplishing almost any task. Several points can be made about the program.

1. The bank must train its employees in social membership because of the overthrow of the traditional school system of Japan after the occupation. The training the bank provides is necessary to provide highly socialized and effective employees who can mesh well with a management structure molded to traditional Japanese values.

2. The emphasis of training is on spiritual strength or composure. The core of this scheme of education is the concept of heart, or spirit, representing a broad area of individual psychosomatic unity. The goal of composure that underlies this training can be achieved only when there is a harmony of mind, body, and spirit. Then both the mind and the body can operate properly and efficiently. This training makes employees aware of the interrelationship of physical and mental aspects of both composure and disturbance.

3. Spiritual strength or composure is not so much an end in itself; rather, it is a basis for effective action. Particularly important is the ability to overcome difficulties that test one's will, difficulties such as fear, disillusionment, boredom, loneliness, and failure.

4. Perseverance and composure, the ability to carry on, is imparted through tests that deliberately produce emotional wavering within the individual and present the opportunity of quitting, thus eliciting a spiritual struggle to carry on—for example, the endurance walk.

5. An individual's difficulties are believed to stem from incorrect attitudes. Therefore the training aims to teach the acceptance of necessity and responsibility.

Instead of fighting life's requirements, such as work, the most satisfactory attitude is to acknowledge and accept them as necessary parts of life.

6. The dimension of accepting/resisting is crucial to spiritual training. The individual is taught to display an accepting attitude to all of life's necessities, especially social responsibility. "The requirements of a social system and the interdependent quality of society, both of which make the diligent performance of every role important, are taught as the basic facts of life."[5]

To conclude, spiritual education aims to help the bank trainee achieve contentment by developing an ordered and stable psyche free from confusion and frustration. This is achieved through a gradual conquest of one's primitive self and by subordinating oneself to society. Spiritual education uses real events—experience—to attain this goal.

NATIONAL CULTURE, BUSINESS CULTURE, AND CORPORATE CULTURE

Let us restate our objectives.

Gaining access to another organization's backstage culture is an important task for managing international operations. One important technique for getting backstage is understanding the series of training experiences for people in that organization. Our extended case study—of the series of cultural trainings in Japan—illustrates the point that codes for behavior are progressively specified in national culture, business culture, and corporate culture. A child first learns ways of doing and understanding via childhood experiences (for example, the childhood games); these ideas are reinforced later in life (for example, by manga). After training in some professional culture, individuals may join an organization that further trains them in the corporate culture. (See Figure 3-1.)

Now we shall see how this series of cultural trainings fit together.

FIGURE 3-1

SERIES OF CULTURAL TRAININGS

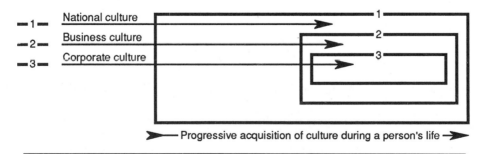

The Fit between Spiritual Education and Japanese Culture

So far, we have examined the bank's training program in isolation without trying to connect it to the Japanese society and culture of which it is a part. However, two of its main ideas—that the individual is insignificant, and that the individual realizes full potential only improving by the welfare of the group and society—are at the heart of the Japanese tradition.

Writing on Japan's managerial system, Yoshino explains how an approach so different from Western principles of management is nevertheless highly effective and efficient because it is congruent with Japanese culture.[6] In this view, the Confucian system of values underpins the system.

Great importance is attached to the collectivity. The individual cherishes membership in a group, and the group serves as the frame of reference for individual thoughts and actions.

An allied concept is *ie,* or house, which is an inseparable aspect of the family. The house has a head, and its members are blood relations of the head or unrelated persons who are part of the house through the head's consent. The house is in fact a name group, not a blood group. And the *ie* serves as the model for structuring all types of secondary groups; that is, unrelated individuals are to function together in harmony, as if they were kin.

Within the collectivity, absolute loyalty is stressed; duty comes first, and one must suppress personal feelings should they hinder fulfillment of one's duties. Complementary ideas—*giri* and *on,* obligation and benevolence—point to the obligation of those occupying superior positions in the hierarchy to be benevolent to their inferiors.

Compliance with this code is enforced by shame. Personal shame arises out of society's disapproval of one's behavior; "we-group" shame arises from bringing dishonor to one's collectivity. Since one is defined in terms of one's *ie*—one has no identity apart from it—the fear of being ostracized from the group compels conformity to group norms and values and striving for group goals. In turn, as long as the individual conforms to group norms, is loyal to the group, and is content with one's status in its hierarchy, the group bestows maximum security on the individual.

With these concepts in mind, the goals of the Japanese bank training program seem more appropriate. By socializing the trainees to regard themselves as immutably a part of the bank, management helps trainees become more committed to mutually sought goals.

The Incorporation of Japanese Cultural Concepts in Japan's Managerial System

The overall program of recruitment and training (including socialization into a corporate culture) jibes with the wider frame of reference that is the business culture. Some general features of Japan's managerial system are now considered.

- Central to Japanese business ideology is the emphasis on duty to the nation and service in the public interest as well as the profit motive.

- Management is heavily involved in the lives of the workers. One-third of the population has lifetime employment: guarantees against dismissal as well as regular wage or bonus increases to keep pace with the cost of living and the demands of a worker's growing family. Wide-coverage social security provisions for employees appeals to the mass of workers coping with the insecurity and isolation of urban life.

- Group-orientation: People are hired by age groups (cohorts). There is some competition among adjacent cohorts during the first five or so years; cohorts receive steady, small promotions and pay raises according to length of service.

    The homogeneity of Japan's managerial elite helps form groups; groups tend to be homogeneous in age, educational background, and work experience. (Forming groups in the United States requires harnessing the heterogeneous backgrounds of managers in a firm.)

    Organizational structure is defined and work is assigned to groups rather than to individuals. An organizational unit's responsibilities are defined only in very general terms due to the traditional view that a task should be performed through the cooperative effort of the members of the organization. Working together harmoniously to accomplish collective goals is more important than individual performance.

Some companies have recognized that ambitious young employees of outstanding ability feel frustrated by this strict regime. Some programs now permit more individual flexibility in relation to performance.

This brief account of Japanese business culture should be taken in the proper perspective. Individual Japanese firms such as Nissan and Mitsubishi have corporate cultures that differ significantly within the general frame of Japanese business culture, just as individual American firms such as IBM and Ford have significantly different corporate cultures within the general frame of American business culture.

Corporate Culture (the Japanese Bank's Training Program)

In the light of the admittedly rudimentary accounts of Japanese culture and business culture, the emphasis on spiritual training in the Japanese bank's training program should now be easier to grasp.

The Japanese managerial system relies on the internalization of the group's goals by every employee and on the ability of employees to work harmoniously to attain group goals. These values were originally taught in the traditional Japanese educational system, a system disbanded during the occupation. It now becomes necessary to reinforce values inherent in the culture and generally present in the business culture by means of active socialization in the spiritual training program. The training seeks to assure that the individual will make the best efforts possible on behalf of the group and leaves it to the individual to acquire the technical competence necessary to carry out activities implementing group goals.

CONCLUSION

Corporate educational systems specify and refine the more general behavioral codes of the business culture and the culture. Culture, at whatever level, is not static, but cumulative and changing. Japanese paternalism, lifetime employment, and absolute loyalty to a firm are by no means universal in Japan in the early 1990s due to greater unionization, changing global competitive conditions, industrial legislation, and the impact of Western firms. Corporate socialization programs must be revised to accommodate changes in the wider systems of culture.

WHAT IS EDUCATION?

Let us turn our attention to the educational environment facing the multinational corporation. The central point is that educational systems are culturally specific. Even when similar information is transmitted through education, as it commonly is in developed nations, the emphasis on educational materials differs according to different systems of cultural values. When ecological, technological, and productive requirements of societies differ, educational requirements vary accordingly. In general, educational systems must align with cultural assumptions about human behavior, about relationships between humans and the natural environment, and about relationships between humans and divinity. This principle must be heeded when nations change their educational systems and when corporations plan employee training programs.

Education and Socialization

The cultural process of education is best approached as a part of the broader process of an individual's socialization. Socialization is cultural learning. This instruction in what is socially defined as normal, right, effective, and efficient limits the range of variation of potential human actions. Some socialization is manifest: explicit, often verbal, and intended by the instructor. This process defines a range of variation of behavior that is socially permitted. Other socialization is latent: implicit, often nonverbal, often unintended by the instructor. What is learned in this process of latent socialization expands the range of variation of behavior to include a wider range of action known to be improper but possible. See Figure 3-2.

To Americans, for example, ripe apples are classified as an edible food. Unripe or rotten apples are classified as inedible: it is possible to eat them, but not proper to eat them. Beyond this wider range of variations are actions that are humanly possible but considered inhuman by persons in a culture. Most Americans, for example, consider roast snake neither edible nor inedible. Roast snake is not thought to be food that humans should even consider eating.

Agents of informal socialization are the family; peer groups; religious, legal, and political institutions; business; media; and art. The overall function of socialization is to instruct people with cultural understandings and orientations that are sufficiently shared to allow coordinated and predictable human activity.

FIGURE 3-2

SOCIALIZATION: VARIOUS LIMITS TO HUMAN ACTION

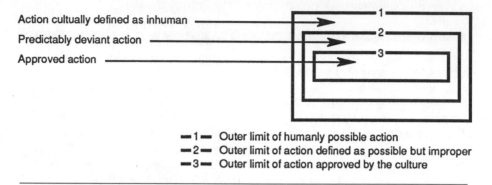

Action cultually defined as inhuman

Predictably deviant action

Approved action

— 1 — Outer limit of humanly possible action
— 2 — Outer limit of action defined as possible but improper
— 3 — Outer limit of action approved by the culture

Functions of Education in Relation to Economic Development

The *affiliative* function of education is social learning concerned with shared expectations for human behavior. There is a social distribution of knowledge in society. People in different occupational cultures have different expectations about one another's behavior. This kind of learning is imparted in every social institution in which the individual interacts.

The *instrumental* function of education is both economic and political. How to chart a career path and deal with the prevailing political-economic order is knowledge imparted both formally (through education) and informally (through social contacts). The mix of formal and informal education differs from society to society. When social relationships are organized mainly through kinship relations, then informal education is more prevalent. When social relationships are organized predominantly through contractual relations, then formal education is more prevalent. Regarding political education, societies differ in the mix of allegiance to the social givens of existence (religion, race, ethnicity, region, language) versus allegiance toward the more abstract collectivity, the nation.

The *figurative* function of education relates to what we shall call the recentering function of religion and values. (This topic is discussed in Chapter 5.) Emotional commitment to the abstract codes for behavior of society is not automatic. In traditional societies, religion, myths, and folklore are forms of knowledge that attempt to locate the role of humans in the universe. They convey a sense of tradition—that is, a connection between past, present, and future members of society. These forms of knowledge overcome the existential malaise that is so common in modern societies. They provide a sense of priorities (values) and ethics to guide the conduct of people in their daily affairs. Figurative, or mythopoetic, social learning is not absent in modern societies: Myths and heroes are presented in mass media drama and sports.

For the educational system to carry out its mission, the three functions must be integrated. When individuals have incorporated a consistent set of expectations that are both well motivated within the psyche and reinforced positively in social relationships, then coordinated, effective action is facilitated.

A comprehensive examination of a relatively well-integrated educational system on the national level would require a book in itself. Our four-step case study of Japanese childhood games, continuing education with comic books, professional training, and a Japanese corporation's training program may serve to illustrate a method of integrating these functions.

One society's method cannot be an overall model for another society. What constitutes appropriate education is a function of the objectives of a social entity given its natural and human endowments, its level of technical and economic development, and its ideology.

INTERNATIONAL DIFFERENCES IN EDUCATION

Education in Traditional Societies

Societies face the problem of how to bring up their children to become adequate adult members of society. Education in traditional societies is too frequently stereotyped as serving only to replicate the customs of the ancestors from one generation to the next, as inciting backward-looking traditionalism, and as lacking in formal methods of instruction.

To more accurately understand the impact of a particular society's educational system on economic development, we consider four variables.

- The educational system may be based on a science of the concrete or on a science of the abstract.[7]

- The educational system may be predominantly an oral tradition or predominantly literate.

- A traditional system may have been modified by the imposition of a colonial educational system.

- Current political ideology affects the potential of the system.

The Science of the Concrete and Systematic Knowledge

Western-educated persons often undervalue oral traditions with the stereotype that oral traditions are good for telling stories around campfires. This is a false view: Oral traditions transmit systematic knowledge with the format Levi-Strauss calls the *science of the concrete*. Oral traditions organize, preserve, and transmit knowledge by reference to clearly sensible (perceivable to the senses) attributes. Sailors in the state of Maine know that "red sun in the morning, sailor take warning; red sun at night, sailor's delight" is a concrete, sensible prescription to guide action in the absence of abstract measurements of climatic pressure, temperatures, and wind speeds. When farmers in northern Sri Lanka say "Plant long-tooth rice when the first rains come, plant it with care; plant short-tooth rice when long-tooth rice sprouts, scatter it roughly," they too are using the science of the concrete.

Classification of the world by concrete, sensible attributes allows experimentation. What difference if (hypothetically) the ancient Babylonians transmitted the formula for a certain type of pottery as "three parts red-horse clay to one part gray-mule clay" instead of proportions based on magnesium and aluminum oxides. The proof of the efficacy of the science of the concrete method of transmitting cultural knowledge is evident in the human inventions created well before the scientific method—that is, during the neolithic revolution: pottery, metalworking, domestication of plants and animals, and more.

It was not until the 17th century that widely impacting technological advances were made with a *science of the abstract*. This science differs from the *science of the concrete* in that it analyzes phenomena in terms of attributes that are not always perceivable to the unaided senses—classifying, for example, the internal properties of chemical elements and charting their physical interrelationships. This more recent science permitted the technological advances known collectively as the Industrial Revolution.

Non-Western Literate Traditions and Formal Educational Systems

A second factor regarding the potential of a country's educational system for economic development is the longevity and continuity of a literate educational system. In China and other Far Eastern countries, formal education and competitive examinations within kingdoms were the means of recruiting for the imperial bureaucracy. In practice, this system recruited only from the landed aristocracy. Literacy and the right to rule went hand in hand.

Writing facilitates the preservation of knowledge with greater accuracy and over a greater span of space and time. Even if the written tradition preserves knowledge of the science of the concrete variety rather than the abstract variety, systematizing knowledge and introducing alternative systems of thought become possible. There were 64 traditional sciences in India. Some correspond to modern sciences (medicine); others do not (dice playing). Nevertheless, systematic academic thought has been present for two millennia as in the Sankam (academy) of Tamilnad, South India.

In literate societies, the acquisition of modern sciences has undoubtedly been facilitated by these traditional sciences. Further, Western scientists have been learning (witness the Western use of acupuncture) the advantages of some of these ancient sciences. In sum, in regions where literate traditions and formal education have existed, potential for development should exceed that of previously nonliterate, non-academic regions.

Colonial Influences on Education

On the other hand, an existing educational system may hamper attempts to modernize society. In less-developed countries, educational systems were originally set up by colonial rulers. The languages used were foreign ones: Dutch, English, French, Portuguese, Spanish. Curricula were liberal because the goal was to train well-rounded natives who would occupy the lower ranks of the civil service. Parallel to this limited Western system was the indigenous (formal or informal) educational system that concentrated on traditional skills. Both systems are ill-adapted to the needs of modernization.

Even in countries where only one child in a thousand is likely to enter a university, the elementary and secondary levels tend to be distorted toward a linear curriculum that prepares its students solely for university entrance. The vast majority, who will not gain higher education, is ill-equipped to cope with the practical world. A direction of reform might imitate the model of Korean education. In South Korea, students take highly competitive examinations. Some students are tracked toward universities and others toward technical and practical skills needed in the work force.

Ideology and Education

Modification and development of educational systems may also involve ideological questions. School systems inherited from colonial times may unconsciously disseminate such elite values as disdain for manual labor and a benign acceptance of a social order in which glaring inequalities in the distribution of wealth are present. An important developmental goal for less-developed countries is to achieve minimum standards of living for the entire populace. It is necessary to instruct civil servants to empathize and help implement this goal.

Less-developed countries with large public sectors and state-owned productive facilities may be drawn to a similar politicization of education, especially in the management sphere. Bureaucrats who operate state enterprises need a sound business education if the enterprises are to work effectively. But the ideology of private entrepreneurship common in Western management education may not be appropriate for public servants—the more talented ones move to the private sector and start their own firms. Less-developed countries with large public sectors may then want to instill a sense of national purpose by combining some socialist ideology with business education.

Politicization of the education system reflects a choice between the state's interest and individual freedom. Certainly, less-developed countries have a choice between a command system of education and a market system. In a market system, educators choose what to teach and students choose what to learn. The command system is more restrictive but also more efficient: low cost, economies of scale, fewer teachers, fewer books. A command system can be more effective for targeting developmental goals. The mix of command system and market system of education should change during different phases of a country's socioeconomic development.

Differences in Formal Educational Attainment

The most obvious international difference in education is the extent of the educational attainment of the populace. A second difference is that the different educational mix of levels (primary, secondary, university) of educational training produces a different distribution of competencies at the university level. Different mixes of levels and of competencies are appropriate for societies at different stages of socioeconomic development.

The extent of formal education differs from country to country. Members of every culture are socialized into becoming adults with a role in their society. Formal education becomes necessary as a supplement to socialization when the society grows and becomes specialized and complex in its division of labor. Table 3-1 provides statistics on educational attainment around the world.

TABLE 3-1

ESTIMATED SCHOOL ENROLLMENT BY LEVEL OF EDUCATION (1985)

	Gross National Product Per Capita in 1986 Dollars	*Students Enrolled as a Percentage of Their Age Cohort*		
		Primary Education	*Secondary Education*	*Higher Education*
China	$ 300	124	39	2
India	290	92	35	NA
Other low-income countries* (37)	200	67	22	5
Middle-income countries** (34)	750	95	41	11
Industrial market economies (19)	1,890	102	93	39
High-income oil exporters (4)	6,740	86	56	11
Centrally planned economies (19)	12,960	102	92	27

Figures are greater than 100 percent when pupils older or younger than the standard age are attending school.

*This category corresponds to the UNESCO classification of least-developed countries.

**This category corresponds to UNESCO categories of less-developed countries and newly industrialized countries and advanced developing countries.

Source: *World Development Report, 1988* (World Bank, 1988): 222, 223, 280, 281.

During the 1960s, many less-developed countries expanded the facilities for formal education. Among industrial nations, where formal schooling has been available for some time, the trend is to increase the amount of time spent in schools. The range of educational attainment currently varies from a high rate of literacy in the United States to a high rate of illiteracy in Nepal. The distribution of educational attainment among the three levels of education is also significant: only in North America, Europe, and Oceania are about one-third of the total enrollments at levels beyond primary education. Total school enrollment all over the world has increased at a faster rate than has population. The biggest increases are observed in Africa and Asia, regions with many less-developed countries and very intensive efforts to spread education.

Considering the role of education in the world economy, Table 3-1 also differentiates five categories of countries. Classification into low-income, middle-income, and industrialized countries as well as oil-exporting and centrally planned economies gives more information than the ideologically charged classification of First, Second, and Third Worlds (for a complete listing of countries with gross national product information, see Appendix). We note one overall correlation between educational attainment and economic performance: the figures on students enrolled in secondary education as a percentage of their age cohort correlates with overall economic performance.

POLICY IMPLICATIONS: COUNTRY POLICIES REGARDING EDUCATION

Infrastructure for development is not limited to the quality and quantity of transportation, communications, and utilities facilities present in a country. Human resources developed through education are also part of infrastructure. In this section, we discuss country strategies regarding education policy.

The Concept of Functional Literacy

UNESCO has set up an educational program to help less-developed countries that wish to improve their educational systems. The unspoken premise is that formal education leads to economic development. The UNESCO program's major themes and objectives are as follows:

1. Functional literacy for adults.
2. Equal male-female access to education.
3. Training of middle- and higher-level personnel for development.
4. Democratization of secondary and higher education.
5. Transition from selection to guided choice in secondary and higher education.
6. Adaptation of education (both general and technical) to the needs of the modern world, especially in rural areas.

7. Development of educational research.

8. Preservice and inservice teacher training.

It is significant that the program concentrates on *functional literacy*. Literacy alone may not be very useful. Learning to read is all very well, but reading is a skill that can be quickly forgotten if not exercised frequently. Functional literacy is literacy geared to the daily lives of the students so that what they learn in the classroom is soon applied in their daily lives.

Functional literacy is a work-oriented literacy. It emphasizes the use of reading, writing, and arithmetic in daily life and work. Attaining literacy is thus combined with job instruction. A farmer first learns an agricultural vocabulary. Thus promoting literacy also aids industrial and agricultural development projects. In this vein, Ecuador has developed a "School for Everybody" almanac: the almanac features stories about the indigenous cultural heritage, charts showing how to tell a cow's age by its teeth, and so forth. Brazil's Mobral program is primarily an adult-education program for illiterate workers and peasants. Established in 1970, it is inexpensive to administer (about $10 per person) because of simple facilities—scanty classrooms—and committed teachers who work for low salaries. Classes are held in the evening, after the work day has ended. Because the aim of the program is increasing productivity in the fields and factories, the emphasis is on such practical matters as reading, counting change, and composing letters.

A key problem in developing literacy programs is language choice. Learning takes place best in the native language, but the languages of science and commerce are mostly European and Japanese. Educational programs must be bilingual for most less-developed countries, treading a thin line between nationalistic sensibilities and development imperatives (recall the discussion in Chapter 2).

The Optimal Education Mix

A. L. Peaslee argues that education gives impetus to economic development. Having analyzed historical data from what are now the more advanced nations, he examines the association of (1) ratios of elementary, secondary, and higher-education enrollment to total population and (2) levels of economic development. He relates the several levels of education to economic growth, with lags of 8–12 years. From this analysis he suggests a regime of educational investments (the optimum educational mix) likely to foster growth in developing nations.

Primary Education. "Among the first 35 countries in per capita gross domestic product in 1958, all but six had a record of 10 percent of their population in primary schools by 1920 or earlier."[8] (The other six had either reached this level by 1938 or have hovered around there since.) Further, "of the more than fifty countries that had not reached the over 10 percent point, only one—Colombia—had attained by 1958 production above $300."[9] Sustained growth generally starts when 30–50 percent of the school-age population (ages 5–14) are in primary school. Almost all nations that achieved high rates of primary enrollment were subsequently among the world leaders in production per capita.

Secondary Education. Secondary school enrollment has a growth impact only after an 8–10 percent primary enrollment ratio has been reached. Peaslee cites the example of India, which had 4.3 percent of its population in secondary schools in 1962, a level that compares favorably with many European countries; but India's primary enrollment covered only 6.2 percent of the population; India's per capita income in 1963 was only $76.

Higher Education. "The association of higher education enrollment ratios with subsequent growth in real income per capita (after more or less universal primary education has been established) is impressive.[10] He cites evidence from Kuznets, Colin Clark, Angus Maddison, and the U.N. World Economic Survey of 1961 as support for these findings.[11]

Educational Policy for Developing Nations

Peaslee's regime for an optimum education mix for developing nations requires local modifications in behavior patterns, capital formation, and natural resources.

> Thus, for an optimum mix, a policy framework for expansion of enrollment of an economically undeveloped country would begin with ten years' concentration on primary education, which hopefully could bring enrollment up from around 2 or 3 percent of the total population to over 10 percent. Then somewhere in the neighborhood of five years could be spent expanding secondary enrollment from about .5 to 2 percent. In the final ten years (while expansion was continued for primary and secondary enrollments), the emphasis could be focused on expanding university enrollments from say .075 to .3 percent. As far as education's impact on economic growth is concerned, the record of countries that have achieved development indicates that this type of enrollment expansion would be most conducive to increase in real income per capita.[12]

There are several practical difficulties with Peaslee's plan. First, work-force needs must be estimated from projected future levels of economic activity. Such projections are difficult because the level of activity is dependent on exogenous factors such as the growth of export markets or the quality of the monsoon. The work-force education plan must continually be revised, at least on an annual basis. Second, the plan makes sense only if a strict system that decides which students may continue in school is installed. Since education is an important path of upward social mobility, such a plan in effect would decide who would receive greater benefits of development. In multiethnic nations, this system can have serious political consequences if the method of decision is biased. Third, in practice, it is doubtful whether developing nations can wait for certain target levels of literacy to be reached before tackling higher levels of education. Rather, a work-force education plan must strike on several fronts. It must not solely rely on Western college preparatory schools at the secondary level but must establish vocational schools in areas responsive to the nation's developmental needs.

Adult education is another component of work-force planning. Adult education plays an increasingly important role in countries faced with a rapidly changing technological and social environment. As countries develop, workers may change jobs and require retraining.

A good model is Taiwan. Educational budgets are set in five-year plans attuned to economic development needs. Agricultural schools were advanced during one five-year period, technical schools during another. There is company involvement in education. On-the-job training is subsidized by tax rebates. Note that Taiwan is a small, controllable economy. Taiwan is about as large as a district in one of India's states. Larger nations, then, may wish to designate development regions with separate educational and development plans.

Host-Country Use of Foreign Firms and New Technology in Developing the Educational System.

Government-run schools are not the only vehicle for developing the educational system. On-the-job training is a valuable supplement to standard education. Company-sponsored continuing education programs benefit the state by saving government expenditures. Such education may be narrow in scope, but it is certainly appropriate education. While deciding on the technological process they will employ in the host country, the company can also plan for an employee training program that will support the processes. More advanced technology can be introduced in the future when employee skill level improved. Developing countries favor the progressive introduction of more advanced technology. The company is then practicing and not just preaching good corporate citizenship. There are benefits in both directions.

The Brazilian government enlists the aid of foreign firms to educate its citizens in technical and mechanical skills. Since 1966, companies with more than 100 employees must provide free primary education for workers and their children, either by maintaining schools of their own or by paying a payroll tax. Several multinational companies have responded to this scheme. For example, Volkswagen has set up an educational fund that provides loans for adult education. Massey-Ferguson imported an eminent geneticist to aid the Brazilian association of wheat farmers in developing a highly productive and plague-resistant strain of wheat. This firm also set up a center that trains farmers in the use and maintenance of farm equipment. By helping increase wheat production, Massey-Ferguson is creating a large market for its machinery. Commercial self-interest is combined with host-country interests.

Argentina has a well-developed technical school system. Six-year secondary schools grant technical certifications in such areas as chemistry, electronics, and mechanics. In addition, 90 mobile trade schools each teach a single trade. Each unit remains in one location for two or three years. When it moves on, its site is occupied by another unit teaching another trade.

Other schools have been established by corporations. Firms receive tax incentives and are encouraged to set up schools tailored to meet their needs. Employers avoid payroll tax by operating their own schools. All costs are covered by the firm. The curriculum is equally divided between general subjects and vocational training. IKA-Renault sponsors one school; its graduates are eligible to enter the university. Ford plans to offer university-level courses within its company school system. An advisory council composed of representatives of industrial organizations and trade union locals helps in promoting and planning technical education.

India is another large country with a pressing need for better education. A satellite TV program was used during the late 1970s to reach villagers. Most of the programs concentrated on agricultural development—teaching better farming methods and promoting cooperative movements in agriculture—and on family planning. This program aimed to build a common base of knowledge throughout a sprawling country. Corps of parateachers (relatively more educated villagers) helped implement the program. Satellite TV cuts the cost of communication. Satellite TV is a technology of education especially feasible for large populations. The greatest administrative problem is a lack of funds for programming.

Visual instruction is an important tool for educational development in developing countries because it is accessible even to illiterate persons and because it can be entrancing to the audience. Spitz Space Systems has developed an advanced form of planetarium that aids mass education in several developing countries. The astral projection system allows a viewer to be located at any point within 9.3 billion miles of the earth (normal planetaria locate the viewer at any point on the earth's surface); a computer-assisted system of film projectors and sound systems augments the presentation. Educational programs are adapted to the local cultural traditions. Education need not be dull.

The Brain Drain

The *brain drain* is a flow of highly trained personnel from developing nations to industrial nations. Small economies have trouble providing competitively priced jobs for all their educated personnel. The level of brain drain is debatable. A 1982 study by UNCTAD (U.N. Conference on Trade and Development) demanded compensation to developing nations who have lost such personnel and calculated that the losses be valued at billions of dollars annually. Countries receiving the educated migrants dispute the value. It is harder to deny that the migrants are among the most talented persons trained in developing countries; as such, their departure is a loss.

The situation has reversed in the Asian NICs (newly industrialized countries) of South Korea, Taiwan, Hong Kong, and Singapore. South Korea reported that the global recession in the early 1980s had a favorable impact on reversing the brain drain. Government officials formerly expected that 80 percent of the students who received training abroad (principally in the United States) would not return to the country; in recent years, the rate of loss has been closer to 20 percent. This is important because NIC industries had boomed during the 1970s due to cheap factory labor. More recently, other countries in the region, especially China, have stolen the most labor-intensive work. (For more details, see the first section of Chapter 6.)

Educational Policy for Industrialized Countries

The Optimal Education Mix for Developed Nations

A different regime is relevant for newly industrialized countries (the more advanced developing nations) and for fully industrialized countries. Such countries differ first in the percentage of the age group engaged in higher education. Within the 20–24 age group, enrollment is 43 percent of United States citizens, 19 percent of French citizens, 15 percent of Belgian citizens, 14 percent of Irish, Dutch, and British citizens, and 11 percent of German citizens. Could the United States afford to have that 43 percent of the 20–24 age group competing in the economy for jobs? Countries differ also in the distribution of the products of higher education. Over the last 20 years, the number of accountants and lawyers produced by the United States free-market education system has increased, while the number of engineers has declined. Over the same period, the trends in Japan are precisely the opposite. No wonder Japan is currently praised for the excellence of its basic manufacturing skills. Further differences can be seen in countries' strategies of research—an input into the educational system. This topic will be addressed in Chapter 6.

Industrial nations now face the prospect of restructuring industry in the face of global competition. The changing educational needs are now more profound than they were in the past. Previously, competition was defined domestically; thus the rate of competitive technological changes was less rapid than it is today. How is the burden of retraining to be accomplished? For a while the U.S. government addressed this problem with its program of Trade Adjustment Assistance. Under this program, industries significantly afflicted by international competition were granted funds ostensibly to retrain workers (and thus shift workers from declining to rising industries). Unfortunately, the funds were used primarily for extending unemployment benefits to workers fired or furloughed due to cutbacks in production. There is now greater awareness in federal circles of the need for a comprehensive industrial policy in which industries are to be targeted for development. A comprehensive educational policy is required to implement industrial policy.

Host-Country Use of Foreign Firms and New Technology in Developing the Educational System

Innovative educational schemes that enlist the aid of corporations are not restricted to developing countries. France passed a vocational training law in 1972 that provided for apprentice training and continuing education for workers, either in government centers or within companies at schools set up for this purpose. All companies with more than 10 employees must conform to this regulation. The apprentice program provides for a two-year contract. Employers must provide apprentices with a complete training course including on-the-job instruction and a minimum of 360 hours of classroom training. The apprentice has the same status as a regular worker; this program is open to primary school graduates aged 16–20.

All firms with more than 100 employees must also provide time off for continuing-education courses. Executives may receive time off for teaching. These programs are funded by a payroll tax; company expenses are tax deductions. Some resistance has arisen from union leaders, who feel the programs are instituted by management solely to increase productivity. Workers are sometimes reluctant to sign up because they originally hated school, because they are afraid of failing, or because they doubt whether their efforts will result in promotions and higher pay. Strategies for motivating workers must be improved if these programs are to be implemented successfully.

Sweden was one of the first industrial nations to institute such training programs. Here the initiative came from the trade unions, headed by Gosta Rehn. The Rehn plan created an autonomous agency that worked with government, industry, and labor unions. This agency made employment projections to assess future job redundancies and job opportunities in the economy. Projections were used in programs to retrain workers, promote their mobility, and help shift attitudes necessary for changing jobs and professions. As a result, despite industrial transformations, Swedish workers' skills, job satisfaction, and standard of living have improved.

England also has a training act to ensure an adequate supply of properly trained industrial personnel, improve the quality and efficiency of industrial training, and spread the cost of training among firms. Companies must take the initiative to set up training programs suited to their needs. Programs are evaluated by a board, and tax rebates may be allowed.

POLICY IMPLICATIONS: COMPANY POLICY REGARDING EDUCATION

Multinational corporations directly educate persons affiliated with the organization and indirectly educate persons when they support host-government educational programs. We now address six major points about company educational policy.

Impacts of Education on the Corporation

Educational levels affect the quality of people available for employment; hence they partially determine efficiency and productivity. To Farmer and Richman, educational levels affect virtually every aspect of managerial and industrial life. In particular, they bear on the entire staffing function, the size of industrial enterprises and their overall organizational structures, degrees of decentralization, degrees of specialization, types of processes, techniques and technology used, costs of production, and overall productivity of firms and their management.[13]

Corporate Training as Innovation

Although the purpose of a corporation's direct educational program for workers or managers is to facilitate relationships within the firm, the corporation should remember that to be effective, such education should take account of the previous socializations experienced by the individual. As we observed in Chapter 1, every individual undergoes cultural socialization, and many undergo business culture socialization. From the point of view of the employees, their corporate education is an innovation. Innovations are communicated well when they do not go strongly against the grain of the recipient's previous orientations.

Selection, Training, and Monitoring Systems

In formulating corporate educational policy, the corporation should also decide on its goals: Whether training workers or managers, is the corporation trying to impart just technical skills, or is it also attempting to socialize employees into the corporate culture. All corporations must coordinate and control the activities of their employees, and each must decide how much to invest in each of the related processes of selection, training, and monitoring of employees. Added expense in selection and training may reduce the expense of monitoring workers.

Emphasis on selection and training may be termed *cultural control*. Recall the example (in the introduction to Part I) of the Mersk company whose fine coordination of activities under diverse and stressful conditions is made possible by a strong program of selection and training. Because they share understanding, even at a distance, close monitoring of activities is not very important.

Emphasis on monitoring activities may be termed *bureaucratic control*. Many companies rely on strict policy and formalized reporting procedures that permit standardized accounting for performance of units located in various countries. This regime has its costs: lessened responsiveness to unique cultural conditions. This outcome is hardly surprising, given that the grid of policy and reporting procedures constructed to apply to conditions in the home country is less applicable abroad.

Adaptation of Training Techniques

Remembering that all workers are socialized in their culture even if they are not formally educated, some worker-training techniques must be adapted for use in world regions where formal education is not highly developed. Learning by observation and imitation is a more highly developed art in less-developed nations. Training programs can profit from this resource. Demonstration laboratories can be set up on the shop floor. Master machinists can demonstrate the use of machines rather than instruct via abstract drawings or textbooks. Learning occurs in the situation, not from the rote learning of abstract propositions. Further, innovations can more easily be communicated in the native language. For initial training in technical skills, learning in the native language prevents misunderstandings. Using culturally specific analogies, connections can more easily be made. For more advanced training in technical skills and for corporate socialization, training can shift to the corporate language.

Government Requirements

Multinational corporations resident in developed countries may face both nationalism and national requirements for employee retraining, as in the previously cited cases of England and France. The company may choose to have centralized locations for training employees from many countries or it may send instructors to the various subsidiaries. This choice should reflect the mixture of goals of education (technical skills and corporate socialization). If technical skills are the major objective, the education system can be decentralized, with instructors sent to the subsidiaries. If a global corporate culture is an aim, and if the company prefers to control activities not just bureaucratically but by having employees share cultural understandings and expectations, then centralized training may be effective (and efficient due to economies of scale). The scale of such training programs can be staggering. Almost every day of the year, 5,000 persons are engaged in training programs run by IBM of Europe.

Training and Reward Systems

Training programs should be established with reward systems in mind. Reward systems should also recognize the impact of the individual's socializations before he or she entered the firm. Despite its desire for consistency, corporate headquarters may wish to modify reward systems in foreign operations.

American firms generally use economic rewards (bonuses, stock options) and noneconomic rewards (autonomy, responsibility, and opportunities for psychological growth). The manager's job in America is high paying, insecure, and competitive; the payoffs from success are high. Such rewards are feasible in the context of the American value system of individualism, competition, and materialism.

In Japan, by contrast, there is greater valuation of the collectivity, of fulfilling one's duties as a member of a group, of competition of the group vis-à-vis other groups. These are key Japanese values. Duty comes first, and putting personal feelings above one's duties is viewed with contempt.[14] With these values, longer term evaluation and reward by seniority as well as performance is more appropriate.

Summary

Let us relate this discussion of company policies on education to the three stages of intercultural management. The first stage is environmental assessment (see Chapter 7). In different business situations, the relationship between headquarters and its subsidiaries or the relationship between a provider of service and international clients may call for different cultural policies on the part of top management.[15] Having formulated an appropriate cultural policy (recall Chapter 1), it is necessary to implement the policy. A corporation's policies regarding selection, training, and monitoring of workers and managers are among the techniques used to implement its cultural policy.

QUESTIONS

1. What is the relationship between education and socialization?

2. Would any elements of the Japanese bank training program be successful in the United States? Why or why not? Should a United States firm in Japan adopt Japanese managerial practices? Why or why not?

3. Obtain some statistics for the period 1960–1990 on the involvement of women in education in some LDCs and NICs such as Morocco, Nigeria, India, and South Korea. Examine whether this can be related to trends in growth of GNP per capita.

4. Discuss the relationship between colonialism and the educational systems of many developing countries.

5. Why does educational performance (as measured by literacy rates) correlate so closely with level of economic development?

6. What is functional literacy, and why do so many developing countries emphasize it?

7. How do host countries use foreign firms to contribute to their educational programs?

8. What problems face multinational firms when entering host countries that have low educational achievement? How can firms respond to these shortcomings in the host countries?

9. What effects do you think that satellite TV will have on educational practices in less-developed countries?

10. Is there an educational elite in the United States? Is it growing or diminishing in importance? How powerful is it?

11. Various Japanese companies now send their employees to week-long camps that reinforce the skills of upper-level executives; people relearn how to pay attention to detail and relearn the importance of humility. Executives pledge to correct their shortcomings. They are given ribbons of shame, which are removed only after they pass rigid tests (only 30 percent pass all the tests). The day starts at five in the morning with calisthenics and ends at nine at night with testing. Throughout the 13-day ordeal, trainees are told that management is getting weak and losing sight of goals: quality and excellence of employees as well as product. [Richard Phalon "Hell Camp," *Forbes* (January 1984): 56–68.]

    Compare the impact on employees of a training program that strives for quality and excellence of employees as well as product with quality improvement programs that focus mainly on external performance: "Quality is Job 1" or "Satisfy the Customer!"

Discuss the notion that a company should not only educate their personnel to perform in ways the company desires but should also treat their personnel like customers.

12. You are consulting for the Ministry of Education of a small Third-World country that achieved independence from a colonial power in 1947. A colonial education system exists alongside the indigenous one. The country wants to design three five-year plans to develop their educational system. The World bank will grant the country $20 million at the beginning of each five-year period. For each five-year period, state what percent of the grant would you allocate toward

a. Elementary education
b. Technically oriented secondary education
c. College preparatory secondary education
d. College and post-graduate education
e. Adult education and worker training

ENDNOTES

1. Thanks to Elizabeth Miley, B.A., Michigan State University, for her work on manga. Other references: Beth Hughes, "Japanese Comics Causing Big Blast in American Market," *Minneapolis Star Tribune* (March 23, 1988); Bruce Irving, "Mad About Manga," *Northwest* (March 1988): 30, 55, 61; Shotaro Ishinomori, *Japan Inc.* (Berkeley, CA: University of California Press, 1988); Frederick Schodt, *Manga! Manga! The World of Japanese Comics* (Tokyo: Kodansha, 1986).
2. Thomas P. Rohlen, "Spiritual Education in a Japanese Bank," *American Anthropologist* 75, no. 5 (October 1973): 1542–1562.
3. Ibid., 1543.
4. Ibid., 1555.
5. Ibid., 1558.
6. M. Y. Yoshino, *Japan's Managerial System, Tradition and Innovation* (Cambridge, MA: M.I.T. Press, 1968), passim.
7. Claude Levi-Strauss, *The Savage Mind* (Chicago: University of Chicago Press, 1966).
8. A. L. Peaslee, "Education's Role in Development," *Economic Development and Cultural Change* 17, no. 3 (April 1969): 293–318.
9. Ibid., 294.
10. Ibid., 299.
11. Ibid., 302.
12. Ibid., 305.
13. Richard N. Farmer and Barry M. Richman, *Comparative Management and Economic Progress* (Homewood, IL: R. D. Irwin, 1965), 65.
14. M. Y. Yoshino, *Japan's Managerial System, Tradition and Innovation* (Cambridge: M.I.T. Press, 1968), passim.
15. Kenneth David, "Planning the Project," in Thomas L. Brewer, Kenneth David, and Linda Lim, *Investing in Developing Nations: A Guide for Executives* (New York: Praeger, and Washington, D.C.: Overseas Private Investment Corporation, 1986), 30–50.

CHAPTER FOUR
Religion

In this chapter, we are concerned with the impact of religion on polity and economy and policy implications for international business management. Religion has relevance to human activities. Lucy, a character from the Peanuts cartoon series says, "I believe in the goodness of mankind. And if you believe...[as she watches a rowdy fight between two children and Snoopy]... who needs proof?"

In other words, things believed true are true in their consequences. Stated more formally,

> From the standpoint of pure reason the absurdity of religion is undeniable, [for we are] reducing *all phenomena referring to a non-empirical reality ...* to one category, *the religious.*
>
> When we call it an absurdity the term is not used in a pejorative sense. *The unprovable is not by definition untrue or irrelevant ....* Once we accept the absurdness of the situation we are cautioned, cautioned not forthwith to reject religion as an illusion, but to concede that apparently we are up against something very important.[1] [Emphasis added.]

We must not make too little of religion. Religion is something very important. After all, for thousands of years, great events have been mobilized in the name of religion: Christian Crusades, Islamic conquests, the settlement of American colonies by dissenting religious groups. When religious motivation is aroused, significant social mobilization is possible. International managers are concerned with disruptive political changes in a foreign society. Every social movement begins with civil discontent. A movement becomes volatile when it is accepted by the followers as divinely justified. The overthrow of the Shah of Iran began with civil discontent. The movement became mobilized in the name of Islamic fundamentalism. One objective of this chapter is to note, for different religions, the potential of religious figures and institutions for mobilizing social movements or for stemming the rise of social discontent.

Certainly, religion is a mainspring of culture. In any culture, some reference to an unprovable order of reality (divinity, historical dialectic, nationalism) justifies patterns of authority and patterns of equal or unequal exchange among the members of society. Educational systems, political organization, and social relations such as the role of women are all significantly affected by a society's religion. We can speak of Buddhist or Christian or Hindu art, and of the absence of Muslim representational art.

Religion also has an impact at the practical level of the business firm.[2] Religious seasons always affect consumer demand. The international firm must know which seasons are coming up and how they will affect business.

On the other hand, we must not make too much of religion in the sense of expecting to predict macroeconomic patterns from the sole fact of a society's religion. Early studies, such as Weber's connections between religious dogma and movement toward (or resistance to) capitalism,[3] must be viewed with some caution. Religion is not the unique explanation. If this-worldly religions such as Protestantism always incite capitalism, and otherworldly religions always resist capitalism, then the predominantly Protestant United States has nothing to fear competitively from countries such as Japan and South Korea, countries that adhere to a supremely otherworldly religion, Buddhism, as well as to a this-worldly religion, Confucianism.

Since Weber wrote early in the twentieth century, anthropologists have learned to distinguish the transcendental Great Traditions of the major world religions from the pragmatic Little Traditions of these same religions.[4] Weber's overall descriptions of a this-worldly religion, Protestantism, as opposed to otherworldly religions, Hinduism or Buddhism, relate to the Great Traditions of these religions. We must be cautious about predicting macroeconomic consequences from the direction of dogma in the Great Tradition, for Great Traditions most strongly affect the relatively small group of religious virtuosos such as renouncers, ascetics, and monks. Little Traditions are localized beliefs that condition the orientations and practices of the vast majority of the population.

Both traditions are of relevance to the international manager. The Great Tradition is important for understanding major ideas and events that affect business operations. For example, scheduling production during the Hindu Tai Ponkal festival is as bad an idea as scheduling production during the Christmas festival. The Little Tradition of a community can also have a powerful impact on a firm's operations. A foreign firm in Sri Lanka did quite poorly because its major retail outlet was located next to an ancient, gnarled tree known to be the residence of a fearsome demon.[5] As the following focus case shows, understanding a country's religion is one key to understanding events that may affect business operations.

WHAT IS RELIGION?

To understand the motivations and priorities of a society's people, one must understand their religion. *Religion is a socially shared set of beliefs, ideas, and actions that relate to a reality that cannot be verified empirically yet is believed to affect the course of natural and human events.* Because such belief conditions people's motivations and priorities, it affects their actions. All religions deal with certain generic problems: (1) problems of meaning, (2) problems of motivation, (3) problems of social conflict, and (4) problems of skepticism.

FOCUS CASE:
Confucianism, Education, and Student Extremism in South Korea[6]

In the wake of business success of Far Eastern countries, success certainly aided by very strong educational systems, the connection between the Confucian tradition and education has drawn attention. The South Korean version stands out for its particularly strong sense of education's moral and political importance. Both student protests and genuine input from academics to certain directions of government policy testify to the impact of education in South Korea.

Neo-Confucianism, a stricter and more moralistic interpretation, developed early in the Yi Dynasty (1382–1910); it was used to centralize the country and cast an aura of legitimacy on a new dynasty that had just overthrown the previous one. Critics of the post–Korean War regimes note a parallel with anticommunist and nationalist indoctrination both inside and outside classrooms.

Neo-Confucianism of the Yi period was a universal system of principles—tying together education, morality, and social ethics—with political underpinnings. By this system, the highest possible goal for each student would be to serve in the government. The fiercely competitive, highly centralized examination system for scholar-officials in the Yi Dynasty has a modern counterpart in the annual nationwide university entrance exams in which students compete for places at Seoul National University.

Much power was vested with the *yangban* (educated) class, some of whom were public officials. Even those scholars not holding office regularly marched through the streets with petitions to the court that criticized ranking officials or royal decrees. Provincial yangban also set up academies from which they criticized local officials as well as the central government. What is central to the situation was the religious and moralistic tone of political criticism, for, as William Henthorn wrote in his history of the country, the yangban style of political action *"was not lacking in religious overtones, and it was carried out with all the intensity and self-conviction of a holy war."* Again, there is a modern parallel. In recent years, students have continued to influence the flow of political debate, forcing the government to respond to their demands through increasingly uncontrollable campus demonstrations. International media have publicized the violent confrontations between students and armed forces on some of these occasions. What is not publicized (as Kenneth David noted when a visit to colleagues at Seoul National University coincided with a peaceful student demonstration in 1982) is that the government employs the moral authority of professors to help moderate these protests: Professors are required to attend and watch the student protests.

Problems of Meaning

Religious ideas provide "answers" to unanswerable problems of meaning: ignorance, suffering, and injustice.

The Zande people of eastern Africa can explain rationally that a wooden granary can collapse if the timbers have been eaten by termites. They can well understand that a person might rest under the granary as shelter from the mid-day sun. But they (or anyone) cannot explain why these two explicable chains of causality overlapped in time. They cannot explain why the granary collapsed just when that person rested under it.[7]

The unfortunate event presents a problem of ignorance (why did it happen?), a problem of suffering (why did my friend have to die?), and a problem of injustice (why did such a good person die instead of the thief who lives next door?).

The religious solution to these problems is to refer to an imagined, unverifiable order of reality endowed with power to affect events. The Zande people call this power witchcraft; Westerners call it the will of God, or fate, or fortune. Different unverifiables for different folks.

Problems of Motivation

Religious thought and action help people deal with the difference between what they want to do and what society expects them to do.

Aggressive behavior is forbidden in the Ifaluk atoll in Micronesia. Ifaluk has a high population density, 250 people living in one-half square mile. The inhabitants have no place to go to let off steam. They have no intoxicating drinks to help them forget their problems. Religion provides an outlet for aggression. Ghosts on Ifaluk are hateful creatures, the cause of all misfortunes. Periodic-ally, the inhabitants hold a ritual during which people are allowed to violently smash objects representing the ghosts.[8]

Problems of Social Conflict

Religious thought and action help contain conflicts stemming from the unequal distribution of power, prestige, or material wealth in society.

When the Incas conquered the Peruvian highlands, they co-opted features of the local religion in order to avoid recognition that they were appropriating goods from the highlanders. The highland villagers traditionally cultivated one farm plot collectively, with ritual and festivity. The produce from this plot was offered to their village god. The Inca colonials proclaimed the high god of the Incas was the older brother of the village god. In the highland tradition, younger brothers give gifts to older brothers. Henceforth, the produce of this plot was to be given to the high god of the Incas. You can't fool all of the people all of the time, but the Incas faced far fewer highland rebellions than did the next conquerors, the Spanish. The Spanish made no pretense of justifying their ap-propriations. They uprooted the highlanders and settled them in large haciendas.[9]

Problems of Skepticism

Religious thought and action help people with the leap of faith—in order for them to believe that a powerful though unverifiable reality does exist. Because the powerful reality is unverifiable, humans are skeptical. To incite belief, religions devise socially understood means of communicating with that order of reality. Despite the variety of unverifiable orders (single god, many gods, spirits, etc.), religions have a similar method of communication: mediation.

In the ordinary sense, mediation refers to a party who is neutral to both sides of a conflict—for example, a mediator of conflict between labor and management. In the religious sense, however, a mediator is a figure who is part of ordinary, everyday reality and part of the unverifiable reality. In the New Testament, Jesus of Nazareth is referred to both as the Son of Man and as the Son of God. In other religions, diviners elicit information from the beyond and communicate it to humans. Shamans are possessed by the beyond.

Let us retrace our steps. Human problems are "solved" by reference to a powerful but unverifiable order of reality. Belief in that reality is incited by the process of communication called mediation. Once the religious system is established, it is the final point of reference for a culture's shared system of values, which in turn affect human behavior.

INTERNATIONAL DIFFERENCES IN RELIGION

Religions in the World

Because religion has some impacts on a society's economic performance and political organization but operates mainly through the culture's system of values, the focus of this section is descriptive. That is, we will present a broad picture of major world religions and the general correlations of religions with economic performance. More details on the impact of religion will be examined in the following chapter on values.

The *World Christian Encyclopedia*[10] is the first census of all religions on Earth. As is shown in Table 4-1, the global composition of adherents has been shifting drastically during this century and, if the author's projections are accurate, should continue to do so.

Each nation has a unique religious profile. Banks and Textor classify countries into fourteen categories of religious configurations.[11] A detailed country-by-country survey is beyond the scope of this book.

Nor is a survey of all religions possible. We will discuss the five major religious traditions whose adherents (according to Table 4-1) represent three-quarters of the world's population: Buddhism, Christianity, Hinduism, Islam, and the nonliterate religions listed as folk, tribalist, and shamanist in the table. Thirteen of the fourteen categories identified by Banks and Textor involve only these five religions, either singly or in combination. The omission of religions such as Judaism, Parsi,

TABLE 4-1

ADHERENTS IN MILLIONS AND AS A PERCENTAGE
OF THE WORLD POPULATION

	Year 1900		*Year 1980*		*Year 2000 (est.)*	
Literate religions						
Buddhism	127	7.84%	274	6.29%	359	5.73%
Christianity	558	34.44%	1,433	32.90%	2,020	32.27%
Roman Catholic	272	16.79%	809	18.58%	1,169	18.67%
Protestant &						
Anglican	153	9.44%	345	7.92%	440	7.03%
Eastern Orthodox	121	7.47%	124	2.85%	153	2.44%
Other	12	0.74%	155	3.56%	258	4.12%
Hinduism	203	12.53%	583	13.39%	859	13.72%
Judaism	12	0.74%	17	0.39%	20	0.32%
Islam	200	12.35%	723	16.60%	1,201	19.19%
New religions	6	0.37%	96	2.20%	138	2.20%
Other*	13	0.80%	17	0.39%	61	0.97%
Nonliterate religions						
Chinese folk religion	380	23.46%	198	4.55%	158	2.52%
Tribalist &						
shamanist	118	7.28%	103	2.37%	110	1.76%
Nonreligious & atheist	3	0.19%	911	20.92%	1,334	21.31%
World population	1,620	100.00%	4,335	100.00%	6,260	100.00%

*including Sikh, Confucian, Shinto, Baha'i, Parsi

Source: *World Christian Encyclopedia,* Oxford University Press, 1983.

(Two thirds of the 1,010-page World Christian Encyclopedia consists of detailed statistics on all religions, country by country. International managers may wish to consult this volume as they consult international statistical yearbooks on trade, labor, and such.)

Confucianism, and (as it has many aspects of a religion) Communism would be inappropriate in a volume on comparative religion, but this is not such a text. We will begin with a look at the so-called nonliterate religions.

Nonliterate Religions

The term nonliterate religion is chosen rather than a variety of terms such as animism, spiritism, tribal religion, or folk religion. The term is accurate because such traditions are transmitted orally. Despite an immense variety of forms of non-literate religion, a family resemblance is present. Nonliterate religions are religions in which the transcendental power is imagined to reside in observable, natural phenomena, in spirits, or in a transcendental force (as popularized in the *Star Wars* movies) known in various societies as Mana or Wakanda. These powerful objects, spirits, or forces are held to aid or afflict humans. They are within reach of human supplication or coercion.

Figure 4-1 lists 31 countries where a significant component of religious life is a nonliterate religion. Most of these countries are in sub-Saharan Africa; five are in Latin America. In both areas, nonliterate traditions are mixed with Catholicism or Protestantism. The only Asian country represented is Laos, where Buddhism is the official state religion.

FIGURE 4-1

POLITIES WITH SIGNIFICANT COMPONENT OF NONLITERATE RELIGION

Bolivia	Ecuador	Laos	Sierra Leone
Burundi	Ethiopia	Liberia	South Africa
Cameroon	Gabon	Malagasy Republic	Sudan
Central African	Ghana	Mali	Tanzania
Republic	Guatemala	Niger	Togo
Chad	Guinea	Nigeria	Uganda
Congo	Haiti	Peru	Upper Volta
Dahomey	Ivory Coast	Rwanda	Zaire

Source: Arthur S. Banks and Robert B. Textor, *A Cross-Polity Survey* (Cambridge, MA: M.I.T. Press, 1963), FC56.

This geographical picture is misleading because nonliterate traditions are a component of all religions.

The Little Traditions of both Hinduism and of Buddhism in Sri Lanka, for example, include varieties of spirits, ghosts, demons, and fierce gods who have been incorporated into the lower ranges of the respective divine pantheons. Hindu and Buddhist villagers in Sri Lanka practice an integrated peasant religion in which higher, purer gods are called on (by means of devout, pure offerings in temples) to coerce the lower, less-pure gods to control the ghosts or demons who are afflicting the worshiper. Many peasant Christian traditions treat saints in ways similar to the lower ranges of the Buddhist and Hindu pantheons.

The Japanese Shinto religion celebrates mountains, rock formations, springs, rivers, and islands thought to have immanent power. Powerful healing springs are also venerated by Roman Catholic Christians (Lourdes in France and Saint Anne de Beaupré near Quebec) and by Hindus (Keerimalai in northern Sri Lanka). The Tao of the Taoist religion of China resembles the Wakanda force of North American Indian religions or the Mana force of Melanesian religions.

Notions of sympathetic magic are not restricted to primitive or peasant people. One form of sympathetic magic is contagious magic where things once together continue to affect one another. Sorcerers, for example, use a strand of a man's hair to afflict him. Similarly, bowlers use "body English" to correct the path of a wayward bowling ball.

Elements of Nonliterate Religion

Ancestor Worship. Apart from the Buddhist doctrine of no-soul, *anatta,* all religions believe that human souls exist after death. Nonliterate religions and literate religions alike include beliefs that souls are still part of the environment and are capable of influencing human events. Their actions are most typically defined as benevolent. However, if the living refuse to honor them, they are likely to be dangerous and harmful. Ancestral spirits may become part of very mundane events.

> Among the Lugbara the dead remain an integral and important part of the social structure, and their role is little changed from that of a living lineage elder. Their personalities do not appreciably worsen, and they are not the objects of general fear that they are in many societies. The only social significance of their death is that by dying they gain the power to bring sickness to rebellious kinsmen and become, thereby, the ultimate sanction for proper lineage behavior. Lineage elders may invoke certain ghosts when their authority is challenged, or ghosts may voluntarily interfere to right an injustice, but usually do so in response to the grumblings of the offended.[12]

> Among the Plateau Tongas of East Africa, individuals are supposed to have several spirits, or mizimu, which are liberated at the time of death. Some mizimu are associated with a person's maternal kin while others are associated with one's paternal kin. By continuing to pay more attention to the maternal mizimu than to the paternal mizimu, the Tongas emphasize matrilineality over patrilineality.[13]

It is sometimes suggested that ancestor worship implies a strong conservatism and orientation to tradition because adherents feel it is safer to behave as the ancestors did than to do new or different things. From these accounts, it should be clear that ancestor worship is very closely tied to the preindustrial social structure. When workers or managers move into a different social structure, such as an industrialized urban setting, continued reverence for ancestors does not automatically imply a traditional orientation.

Spirit Worship and Magic. Spirit worship is the attribution of existence and power to nonhuman objects such as animals, trees, rocks, and rivers. Humans do not so much worship natural spirits as feel a harmonious connection between themselves and these natural phenomena. This orientation to nature does not, however, preclude a very pragmatic orientation to changing human events. Witness the speech by Chief Sealth (Seattle) in 1854, when the tribal assembly was preparing to sign treaties with the whites who were settling the area near Seattle.

The Great Chief in Washington sends word that he wishes to buy our land. The Great Chief also sends us words of friendship and good will. This is kind of him, since we know he has little need of our friendship in return. But we will consider your offer. For we know that if we do not sell, the white man may come with guns and take our land.

How can you buy or sell the sky, the warmth of the land? The idea is strange to us. If we do not own the freshness of the air and the sparkle of the water, how can you buy them?

Every part of this earth is sacred to my people. Every shining pine needle, every sandy shore, every mist in the dark woods, every clearing and humming insect is holy in the memory and experience of my people. The sap which courses through the trees carries the memories of the red man. The white man's dead forget the country of their birth when they go to walk among the stars. Our dead never forget this beautiful earth, for it is the mother of the red man. We are part of the earth and it is part of us. . . .[14]

From the outsider's view, the connection between humans and their nature is sometimes perceived as a false science, a magical manipulation of natural phenomena and spirits imagined to have power over human events. Humans tend to want to explain events in their lives. We may recall that Western civilization has posited a series of explanations for the unfortunate event called illness. In Elizabethan days, the humours caused it. Later, glands caused it. Now biologists know that microbes and toxins and viruses cause it.

Cause-and-effect relationships have been updated to apply to modern products and techniques. During Vern Terpstra's years in Zaire, he observed the persistence of such beliefs. Along with modern educational activity, traditional witchcraft was practiced. European products often received a magical interpretation. For example, a number of Africans affected the wearing of glasses. Because many Europeans wore glasses, it was felt that the wearing of glasses enhanced the intelligence of the wearer. For another example, dispensaries established by Europeans were successful in replacing the witch doctor because the white people's medicines, especially penicillin, were better magic than the *dawa* of the witch doctor. Some consumer-goods marketers in Africa have not hesitated to imply that possession of their products gives magical qualities to the owners. Of course, the same is true for some marketers of health and beauty care products on American television.

Business Implications of Nonliterate Religions

The previous discussion allows us to modify the general Western view that peoples adhering to nonliterate religions are tradition bound and conservative. The point is to understand the logic of their beliefs and learn how to work with it. Recalling the introductory comments on the functions of religion in general, we note that spirits have social purposes. For example, most people have a tendency to express fear and hostility at technological change. In nonliterate religions, spirits are an idiom for expressing fear and hostility. In the following account, Hawaiian beliefs in curses were forwarded as an explanation of truck accidents at a construction site.

Herbert Ikeda, president of the Pacific Truckers Association, said there were strange goings-on at the construction site, Kalaepohaku, an ancient Hawaiian burial ground. The problems began Monday when truckers began hauling dirt to a little valley where workmen were building a baseball field for the Roman Catholic college. A truck sent to pick up a water hose was involved in an accident. A second truck overturned. When a third truck overturned Thursday, the construction crew vowed not to return to work until the site was blessed.

Ikeda asked church officials for permission to bring a kahuna to the ground to lift the curse. A kahuna, Hawaiians believe, possesses secret knowledge passed from generation to generation which enables him to be a prophet, priest, and doctor.

When Ikeda couldn't locate a kahuna, the church offered to help. The Rt. Rev. Msgr. Charles A. Kekumano, who is of Hawaiian ancestry, went to the site early Friday. He sprinkled holy water on the ground and said prayers in both Hawaiian and English. The workers returned to their jobs.[15]

People want explanations for unfortunate events. The Hawaiian workers walked off their jobs, convinced after three truck accidents that the construction site for Chaminade College was jinxed. Explanations for unfortunate events are culturally specific. The workers asked their boss to locate a Hawaiian kahuna to lift the curse, but settled for the services of a Roman Catholic monsignor and went back to work.

Are Americans immune from expressing fear and hostility at technological change? They treat machines in human or animistic terms.

Many Laurel and Hardy movies dramatically express aggression at a technological change that was then sweeping the country. Laurel and Hardy very frequently smashed up automobiles. Charlie Chaplin waged war against the assembly line in the movie *Modern Times.*

More recently, both awe and fear have been expressed toward the computer. In companies, access to computers has become a sign of greater power in decision making. In order to justify decisions that have already been made privately, computer printouts are used as if they possessed more-than-human authority. Fear of computers is represented in very animistic terms: there are "bugs" in a program. Computers are personified. Computer manufacturers attempt to overcome consumers' fear of computing by inventing software that is "user-friendly."

Technologically advanced societies are by no means free of beliefs and fears that are similar to those commonly ascribed to "primitive" peoples.

The lesson for international managers is to reject the view that what *they* do is weird and irrational but what *we* do is necessarily practical and rational. The manager must learn their logic and work with it.

Hinduism

I find that someone like me lives in two worlds—the world of international business and modern technology, and the world of yesterday.

Prakash Lal Tandon, Indian executive

Geographically, Hinduism is easily located. Hindus comprise almost 85 percent of the population of India. Other long resident Hindu populations are in Bali and in northern Sri Lanka. In the course of British colonial rule, Hindus migrated west to the eastern and southern edges of Africa, to the Caribbean, and east to various Southeast Asian countries such as Malaysia and Fiji. After the emergence of new nations in Africa, many Hindus migrated to the United Kingdom. According to the *World Christian Encyclopedia,* there are over 583 million Hindus.

Although Hinduism is popularly identified with the Aryan civilization of northern India, it is more accurately described as the confluence of two civilizations. The Indian subcontinent is the meeting place of the Aryan invaders from the west (Persia) and the indigenous Dravidian civilization of southern peninsular India. Both civilizations assimilated and codified local and regional Little Traditions of nonliterate religions. They borrowed from one another. The bewildering variety of practices that is Hinduism is the result of thousands of years of assimilation of religious practices from a variety of sources.

Because it reflects social practices, Hinduism differs from region to region, class to class, rural illiterates to urban intelligentsia. There are few beliefs or institutions common to all Hindus. The great dynastic temples, for example, are mainly found in the south of India. Wheat is a sacred food in the north, rice in the south. Almost every belief considered basic to Hinduism has been rejected by one group or another. Even the near-universal veneration of cows and the prohibition of eating beef is violated in the Tantric tradition. Hinduism, then, does not have a singular, identifiable creed but a set of creeds that bear some family resemblance.

Elements of Hinduism

We shall note a few elements of Hinduism to give a flavor of its orientations and priorities.

The Hierarchy of Natural Substances. A basic notion of Hinduism that conditions the social practice of Hindus is the idea that all units of creation (gods, humans, plants, animals, inanimate substances, whatever) are composed of natural substances that are not only different, but also inherently unequal. All units in a domain (gods in a pantheon, castes of humans, species of animals) are ranked according to the power and purity of their substance. That is, higher forms in any domain are purer and more powerful than the lower forms in the domain.

Further, this logic of natural substances holds that substances affect one another immanently. The power of a village deity affects the people and their behavior, the village land, and its crops. Virtuous or wrong behavior is believed to affect, for better or worse, the quality of the crops. The circle is closed because the crops are food to the people and offerings to the gods. Religious thought and common sense are strongly marked by a logic of ranked natural substances that immanently affect one another.

The Caste System and Dharma. The hierarchy of natural substances is elaborated in the most salient feature of the Hindu social order: *caste* and *dharma.* Although there are over 3,000 named castes and subcastes in India, there are at most 40 within any local rural area. Caste is the basis of the social division of labor. There are dominant landowning castes, priestly castes, artisan castes, fishing castes, and serving castes. What is distinctive about the Hindu ideology of rank is that humans of the purest caste, the Brahmin priests, are usually not the most powerful. This is in contrast to Western ideologies of aristocracy, where the monarch is both the most powerful of humans and the closest to God and therefore rules by divine right.

Caste is tied to the division of labor by the logic of natural substances. Within each caste, a person's substance is deemed to be coded with the aptitude for a certain kind of work.[16] In the United States, when a runner wears an exercise outfit stenciled ''Born to Run,'' the message is metaphorical. In Hindu areas, some people are (nonmetaphorically) held to be born to rule, others born to craft gold, others born to plow, and so forth.

If this notion is understood, the international manager can understand Hindu ideas that restrict individual mobility but specify duties (dharma) appropriate to castes (as well as to genders and different stages of life). Dharma denotes that there is appropriate conduct for each caste. Especially in the traditional agricultural sector, duties among castes were categorically defined as nonnegotiable rights and duties. On the other hand, castes in more mercantile sectors—merchants, artisans, and fishermen—maintained more negotiated, contractual relationships.[17]

In former days, the result was a well-defined and highly stratified social order. Rigid stratification fostered an ambiguously exploitative situation. The superiors in the system prospered. Their actions were constrained, however, because their honor was defined in part by the well-being of their servants. Then low castes had more covert influence than was apparent.

In current times, the implications of the caste system for the economy are also ambiguous. Caste membership can bias educational and career opportunities. When caste rank outweighs personal ability and performance in personnel decisions, the economy suffers. Poor low castes have problems similar to poor minorities in the United States. The government, however, reserves seats in institutions of higher learning for scheduled castes and tribes. Further, traditional rules of conduct separating castes are often neutralized in the work setting. Occupational cultures among professionals such as engineers often outweigh caste identifications. Even if these categorical differences are overcome at the workplace, they remain in force at the home and the club, contexts of affiliation that are essential in Western managerial behavior.

Karma, Samskaras, and Nirvana. Although the word *karma* literally means action, the notion implies cause and effect. In a further extension of the logic of natural substances, the notion of karma is connected to the notion of reincarnation. Good and bad actions during this life are held to affect one's substance for better or for worse. The longer-term result is rebirth that is higher or lower in the hierarchy of beings. One way to improve one's natural substance is to perform the *samskaras,* life-cycle rituals held at birth, puberty, marriage, and death. When properly performed, these rituals are held to improve (or, as they say, polish) the natural substance.

Foreigners are sometimes taken aback at the heavy sums spent by Hindus on life-cycle rituals. Their life-cycle rituals are not only occasions for displaying one's social prominence, but also an investment. The long-range spiritual strategy is to improve one's body and spirit to the point where one escapes the cycle of rebirths and attains the state of endless serenity, truth, and bliss called *nirvana*. Hindus are rational maximizers, as are all humans. The question for the international manager is to find out what is on the agenda for maximization in the culture.

Economic and Business Implications of Hinduism

Depending on how you look at it, Hinduism can be interpreted as either resistant to change or the most dynamic of religions.

The view of Hinduism as resistant to change stems from the concept that Hinduism is not a religion segregated from daily life. Traditional religions are inextricably woven into daily life:

> Hinduism has no dogma; it is not even a religion when you come to think of it; it is a way of life. This in itself makes the task of change harder. You are not up against dogma, you are up against a total way of life, which is more difficult to change than dogma.[18]

Yet, Hinduism can be seen as quite dynamic. What distinguishes Hinduism from other world religions is its syncretism. As we noted earlier, Hinduism has drawn together a variety of nonliterate religious practices and beliefs. Hinduism is the result of the confluence of two major civilizations. It has accumulated ancient and modern practices and developed rival philosophical systems, a luxuriant mythology, and a set of epic legends. Hinduism has also been influenced by later world religions: Buddhism, Christianity, and Islam. Indeed, a major reason for the durability and strength of Hinduism is precisely its ability to assimilate and adapt. Hinduism has evolved far more over the last 2,000 years than has Christianity. Under an appearance of immutable, changeless tradition, it is, ironically, the most accommodating of religions.

Opposing views on the impact of Hinduism on the economy appear to correlate with the focus of the author, whether the studies were aimed at the rural masses or at urban elites. Those who focus on the rural sector often hold that Hinduism and the traditional Hindu value system are antithetical to change and development. For example, Nair relates the static, limited aspirations of rural peasants to traditional beliefs.[19] By contrast, Prakash Lal Tandon, a prominent Indian executive, is more optimistic. He sees the educated Indian as capable of living in two worlds— work, and the rest of life—that can be compartmentalized.[20] Srinivas and Shah say that the older Weberian ideas (mentioned earlier in this chapter) about the negative impact of Hinduism are based on a partial view of Hinduism. They note that some elements of Hinduism are not antithetical but favorable to economic development. They cite the positive economic motivation among Jains, Lingayats, and Madhvas, and the occupational ethic among the merchant and artisan castes. They note that exposure to Western ways has occurred for the last two centuries, especially under the influence of British political and economic activity. This exposure resulted in the growth of a highly Westernized Hindu elite.[21]

Buddhism

Buddhism began in the sixth century B.C. in India and spread first south to Sri Lanka, then eastward to South-east and East Asia. There are small Buddhist communities in Europe and North America. According to the *World Christian Encyclopedia* estimate, there are now 274 million Buddhists. It is the dominant religion in only five countries: Burma, the Khmer Republic (Cambodia), Laos, Sri Lanka, and Thailand. We shall see that the impact of Buddhism differs according to the presence of other major religions such as Zen Buddhism or Confucianism.

Theravada and Mahayana

The division between Theravada and Mahayana Buddhism resembles the division between older and newer forms of Christianity, Catholicism and Protestantism.

Theravada means "the teaching of the elders." Theravada Buddhists are especially oriented to the sacred writings that contain the original teachings of Buddha. Theravada is the older and more conservative branch of Buddhism.[22] Theravada Buddhism is found in the southern countries of Asia: Burma, Cambodia, Laos, Sri Lanka, Thailand, and Vietnam. In these countries, Buddhism is tempered by Little Traditions. Its adherents do not, however, practice another major religion along with Buddhism.

Mahayana means "the greater vehicle." Mahayana Buddhists believe that Buddha did not mean to stop with what is contained in the teachings of the elders, but had in mind a greater vehicle or greater ways that were broad and comprehensive enough for all peoples. Mahayana Buddhists have greater diversity in their religious belief and practices. Mahayana Buddhism is found in the more northerly countries of Asia: China, Japan, Korea, Mongolia, Nepal, and Tibet. In these countries, Buddhist adherents often practice not only Little Traditions, but also one or more major religions in addition to formal Buddhism. In China and Korea, Confucianism and Zen Buddhism are practiced. In Japan, Confucianism, Shinto, and Zen Buddhism are practiced.[23]

Historical Background

The word *Buddha* is not a name but a title signifying the Enlightened One. The title is associated with Siddhartha Gautama, born around 563 B.C. in the north of India. Prince Gautama spent his first two decades in a life of ease and luxury. His father saw to it that his experiences were beautiful and pleasant. One day he left the palace and saw an old man, a dead man, and a begging monk. The harsh realities of the world were brought home to him. Disturbed by human suffering, he left his home, wife, and child to wander as a hermit and find the answer to this problem. After several years of wandering, asceticism, instruction, and meditation, Gautama meditated for 40 days under a sacred tree and became enlightened. His answer was called the Middle Way because it avoids the two extremes of self-indulgence and Hindu asceticism, both of which Gautama tried and found wanting.

Elements of Buddhism

The heart of the formal Great Tradition of Buddhism (common to Theravada and Mahayana) is not difficult to summarize because it consists of Gautama's teachings. Buddhism—being a reformation of, or rebellion against, Hinduism—offers a contemplative ethical system that is simple to state but demanding to practice. The following sections sketch the basic elements of formal Buddhism.

The Four Noble Truths. In Buddhism, enlightenment and nirvana are approached through the realization of the Four Noble Truths:

1. The truth of suffering. All existence is suffering.
2. The truth of the cause of suffering. Desires of all kinds (possessions, sensuality, or whatever) are never fulfilled forever. If you feast today, you are still hungry tomorrow. Suffering is caused by desire.
3. The truth of cessation from suffering. Suffering ceases when desire ceases.
4. The truth of the path that leads to the cessation of suffering. This is the Noble Eightfold Path.

The Noble Eightfold Path. The path identified in the Fourth Noble Truth of Buddhism spells out eight "right" conditions:

1. Right view is understanding and accepting the Four Noble Truths.
2. Right thought is freedom from lust, ill will, cruelty, and untruthfulness.
3. Right speech is abstaining from lying, talebearing, harsh language, and vain talk.
4. Right conduct is abstaining from killing, stealing, and sexual misconduct.
5. Right livelihood is the avoidance of violence to any living thing and freedom from luxury.
6. Right effort is avoiding and overcoming what is evil and promoting and maintaining what is good.
7. Right awareness is contemplating the fact that the body is transitory and loathsome, contemplating the feelings of oneself and of others, and contemplating the mind and other phenomena.
8. Right meditation is complete concentration on a single object to achieve purity of thought: thought free from all desires, hindrances, and distractions and, eventually, free from all sensation.

Karma and Nibbana. Karma is the law of cause and effect of actions. Karma is a Hindu concept to which Gautama gave a distinctly ethical interpretation. Good deeds such as following the Noble Eightfold Path bring good results; evil deeds bring evil results during the current life and during future lives. Karma is held to operate in the physical world as well as in the mental and moral domain. The Buddhist notion of *nibbana* is similar to the Hindu idea of nirvana in that both imply the cessation of becoming, of rebirth, of one's karma—the end of the endless journey. While the Hindu idea of nirvana implies union with the unity of all creation, the Buddhist idea of nibbana implies the joining with the great nothingness beyond creation. Gautama's description of nibbana is as follows:

> There is, disciples, a condition, where there is neither earth nor water, neither air nor light, neither limitless space nor limitless time, neither any kind of being, neither ideation nor non-ideation, neither this world nor that world. There is neither arising nor passing away, nor dying, neither cause nor effect, neither change nor standing still.[24]

Life is suffering. Nibbana is escape from suffering.

The Sangha. Religious virtuosos who fully practice the elaborate religious codes for behavior are often organized into monastic orders. The collectivity of monks is called the *sangha*. Though typically secluded, the monks are highly apparent in the world with their saffron robes and shaven heads. In Theravada countries, entering the sangha is a lifelong commitment. In Mahayana Buddhist areas, many adolescent boys enter the sangha temporarily as novices. It is a ritual of passage to manhood. Only a few remain and become full-fledged monks.

Modifications of Formal Buddhism

The Buddhist case is instructive because it cautions managers against making too much of the formal religion. If formal Buddhism were truly practiced, the impact on social life and on the economy would be devastating: no work and no society. There are several reasons why this does not happen.

Conduct of Monks and Laity. First, monks and lay people observe very different rules for conduct. When they are in trouble or desire a special boon, lay people choose to take a special vow to observe—for a short period—the less subtle restrictions against stealing, murder, adultery, and lying as set out in the Noble Eightfold Path. By contrast, monks in Sri Lanka consider themselves religious virtuosos because they ordinarily follow 227 precise rules for conduct. The rules are very fine grained. For example, as part of the rule against working, a monk cannot even lift a rice bowl while eating.

Integration with Little Traditions. Second, the formal Buddhist belief system has become integrated with Little Traditions in different countries. Buddhism in Burma has incorporated pre-Buddhist, indigenous beliefs in territorial spirits called *nats*. Buddhism in Sri Lanka has incorporated pre-Buddhist demons called *yakkha*. The following examples illustrate the integration of transcendental, formal Buddhism with practical Little Traditions.

Yakkha demons in Sri Lanka are held to be responsible for very specific misfortunes. The yakkha called the Black Prince, for example, causes sexual excitement in adolescents. When this happens to a young novice monk, the youth is not expelled from the monastery. He is given leave to return to his native village, where he undergoes the appropriate demon exorcism. When judged fit, he returns to the monastery.

A Buddhist temple complex includes both the dagoba shrine to Buddha and a temple to a high god. A villager goes first to the dagoba, where he or she praises and makes offerings to Buddha and promises to observe right conduct according to the Noble Eightfold Path. For this, the villager receives merit (pin). The villager then goes to the adjacent temple of the high god, where the merit just received is offered to the god. Then the villager asks a favor of the god—that is, help in some practical problem such as obtaining a job, curing a sick relative, or finding a mate.

In the life of a Sri Lankan peasant, then, there is no boundary or separation between the otherworldly high religion and the practical, this-worldly local tradition.

Political Involvement. Third, even the sangha, the community of monks, are not totally dissociated from worldly action. Monks are politically involved. Despite their ascetic aims, monasteries control large estates and are indeed involved in political process. Monks in Sri Lanka helped lead the political mobilization in 1956 when the Sinhalese community became the dominant ethnic group in the country. Americans may still remember ghastly images of blazing Vietnamese monks who were protesting foreign military activity in their country. Companies operating in Buddhist countries are well advised to study the local Buddhist sangha as one of the most important groups for mobilizing profound social and political action.

Integration with Other Major Religions. Fourth, formal Buddhism is integrated with other major religions in some countries. In Chapter 3, we described a Japanese banking firm's spiritual education program. Its emphasis was on Zen training, not on otherworldly Buddhism. Zen is a religion of contemplative action. Various paths of activity, called *do,* are known to both improve skill and polish the character. Karate-do, for example, is a martial art that aims to achieve a harmony of mind, body, and spirit. International managers who are interested in learning something about Japanese business strategy may want to study a particular Zen path, the game of Go (Go-do). Lack of space precludes a full discussion of the resemblances between this board game and business strategy. It might suffice to say that managers in Japan and in South Korea are known to play this game during their lunch break.

In other countries, both Buddhism and Confucianism are practiced. Briefly described, Confucianism is a religion of everyday ethics. Duty to family, king, and country is stressed. Executive informants in South Korea asserted that the Confucian ideal of duty has become part of corporate culture in that it supports their priorities on work and achievement by groups as well as by individuals. They relate the notion of duty to various contexts, such as the individual's duty not only to accept but also to perform excellently in a personally unappealing job assignment.[25]

Buddhism and the Economy

Some authors argue that the otherworldliness of Buddhism has a negative impact on the economy. For example, Lester describes Theravada Buddhism as more than a religion in a Western sense; it is a life-style, an all-encompassing instrument of spiritual, cultural, and political identity, a way of life that begins and ends with the mold of traditional Buddhist values. Because Buddhism emphasizes wantlessness and contemplation rather than consumption and work, the religion is a drag on economic growth, if not an actual deterrent.[26]

Against this view, we have contrasted the otherworldly Great Tradition of formal Buddhism with the practicality of the Little Traditions also observed by Buddhists. Further, as we noted in Chapter 3, the Buddhist community of monks has maintained a continuous academic tradition for more than two millennia. This tradition has allowed Buddhists to take up Western education with greater ease than is seen in regions with nonliterate religious traditions. Education is, of course, one of the precursors of development. This may mean faster development in the future.

There are conflicting views as to whether Buddhism has positive or negative implications for economic development. It is true that countries in which Theravada Buddhism is the dominant religion are at the lower end of the scale of economic development (see Table 4-2, page 98). It is also true that the countries in which Mahayana Buddhism is an important part of the religious scene (along with Christianity, Confucianism, Taoism, and Shinto) are among the fastest growing in the world economy: Japan, Hong Kong, South Korea, Singapore, and Taiwan.

Islam

According to the *World Christian Encyclopedia,* Islam is the religion of about 723 million people in some 30 countries. In 19 of these countries, as shown in Figure 4-2, it is the dominant national religion.

FIGURE 4-2

MUSLIM POLITIES

Afghanistan	Indonesia	Libya	Saudi Arabia	Tunisia
Algeria	Iran	Mauritania	Senegal	Turkey
Bangladesh	Iraq	Morocco	Somalia	Yemen
Egypt	Jordan	Pakistan	Syria	

Source: Arthur S. Banks and Robert B. Textor, *A Cross-Polity Survey* (Cambridge, MA: M.I.T. Press, 1963), FC58.

The Muslim world extends from the Atlantic shore of North Africa eastward across North Africa, through the Middle East, across the top of the Indian subcontinent, through parts of Southeast Asia, and ends in the Philippines, where there is a Muslim minority. In addition, there are over 50 million Muslims in India. The Fulani, a large minority in Nigeria, are Muslims. Islam is now the second religion of Western Europe (7 million) and of Great Britain (1 million).

The calendar of Islam begins in 622 A.D. with the *hegira,* or withdrawal of Mohammed from Mecca to Medina. During its first two centuries, Islam spread rapidly, largely through military conquest, over the area where it is now dominant. Muslim armies controlled Spain for several centuries and were stopped by the army of Charles Martel at Tours in 732 A.D.

Another factor aiding the spread of Islam was the absence of racial discrimination. Islam promotes the equality of every Muslim, of whatever race or color. In India, for example, many converts were from lower castes who saw a way to sidestep the restrictions of the Hindu caste system. The ideal of Muslim brotherhood is not trivial. Malcolm X, the chief lieutenant of the separatist Black Muslim movement, revised his vision of social change after making a pilgrimage to Mecca. In Mecca, he was highly impressed by the harmony among Muslims of many colors.[27]

Elements of Islam

Islam and Muslim. Understanding these terms is a key to understanding the nature of the religion. The word *Islam* is the infinitive of the Arabic verb to "submit" and is exemplified in the submission of the prophet Abraham to the will of the Lord by attempting to sacrifice Isaac, his son. The word *Muslim* is the present participle of the same verb. In other words, a Muslim is one who is accepting and is submitting to the will of Allah. Perhaps the most common expression in Muslim countries is *inshallah:* "God willing." This stems from the orthodox belief that everything, good or evil, proceeds directly from divine will. (Never refer to Muslims as Mohammedans, a term they resent because it implies they worship the prophet Mohammed. They respect him but do not worship him.)

The Five Pillars. Practical religion in Islam consists of observing the five duties or foundations of Islam.

1. Shahadah, the Profession of the faith. The succinctly stated creed, "There is no god but God, and Mohammed is the prophet of God," has been communicated throughout the Muslim world.

2. Salah, ritual or devotional worship. There are five required periods of prayer during the day. The ritual prayers are in Arabic. Particularly important is the congregational prayer at noon on Fridays, where attendance is incumbent on all adult males. Though the Friday service includes a sermon, Friday is not always prescribed as a day of rest, as are Saturday or Sunday in the Judaic or Christian traditions. Work schedules must allow for these prayer periods, even for Muslim workers in factories in Germany.

3. Zakat, alms giving. Both legal alms and freewill gifts are enjoined on the Muslim. Himself an orphan, Mohammed had a real concern with the destitute. Because alms are a personal charity, government welfare programs have sometimes been constrained.

4. Sawm, fasting. There are 30 days of daylight fasting during the month of Ramadan, the month when the Qur'an (Koran) was laid down. Ramadan is the ninth month of the Muslim calendar. The fast is esteemed as inculcating both self-control and sympathy with the poor and destitute. The fast involves complete abstention from food, drink, smoking, and sexual intercourse from dawn to sunset. Productivity declines throughout the economy during Ramadan, even though total food consumption rises.

5. Haj, the visit to the revered place. Every adult Muslim who can afford it is required to undertake a pilgrimage to the holy city of Mecca. The pilgrimage occurs during the twelfth month of the Muslim calendar. Each year, hundreds of thousands of the faithful from 20 or more countries make the pilgrimage. The returned pilgrim, the hajji, gains personal prestige in the home community. Perhaps the major impact of the pilgrimage is the pilgrim's strengthened sense of the international solidarity and brotherhood of Muslims.

The five pillars of Islam define the basic identity of Muslims—their faith, beliefs, and practices—which binds together a worldwide community of believers into a fellowship of shared values and concerns.

The Qur'an and the Ulama. The core of Islamic theology is found principally in their holy book, the Qur'an. The Hadith, the Traditions, have taken their place alongside the Qur'an as a primary source of Muslim theology, law, and practice.

There are no formal clergy in Islam, but scholars versed in the Koran and the Hadith, the Ulama, play an important role as law interpreters, preachers, and teachers. They are, as we shall see in a subsequent discussion of the Islamic sermon, very important in the process of change.

Sharia. Islam has a pervasive impact on the everyday life of its followers. Islam is not a religion to be practiced one day a week. It is a detailed way of life. As a Muslim scholar put it, "Islam is both belief and legislation which organizes all the relationships of man."[28]

The Sharia, or law of Islam, embraces every detail of human life; this includes not only personal actions, but also social relations and community life, including the state. Muslim nations are, in fact, established as religious states, in contrast to nations that establish a separation of church and state. The Arabic language includes no pairs of terms corresponding to lay and ecclesiastical, spiritual and temporal, or secular and religious. The Muslim name for citizen, mukallaf, means one on whom is laid full responsibility for the performance of his religious duties and observance of the Sharia, which is the pattern of communal order.[29] Extreme applications of fundamentalist Muslim principles have occurred in several nations. Two examples are Libya and Iran.

A nonsmoker and nondrinker in the strictest Muslim manner, Gaddafi closed all nightclubs, bars, and casinos. He restored the practice of amputations for thievery, in accordance with Koranic law. . . . Gaddafi justifies these actions as a return to Islamic principles of old. "When we do these things," he says, "we purge ourselves of impurity that is a product of imperialism and return to the true values of Islam."[30]

Under the late Shah, Iran became one of the most Westernized of Muslim countries. After the late Ayatollah Khomeini came to power, public behavior according to Sharia precepts was strictly enforced. Muslim women, for example, were no longer permitted to wear sinfully revealing clothing. Popular Western music was banned. Muslim fundamentalism has been exported through Iranian involvement in Lebanon.

The Shia-Sunni Split

As Buddhism has its Theravada and Mahayana divisions, so Islam is divided between Sunnis and Shiites. Sunnis and Shiites agree on the previously discussed fundamentals of Islam. Their differences arose out of disagreement over the rightful succession to Mohammed's authority: relatives or disciples. The Sunnis won the battle on this issue in 680 A.D. Ever since then, there has been ill feeling and occasional violence between the two groups.

Shiites account for only about 10 percent of all Muslims and are the dominant group in only two countries, Iran and Iraq. They are, however, a potentially conflicting minority in most other Muslim nations. The Shiites have a more formal religious hierarchy and have given stronger allegiance to religious leaders such as the late Ayatollah Khomeini of Iran. In general, Shiites are more prone to the orthodox practice of the fundamentals of Islam and the rejection of non-Muslim ways, especially Western patterns of behavior.

Islam and the Economy

Except for the oil-producing countries, Muslim nations are all at the lower end of the economic development scale. Other features of Muslim polities are low density of population but high population growth rates, a high percentage of the population engaged in agriculture, literacy rates below 50 percent, and low rates of newspaper circulation.

Since World War II, there has been a growing concern within the Muslim world of the impact of Islam on change and economic development. In 1969, for example, Malaysian Prime Minister Tunku Abdul Rahman organized a conference of Islamic scholars from 23 Muslim nations to consider ways of accommodating their prophet's teachings to a changing world. Rahman was convinced that the Islamic nations of Asia and Africa had to review "illogical beliefs" that interfered with their economic and social progress. Items on the agenda included discussions on the ban on usury, heart transplants, and birth control.[31]

A few examples will illustrate the constraints posed by Islam and the way they are being modified or endured.

1. Speaking on the Revival of Islamic Business Administration, the finance minister of Kuwait strongly criticized payment or receipt of interest as being contrary to Islam. Arab banks were losing deposits to other banks that did pay interest on deposits. In some countries, the payments are called commissions rather than interest.[32]

2. "Inshallah" (God willing) is an expression of submission to the will of Allah. As a corollary for some Muslims, insurance policies are an attempt to defy the working of Allah's will. As a result, Citibank finds itself financing the uninsured inventories of Muslim merchants. The prohibition against charging interest is circumvented by charging a "commission" instead. However, if the bank must go to a court to collect, the Muslim court will award only the principal.[33]

3. Saudi Arabia built a traffic system for Mecca, the holy city. A Swedish firm had primary engineering responsibility for the project. As non-Muslims, the Swedes were not allowed access to the sacred place. The solution was to use closed-circuit television to supervise the work.[34]

4. The normal weekend in Muslim countries is Thursday afternoon and Friday. Tunisia is a Muslim nation with extensive business relations with Europe. Major Tunisian business firms that deal mainly with European firms follow the European schedule. Under Bourguiba, the pragmatic Muslim Prime Minister, national policy shifted to the European schedule. To have both would be highly unproductive. Even the diligent observance of Ramadan (the month of daylight fast and abstinence) was discouraged. The great drop in productivity and the increase in consumption is considered too costly for the country.[35]

5. The Islamic sermon.[36] Early in Islamic history, the sermon was a channel of political communication, a means whereby the ruling elite informed the public of its programs and policies. During Mohammed's life and for the next century, the political content was quite high. During the first centuries of Islam, preachers developed the sermon into a high art. Gradually, however, the sermons became stereotyped and preachers (ulamas) stopped writing their own sermons and began selecting them from anthologies. Old sermons became increasingly irrelevant to the times of the listeners. Some critics went so far as to attribute the decline of the Muslims to the decline in preaching.

   Since World War II, demands for economic development have required the ruling elites in the Middle East to mobilize their populations into a modern economy. Mobilization of all sectors of the population requires communication between a modernizing elite and the traditional masses.

   After World War II, many ulamas advocated a reform of the Friday sermon toward speaking about contemporary problems. As one reformer noted, "Any subject relating to the welfare of the community may be dealt with in the sermon. It is for the education of the masses, to awaken them to a general sense of duty, to lead them in the ways of their welfare and prosperity. . . ." Thus the sermon has been revitalized in style and content and restored as a channel of communication.

The sermon is a means of mass communication for the elites only if they control it. There has been a reassertion of state control over the mosque and the sermon. In Egypt, mosques and ulamas are under strict state control. Each week, every preacher receives a directive from the Ministry of Religious Affairs telling him the topic of the week's sermon. He can either write his own sermon or use one prepared by the ministry. In Jordan, prior governmental approval is required for all sermons. As a result, ulamas now attempt to integrate the modern developmental policies of their governments with the Koran and with Islamic tradition.

In the sermon, developmental messages are legitimized by reference to Islamic precepts. The sole sources used by the preachers to justify their arguments are the Koran and Hadith, works that the people have partially memorized. The preachers are members of a traditional social group and are usually of humble birth. They wear traditional costumes, live modestly, and dwell close to the people. Sermons are preached in the mosque, an environment with architecture that evokes memories of the great Islamic past.

Christianity

We shall focus on Roman Catholicism and Protestantism individually for several reasons. First, the number of people represented by these branches of Christianity is large enough to warrant separate attention. According to the *World Christian Encyclopedia,* there are 809 million Roman Catholics, 124 million Eastern Orthodox Catholics, and 345 million Protestants and Anglicans. Second, in countries where the two major branches are dominant, the patterns of economic performance differ significantly.[37] The Russian Orthodox and Eastern Orthodox Churches will not be discussed because their belief structure is fairly close to that of Roman Catholicism.

There are two aims to the following discussion. The first is to contrast Catholic and Protestant belief and its possible connection with the motivation to economic performance. The second is to consider political impacts of these religions.

Relevant Catholic Belief and Practice

The Church, the Sacraments, and the Mediators. The Roman Catholic Church has traditionally emphasized the Church and the sacraments as the principal elements of salvation. Jesus of Nazareth, called the Christ, the Son of God, and the Son of Man, is believed to be the ultimate mediator between humans and God the Father. Mary, mother of Jesus, is also defined as a mediator because she was an earthly woman touched by divinity. The Roman Catholic Church holds that apart from these figures, the Church, and the sacraments, there is no salvation.

The Religious Hierarchy of the Church. The Catholic Church has a global hierarchy of holy offices. The Pope, cardinals, archbishops, bishops, and priests constitute a formal hierarchy of authority.

The Religious Order and the Laity. A clear distinction exists between religious orders and the laity, with different requirements and standards of conduct applied to each. The Church and its priests are the intermediaries between God and people. People do not approach God directly, but rely on the priests.

Relevant Protestant Belief and Practice

Despite agreement with Catholic doctrine on many points—for example, the Apostle's Creed—the Protestant Reformation changed both the organizational structure and some beliefs of the Roman Catholic Church. Protestants stress the role of the sacraments, the mediating role of Mary, and the intermediary role of its priests or ministers less than the Roman Church does. Citing the passage, "There is one mediator between God and men, the man Christ Jesus,"[38] Protestants said that people could approach God directly—they didn't need a go-between other than Jesus himself.

Variation in Organizational Hierarchy. As contrasted with the global hierarchy of the Roman Church, Protestant sects differ widely in organizational hierarchy. At one end of the spectrum, the High Episcopalian Church has a stratified hierarchy of holy offices. At the other, Quakers do not even designate ministers separate from laity: Quaker meetings are convened by elders.

Individual Salvation: the Calling. Another reforming change was the elimination of the distinction between the secular and the religious life. Rejecting the idea that the religious orders had a special calling, Luther said, "All of life is a calling [beruf]." In other words, religious significance is attached to the secular life. "God accomplishes all things through you. Through you He milks the cow." The conception of the secular life as a God-appointed task involved the idea that the proper performance of even such a secular task is a religious obligation.

Salvation and Economic Performance. Calvin added the idea that certain people were the elect—that is, predestined to salvation. The believer did not work to achieve salvation, which was a free gift from God. Rather, productivity and income were seen as signs of God's approval and as a sign that a person was among the elect. From the point of view of the adherent, the notion of election is an incentive for high achievement. For superior performance in worldly activities would demonstrate to the world that you were among the elect.

Asceticism and Accumulation. Another incentive to economic endeavors is the Protestant doctrine of asceticism. Wesley noted that "Religion must necessarily produce both industry and frugality, and these cannot but produce riches." The important question was the use to which the riches would be put. Wesley said, "After you have gained all you can and saved all you can, spend not one pound, one shilling, or one penny, to gratify either the desire of the flesh, the desire of the eyes, or the pride of life, or for any other end than to please and glorify God." Spending on personal consumption was thus to be limited. And if one followed the tithing principle, giving one-tenth of what one earned to the Church, there would still be a significant residual accumulation for investment. The result was that Methodists,

Puritans, and Quakers accumulated wealth and not infrequently became what we call capitalists. This strain of thought differs markedly from the Catholic attitude. In Catholicism, money making was considered as socially degrading and morally and religiously dangerous. Thomas Aquinas regarded it as turpitudo—shameful and degrading.

Political Impacts of Christianity

Turning now to political impacts, a major difference between Christianity and the religions previously treated is that both Christian religions have been on both sides of major social movements. In some instances, Catholic and Protestant religious leaders have been regarded as part of the Establishment; in others, they have opposed it.

When are these Churches regarded as part of the Establishment? A similarity between Roman Catholicism and Protestantism is that both branches of Christianity have been for centuries engaged in seeking converts throughout the world. The international manager should recognize that less-developed countries are sometimes ambivalent toward Christianity because it was the religion of the colonial powers. On one hand, Catholic and Christian priests, monks, and missionaries provided access not only to a promise of eternal life, but also to education and medicine. On the other hand, Christian institutions were part of the colonial administrative process. There is strong evidence, for example, that the inquisition at Cartagena, Colombia, prosecuted as heretics people who were rebelling against colonial rule.

As a result, Christianity can be viewed by these leaders as part of the process of dependency (which we will discuss more fully in the chapter on politics) the process by which countries now called less developed actually became less-developed countries. This reaction is not limited to less-developed countries. For example, one of the early aims of the Parti Québecois, the separatist party of French-speaking Canadians, was to reduce the power of the Roman Catholic Church, which was viewed as aiding the English-speaking rulers of Canada.

On the other hand, Christian religious leaders have more recently been involved in liberal or radical activism. One example is the concerted effort by Catholic bishops in the United States to oppose nuclear armament. Another example is Liberation Theology, the grass-roots involvement of religious figures in Central America, where priests and nuns have agitated and sometimes died for the sake of those they consider oppressed.

Another major difference between Christian religions and other major world religions is that both Roman Catholicism and Protestantism have modified religious practices in line with changing norms of social behavior in the wider society. In some orders of the Catholic Church, for example, nuns now are allowed to wear secular clothing and pursue a wider variety of occupations than were previously permitted. A faction of the Episcopalian denomination has lobbied successfully for the entry of women into the priesthood. This direction of change is the exact opposite of that practiced by Christian-oriented cults. Most cults aim to provide refuge from the multitude of life-style choices that now exist in the United States. In these cults, behavior is often very strictly regulated. Behavioral directives are justified by direct reference to the cult leader's vision of the original doctrines of Christianity.

POLICY IMPLICATIONS FOR THE MULTINATIONAL FIRM

When considering foreign operations, multinational firms assess the environment of the potential host countries. International managers should distinguish three aspects of a society's religion or religions in their environment assessment.

First, they should learn to avoid quick stereotypes about the impact of religion on economic development.

Second, they must become informed on details of religious beliefs that, just as in their home country, specifically affect operations. Religious holidays, for example, may affect the production schedule. Other beliefs may affect patterns of consumption.

Third, they should consider the degree of religious heterogeneity in a nation and the impact of religious figures and institutions in mobilizing support for social and political movements. In other words, they should consider the impact of religion as part of the analysis of political risk in the host country.

Economic Development and Religion

Our thesis has been that one should make neither too much nor too little of religion as a factor influencing economic development. To give religion appropriate weight, we present Table 4-2. The table indicates—for 1978 and for 1986—the level of economic development of nations categorized by the numerically dominant religion. The tables show that when country developmental level is measured by GNP per capita, religion is not a sufficient indicator of a country's economic performance. The second and third categories in the table actually shifted position in the eight-year period.

Other factors are at work. In Table 4-2, the figures are organized by geographical region and resource endowments.

- Geographical region, which itself correlates with patterns of colonial domination, helps clarify the GNP per capita data. For example, Catholic polities in Europe are more advanced economically than those elsewhere. Similarly, Protestant polities in the North Atlantic are more advanced than those elsewhere.

- The importance of resource endowments is apparent in the economic gaps between OPEC and non-OPEC Islamic polities. Resource endowments are also an important factor in South Africa's significant advantage over other polities with major nonliterate religious components.

Other ambiguities in the data are evident in the economic performance of the newly industrialized Asian countries—Hong Kong, Singapore, South Korea, and Taiwan. Together with Japan, these countries are called post-Confucianist because their work ethic is derived more from Confucian teaching than from any other source.[39]

TABLE 4-2

DOMINANT RELIGIONS, REGIONS, RESOURCES, AND ECONOMIC PERFORMANCE

	Per Capita GNP in 1978 U.S. $	Per Capita GNP in 1986 U.S. $
Protestant polities—North Atlantic	5,030–12,100	8,870–17,680
Eastern Asian eclectic polities	1,160– 7,280	2,370–12,840
Catholic polities—Europe	1,990– 9,090	3,680–10,720
Islamic polities—OPEC	1,260– 7,690	2,590–13,800
Judaism—Israel	4,120	6,210
Protestant—non-North Atlantic	1,110– 7,990	840–11,920
Catholic polities—non-Europe	480– 2,910	560– 2,920
Islamic polities—non-OPEC	90– 1,200	160– 1,830
Polities with major nonliterate religious component*	90– 910	120– 1,160
Theravada Buddhist polities	90– 490	160– 810
Hindu polity—India	180	290

*Excluding South Africa

Source: Countries are classified by a criterion of 80 percent of the population as done in Arthur S. Banks and Robert B. Textor, *A Cross-Polity Survey* (Cambridge, MA: M.I.T. Press, 1963), 70. GNP/capita figures from *World Development Report,* 1988.

These countries have an eclectic mixture of religious traditions: Christianity, Confucianism, Mahayana Buddhism, Shinto, and Zen Buddhism. Their economic performance is far superior to that of Theravada Buddhist countries.

To what extent is a nation's level of economic development a function of its religious situation?

First, foreshadowing the discussion of dependency theory in Chapter 8, world region is a strong modifying factor when comparing the economic development of nations classified by religion. In other words, historical patterns of colonial domination have affected the economic development of nations. Thus the level of economic development may differ among countries following the same religion but located in different regions.

Second, through its impact on social priorities, religion does affect social action; that is, social codes for behavior are learned in childhood. Value priorities are also learned. These values motivate people to follow the codes for behavior, and religion reinforces these motivated codes and values for the adult. We shall explore the topic of values in Chapter 5.

For now, a valid question, as part of environmental assessment, is to ask how closely a particular religion is tied to the details of social life. Anyone who has seen the movie *Fiddler on the Roof,* with its key line, "Without tradition our life would be as steady as a fiddler on the roof," knows that the religious traditions of rural Jews in Eastern Europe were very closely tied to their daily social life. Traditional religions still exist: nonliterate religions, Hinduism, Buddhism, Islam, and even fundamentalist versions of Christianity. Traditional religions penetrate deeply into the minute codes for daily life.

How? Traditional religions fit well with traditional, preindustrial social relationships. Traditional social relationships are multistranded; that is, a person has multiple dealings with other persons in the community. A traditional social relationship combines activities that, in the current era, we distinguish analytically as kin, economic, political, and religious relationships. Traditional religions tend to limit the development of single-stranded, contractual relationships.

Single-stranded relationships are important for business as practiced in Western industrial countries. A manager has to deal with someone whether or not that person is of similar kin, economic, political, or religious background. To a certain extent, Protestantism—a relatively recent religion in the course of human history and one developed partially due to the breakdown of the feudal order and the rise of mercantile classes—does not incite multistranded relationships but prioritizes contractual relationships disentangled from the wider web of social relationships.

Does this train of thought force us to agree with Weber's ideas on the connection between the Protestant ethic and the spirit of capitalism? Not necessarily. We should recall the distinction between culture and business culture made in the first chapter. Different religious traditions from the wider culture support alternative business cultures. The definition of social relationships differs in other business cultures. For example, part of the success of Japanese firms stems from the establishment of multistranded relationships within the corporation. In such firms, the corporate culture includes a degree of company loyalty that borders on religion. (Even some American companies, notably Amway and Mary Kay, have annual ritualized events that resemble revival meetings.)

In short, there is no one religion that incites productivity better than all the others. What counts is the impact on the specific codes for conduct and priorities in business culture.

Other Religious Factors Affecting Foreign Operations

Part of cultural briefing for a manager assigned abroad should be instruction on the impact of specific beliefs and practices that will affect the manager's tasks.

Major Religious Events

Every religion has its holy days. They vary in number and significance from religion to religion, and occasionally within the same religion. For example, although Italy and the United States are predominantly Christian countries, the number of religious holidays is much greater in Italy than in the United States. The Russians recognize only six holidays. Sri Lanka has 27, including Buddhist, Christian, Hindu, and Muslim holidays.

Religious events impact on both production and consumption patterns. When members of different religious groups work side by side, differing holiday schedules can pose problems. The month of Ramadan, with its daylight fasting, was noted for its negative impact on productivity but positive impact on consumption during that period (just as the Christmas season is known to Western retailers as the annual peak in sales). The Muslim pilgrimage to Mecca significantly affects not only consumption patterns but even trade balances. For example, the 30,000 Nigerians who go each year represent a sizable debit in Nigeria's balance of payments. Further, the government suspects that many pilgrims take advantage of the opportunity to smuggle home gold coin, jewelry, and expensive cloth.[40]

Effects of Specific Beliefs on Consumption Patterns

Specific beliefs also affect consumption patterns. It is well known that many religions restrict the consumption of some items: for example, no beef for Hindus and no pork for Muslims and Orthodox Jews. Such knowledge is sometimes not used.

> When the Japanese approached Calcutta during World War II, the influx of refugees from the area now known as Bangladesh caused a food shortage. Rescue ships were dispatched. The cargo was mainly tinned beef and rice. Both items went unused. For religious reasons, eating beef is not acceptable throughout India. In addition, as part of the belief system, Northern India, unlike Southern India, valorizes wheat, not rice.

Marketing managers must learn not only the blatantly forbidden items but also the more subtle ones.

Whereas Westerners are aware of the Muslim Ramadan festival for its restrictions, local business people are aware of its other ramifications and make full use of this knowledge when planning business activities. An Egyptian restaurant manager, knowing that overall average sales of food and drink are highest during the month of Ramadan, lays away supplies and schedules the staff for night shifts in preparation.

In summary, the international manager may take religion as part of the cultural landscape. When assigned abroad, the manager should study the religions of the host country to note the impact of religion on business culture, political instability, and specific effects on the planning of production and marketing strategy.

Religion and Political Risk Analysis

Political risk is defined as the chance that political events will disrupt business operations. Big firms do not worry excessively about changes in political personnel, such as one junta replacing another; they do worry about events that may change the social and political rules of the game.

Religious Centralization

Religions differ in the extent to which religious figures and institutions can help mobilize social movements that may disrupt a firm's business activity in a country.

We have noted various instances of political activism by religious figures: Buddhist monks protesting in Sri Lanka and Vietnam, Muslim preachers delivering government-approved sermons, Catholic priests working with dissidents in Central America.

A key question to ask here is how centralized is the religious bureaucracy? Fragmented sects, as in Protestantism, are less likely to deliver a unified message to their congregations than are bureaucratically unified religions.

Religious Heterogeneity

Another impact religion has on the stability of business operations is the variety of religions within one nation. Like linguistic heterogeneity, as we discussed in Chapter 2, religious heterogeneity is an indicator of potential strife, division, and instability in a society.

In Northern Ireland, Irish Catholics are fighting with Irish Protestants. In Canada, there is discord between Catholic Québecois and English-speaking Protestants. Independence from Great Britain was achieved at the expense of splitting the Indian subcontinent into one predominantly Hindu nation and one predominantly Muslim nation. More recently, civil protest and violence has arisen between Hindus and Sikhs.

By contrast, the Netherlands illustrates an accommodation between the Catholics and Protestants, who are about equal in number. Each group has its own political parties, newspapers, schools, and unions. While the partial segregation is workable, it does indicate a segmentation of the economy that can affect production operations and especially the marketing program of the firm.

POLICY IMPLICATIONS FOR COUNTRIES

Working against one another, different belief systems frequently impede a country's ability to harmonize its economic goals. Most governments are aware that foreign investors weigh the political risk of candidate countries. As part of its civil-rights, industrial, and developmental policy, the government of a religiously mixed nation may establish policies designed to avoid potential conflicts of beliefs.

Singapore is a small country of widely varied ethnic groups (Malay, European, Chinese, and South Indian)[41] and religions (Islam, Christianity, Buddhism/Taoism/Confucianism, and Hinduism). Although the (mainly Confucian) Chinese are dominant economically, Singapore consciously regulates its image of religious neutrality because it is surrounded by large Muslim polities— Malaysia and Indonesia. Singapore has developed a successful system to build a unified nation. Its citizens tell you clearly that they are Singaporeans (not Chinese or Malays or Indians).

The government acts politically toward these differences in worship in two simple ways: (1) by treating them equally, declaring two national holidays for each;[42] and (2) by encouraging spiritual and moral growth in individuals through religious education in the schools.

Otherwise, the government prefers to keep politics and religion separate through such actions as seminars on the danger of mixing the two for the good of the country, and banning politically active preachers.[43] Native Singaporeans will tell you privately that the government is very stern toward anyone who tries to gain advantage through mobilizing people along religious or ethnic lines. The result is that religious problems are downplayed and thus effectively kept out of the path of national and economic growth.

Multireligious, multiethnic, and multilingual nations are often politically unstable because people easily mobilize along these separatist lines. Neutralizing or attempting to neutralize divisive interactions among such social groupings is a task both for governments and for companies.

QUESTIONS

1. A beverage company markets a brand of soft drink called Three Stars, which has three six-pointed stars on the label and bottle cap. Because of the visual similarity to the Israeli Star of David, this soft drink is banned in Libya. How should the company react to the situation?

2. Choose three nations from different geographical regions where Buddhism or Islam is the major religion. Read encyclopedia articles on these countries to compare the impact of the religion on daily social life in each one.

3. Of the 184 workers at an American-owned plant in the Middle East, 183 are on strike. The nonstriker is a Christian Armenian, also a native of the country. The Christian has made disparaging comments about the Muslims' interruption of work for their prayer times. He, of course, continues to work during the prayer breaks. The Muslim workers have become angry enough to walk off the job and vow to stay out until the Christian is fired. As manager, what would you do? What would you do if the work force were evenly divided between Muslims and Christians?

4. Kachinas are Hopi Indians' holy spirits, sometimes represented by wooden dolls. Thus the Hopis protested when a distillery hit upon the idea of marketing its bourbon in bottles shaped like kachina dolls. "How would a Catholic feel," asked Tribal Chairman Hamilton, "about putting whiskey in a statue of the Virgin Mary?" What would you advise the distillery?

5. A news item reported the following about an American banker and his family in Saudi Arabia:

> The hardest hurdle for Americans to bear is the ban on women drivers. That means, for example, that the Ansells have to hire a driver to chauffeur Louise to shopping and the children to school. And when she goes to one of the few modern supermarkets or the traditional stalls of the market, she must be careful to wear long skirts so as not to offend Saudi morals.

What are the implications for American firms' staffing policies for Saudi Arabia? Should American female executives not be assigned there?

6. Walter Carlson, a competent and experienced refinery engineer, was recently sent to Bangladesh (a Muslim country bordering India) to replace the ailing American chief engineer at a refinery just beginning operations. His arrival in the midst of all the start-up problems put him under considerable pressure. Carlson's assistant was a Bengali (Bangladesh native) petroleum engineer trained in the United States. Late one day, an emergency arose calling for Carlson's attention. He told his assistant to be on the job early the next morning to work on the problem.

"I'm sorry, Mr. Carlson," said the assistant, "but tomorrow is Eid [a major Muslim holiday immediately following Ramadan]. I thought you knew about the holiday."

"I don't give a damn if it's Christmas. You'd better be here early!" Carlson exploded.

This exchange took place in an outer office, and many employees overheard it. An hour later, the general manager of the plant called: "Carlson, the plant is shut down on a walkout. The men say you insulted their religion."

a. What options does Carlson have now?

b. What should he do?

Carlson's boss in New York hears about the incident an hour later by telephone.

c. What options does she have?

d. What should she do?

Two weeks later, the company's board of directors is discussing the incident.

e. What do they do to prevent the occurrence of similar incidents in the future?

7. How many religious holidays occur this month? See the International Holidays section of the Federal Express's monthly *International Newsletter*. Then picture how you would have to plan operations if you were the logistics coordinator of a major steamship freight shipping company with offices in 20 countries.

ENDNOTES

1. J. van Baal, *Symbols for Communication: An Introduction to the Anthropological Study of Religion* (Aasen: Van Gorcum, 1971), 4, 5.

2. A marketing research firm, for example, studied the demand for three products in 45 countries, examining 193 country descriptors in its analysis. The firm determined which descriptors or country conditions were most influential in classifying a country into a particular cluster: "We are surprised by the importance of religion. The clusters are almost uniformly characterized by the size of a religious group. This means not only that the size of these groups was by itself a critical variable but also that it was subtly related to many of the other discriminating country conditions." Charles Ramond, "Predicting Demand for Consumer Products in Foreign Countries" (Paper given at the meeting of the Academy of International Business, Toronto, December 1972).

3. Max Weber, *The Protestant Ethic and the Spirit of Capitalism,* tr. Talcott Parsons (New York: Scribner's, 1958), passim.

4. Robert Redfield, *The Little Community and Peasant Society and Culture* (Chicago: University of Chicago Press, 1960), 42ff.

5. Kenneth David, field research in Sri Lanka.

6. Adapted from "The Echoes of Confucianism in Student Extremism," *Far Eastern Economic Review* (January 15, 1987).

7. E. E. Evans-Pritchard, "The Notion of Witchcraft Explains Unfortunate Events," in *Witchcraft, Oracles, and Magic Among the Azande* (Oxford: Clarendon Press, 1937).

8. Melford E. Spiro, "Ghosts, Ifaluk, and Teleological Functionalism," *American Anthropologist* 54, no. 4 (October–December 1952): 497–503.

9. John Murra, "The Economic Organization of the Inca State" (Unpublished thesis, University of Chicago, 1956); cited in Maurice Godelier, "The Concept of 'Social and Economic Formation': The Inca Example," in *Perspectives in Marxist Anthropology,* tr. Robert Brain (London: Cambridge University Press, 1977), 63–66.

10. David B. Barrett, *World Christian Encyclopedia* (Oxford: Oxford University Press, 1983).

11. Arthur S. Banks and Robert B. Textor, *A Cross-Polity Survey* (Cambridge, MA: M.I.T. Press, 1963), 70.

12. John Middleton, "The Cult of the Dead: Ancestors and Ghosts," Lugbara Religion: Ritual and Authority Among an East African People (London: Oxford University Press, 1960).

13. Elizabeth Colson, "Ancestral Spirits and Social Structure Among the Plateau Tonga," *International Archives of Ethnography* 97, I (1954): 21–68.

14. Chief Seattle, excerpt from speech delivered in 1854 on Bainbridge Island, Washington. Transcribed and translated from the Duwamish language by Dr. Smith, a settler.

15. *Ann Arbor News* (June 21, 1970).

16. This notion is similar to the Lamarckian notion of the inheritance of acquired characteristics.

17. Kenneth David, "Hierarchy and Equivalence in Jaffna, North Sri Lanka," *The New Wind: Changing Identities in South Asia,* Kenneth David, ed., World Anthropology series (The Hague: Mouton, 1977), 179–226.

18. Prakash Tandon, "Maturing of Business in India," *California Management Review* (Spring 1972): 80.

19. Kusum Nair, *Blossoms in The Dust: The Human Factor in Indian Development* (New York: Praeger, 1962), esp. 192–193.

20. Tandon, op. cit., 81.

21. "Hinduism," *International Encyclopedia of the Social Sciences.*

22. Theravada is referred to as *Hinayana,* "The Little Vehicle," by the Mahayana Buddhists, who feel it is too difficult for the mass of mankind.

23. Robert Slater, *World Religions and World Community* (New York: Columbia University Press, 1968), 96.

24. Sacred Books of the Buddhas, cited in James N. D. Anderson, The World's Religions (London: Inter-Varsity Fellowship of Evangelical Unions, 1950), 126.

25. Company interviews by Kenneth David in Seoul, summer, 1982.

26. Robert C. Lester, Theravada Buddhism in Southeast Asia (Ann Arbor: University of Michigan Press, 1972), 98.

27. Malcolm X, *The Autobiography of Malcolm X,* as told to Alex Haley (New York: Ballantine, 1973).

28. Robert Slater, *World Religions and World Community* (New York: Columbia University Press, 1968), 137.

29. Ibid., 219.

30. *Time* (April 2, 1973): 25–26.

31. *Time* (May 9, 1969): 67–68.

32. *The Wall Street Journal* (May 5, 1976): 9.

33. *The Wall Street Journal* (January 20, 1975): 21.

34. *The Wall Street Journal* (September 8, 1975): 13.

35. Author's interview with Dr. Tourki, Dean of the Business School, University of Tunisia.

36. Adapted from Bruce M. Borthwick, "The Islamic Sermon as a Channel of Political Communication," *Middle East Journal* (Summer 1967): 299–313.

37. Major works have been written on this subject. See Max Weber, *The Protestant Ethic and the Spirit of Capitalism* (New York: Scribner's, 1958); R. H. Tawney, *Religion and the Rise of Capitalism* (New York: Harcourt-Brace, 1926); and David McClelland, *The Achieving Society* (New York: Irvington, 1961).

38. 1 Timothy 2:5.

39. See Geert Hofstede and Michael Harris Bond, "The Confucius Connection: from cultural roots to economic growth," *Organizational Dynamics* 16, 4 (Spring 1988): 5–24.

40. *Time* (February 5, 1973): 39.

41. Of 2.5 million people in 1986, 76.3 percent were Chinese, 15 percent were Malay, 6.4 percent were Indian, and 2.3 percent were Eurasian and European, all descended from immigrants.

42. For the Chinese Buddhists/Taoists/Confucianists, two days for Chinese New Year; for the Malay Muslims, one day for the birthday of Mohammed and one day for Malay New Year; for the Indian Hindus, one day for Depavali (Indian New Year) and one day for Tai Pusan (a day of ecstatic devotion); for the European Christians, one day for Good Friday and the other day for Christmas.

43. In 1987, Vincent Cheng—Catholic activist and revolutionary—was arrested after gaining control of the Justice and Peace Commission and the Geylang Catholic Welfare center (*The Staits Times,* May 29, 1987). After making public statements inciting the Muslim minority to unite and fight against the Chinese majority, four Muslim preachers were banned from Singapore and their followers were questioned by the Internal Security Department (*The Staits Times,* August 17, 1987).

CHAPTER FIVE
Values

The most vital fact about beliefs is that people act on them.

Conrad Arensberg

THE PLACE OF VALUES IN SOCIAL LIFE

Social life is not programmed like a computer game in which discrete, unambiguous actions must be performed in different circumstances. People in society often face moral dilemmas, ambiguous circumstances in which several choices of proper norms and behavior are possible. Values are priorities for sorting out the options and, when one has the will and the resources to do so, for implementing one code for behavior rather than others. If you roughly shove someone during a business meeting, that behavior violates usual rules of politeness and civility. When you shove a child out of the way of an oncoming truck, you have placed a lesser value on politeness and a greater value on saving the child's life.

Put another way, values direct a society's people to selectively attend to some goals and to subordinate others. When as a cultural outsider you find that your canons of reasonableness are being consistently thwarted in a particular arena of action, it is a mistake to jump to the conclusion that you are the target of personal animosity. It is worth the trouble to investigate whether the people with whom you are dealing have different priorities. This was the lesson of the interaction between two chief executive officers, one Canadian and one Indian, that was presented in the first chapter.

Values are emotionally charged priorities. The act of prioritizing is not just a flat mental activity; it involves some degree of emotional commitment. How is commitment incited? In fact, values are learned during the purely human process of socialization, along with cultural classifications of reality and cultural codes for behavior. In order to incite commitment to values, elders present them as if they were created and commanded by what the society defines as holy. This connection is important, for humans are frequently skeptical about anything known to be invented by other humans. To avoid skepticism, then, we frequently justify values by the order of reality we call religion.

Values usually relate codes of surface behavior to underlying assumptions about power, rank, and often religion. The following focus cases illustrate this point.

FOCUS CASE:
Brazilian Values on Punctuality and Success

Being on time or not is a surface behavior that is interpreted in relation to success. An American visitor reports his encounter with the Brazilian version of this relationship.[1]

Brazilians rate persons who are always late for appointments as most successful. Now even in the land of amanhã, this was a surprising result. It's one thing to be flexible and another to believe that not getting there on time actually pays. I had hoped to break through the amanhã stereotype, and, instead, found myself in the middle of a Latin joke. I soon realized I was missing the point.

Although I failed to grasp its full implications at the time, my first hint had come on my first day in Brazil. I had an appointment to meet my new *chefe,* or department head. I arrived at her office on time. Neither she nor her secretary was there. In fact, I had to turn on the lights myself to read the magazines in the waiting room. After half an hour, the secretary arrived, said *alô,* asked me if I wanted a *cafèzinho* (the traditional drink of thick coffee and sugar in equal amounts), and left. Fifteen minutes later my new *chefe* arrived, also offered me a *cafèzinho,* and also left. Upon her return, she sat down at her desk and began reading her mail. When she finally called me into her office, she casually apologized for keeping me waiting, chatted for a few minutes, and then excused herself to "run" to another appointment, for which she said she was late. I learned later that she wasn't lying. It was her habit to make lots of appointments for the same time and to be late for all of them. She apparently liked appointments.

Later that day I had meetings scheduled with several students. When I got to my "office" (a table in the middle of an otherwise empty room), two of them were already there and acting quite at home. One had his feet up on my desk while reading a *Sports Illustrated,* which I noticed was only three months old. They seemed unconcerned over my being a few minutes late; in fact, they were in no hurry to begin. They remained equally relaxed when the time allotted for the meeting drew to a close. They evinced no more concern about the time it ended than they had about the time it began.

My last appointment of the day was with the owner of an apartment I wanted to rent. By this time I thought I was getting the picture. As soon as I arrived at his office, I asked his secretary how long I would have to wait. She said that her boss was running about 15 minutes late. Would I like a *cafèzinho?* No, I said, I'd be back in 15 minutes. When I came back 10 minutes later, she told me he'd tired of waiting for me and had left.

I was learning why Brazilians rate people who are always late for an appointment as most successful: they see lack of punctuality as a badge of success—part of the outfit. Important people are expected to be unpunctual. In the U.S., we resent it when powerful people, such as doctors, keep us waiting. But Brazilians of lower status apparently don't mind such unpunctuality.

This case is a good example of differing priorities used to evaluate the rank of others.

FOCUS CASE:
Swiss and Italian Values on Punctuality and Quality

Different nationalities have contrasting priorities on the urgency of time and of the search of quality. The Swiss, Belgians, and Germans are perceived as punctual with a sense of time that communicates urgency. The Latin nations and the Irish have a more relaxed sense of time with a tolerance of the *mañana* tradition. But what happens when these values meet in business?

A major Italian manufacturing company commissioned a specialized Swiss software and engineering company to design, create, and install computerized materials-handling equipment. The first part of the project was devoted to agreeing on software specifications for the computerized equipment.

Two project teams, one Swiss and one Italian, were formed to develop the programming. The early project meetings were courteous and formal as each side struggled toward mutual cooperation, using English as their lingua franca. After three months of meetings, relationships deteriorated markedly. The Swiss engineers complained that their Italian colleagues were always changing their minds, that they never met deadlines and did not seem to think time was important. They complained that the Italians invariably came back within a few days of agreement on provisional specifications, seeking modifications that would optimize performance of the mechanical equipment but delay further programming. The Italians, meanwhile, complained that their Swiss colleagues were inflexible, always insisting on documents by fixed dates. They could not understand why the Swiss were so committed to the provisional agreements on software specification. Was it not better to get the best possible performance from the equipment by delaying a few days and designing the software better? They had little sympathy for their Swiss colleagues' urgency.[2]

This case illustrates clear conflict concerning the priorities given by the two teams to time versus quality of the final product. One would never fault the Swiss for poor quality work, but in this interaction they conflicted with the Italians, who felt freer to spend time to achieve quality work. Fortunately, the two teams decided to experiment with each other's ways, agreeing to live for short periods according to the sense of time dominant in each culture. The Swiss engineers learned to be more flexible about time, and the Italians realized how the discipline of precise time commands respect in Swiss daily life.

THE ROLE OF VALUES IN THE ECONOMY

Every culture has defined priorities for every aspect of social life. In later chapters we will discuss the impact of cultural priorities in the specific areas of technology, social organization, and politics. Here, our discussion will focus on values critical for understanding the economic performance of a society.

In evaluating the potential of a piece of machinery, it is usually sufficient to refer to objective and measurable specifications. An engineer who knows the horsepower, revolutions per minute, capacity, and tolerances can make a precise evaluation of the equipment. In the social sciences, such precision is impossible. From knowledge of measurable dimensions such as topographical features, the natural resource base, or demographic statistics (age, sex, and education groupings), an economist can predict a nation's economic potential with only limited precision.

Although geophysical factors and demographics certainly affect a nation's economy, there is strong evidence that intangible cultural variables affect economic performance more significantly. In other words, inner motivation and culturally shared values largely determine both economic performance and level of development. According to Nair, "A community's attitude toward work can be a more decisive determinant for raising productivity in Indian agriculture than material resources, or, for that matter, even technology."[3]

Old Stereotypes about Values and Performance

We suggest that managers interested in facilitating intercultural communications and negotiations be skeptical about certain old stereotypes—applied to particular world regions—about values that are held to inhibit or facilitate economic performance in those regions.

Myrdal, for example, noted over 20 years ago that some values are inimical to economic development. Often, in Asia, "religiously sanctioned beliefs and valuations not only act as obstacles among the people to getting the plan accepted and effectuated but also as inhibitions to the planners themselves insofar as they share them, or are afraid to counteract them."[4] He found that in the Asian case the following modernizing attitudes and ideals were necessary:[5]

1. Efficiency
2. Diligence
3. Orderliness
4. Punctuality
5. Frugality
6. Honesty
7. Rationality in decisions on action
8. Preparedness for change
9. Alertness to opportunities
10. Energetic enterprise
11. Integrity
12. Cooperativeness
13. Willingness to take the long view.

Myrdal noted that the list was not comprehensive and that individual items were interdependent. He suggested the list did give some idea of the kinds of values related to economic performance.

Michael took a similar stance, holding that American values toward technology and economy were a very favorable factor in America's growth:[6]

1. A belief that progress is the inevitable result of the use of new technologies.

2. A basic optimism about the future.

3. A belief that there are no limits on the degree to which people and resources can be harnessed to, and rewarded by, the expansion of technology.

4. A belief that a healthy economy is one that shows continual growth in the GNP.

5. A belief that people can and should be organized to achieve anything via technology that seems important to achieve.

These accounts, written a while ago, now seem dated. They reflect a particular ideology. They were written at the height of the period when economic development, modernization, and industrialization were unquestioned key goals of major international organizations such as the World Bank. Myrdal's and Michael's lists of values summarize an ideology of economic performance and development based on central values of the United States.

Outsiders should be wary of interpreting actions that seem contradevelopmental as necessarily due to irrational, traditional values. The case of Turkish enterprise reported by Atac, Muderrisoglu, and Aydin instructs us that such actions may be perfectly rational responses that take advantage of the developmental rules that create market imperfections.[7]

> The practice of setting up companies that obtain profits by making and exporting unmarketable or marginally profitable products is only apparently irrational. The point is that if the company sets up a colleague abroad who sends buy orders, then the home office can apply for and receive currency concessions and import licenses (meant to buy materials to support the export business). The profit comes from selling these concessions and licenses in gray or black markets.

New Values

A more recent work, Gerald Cavanagh's *American Business Values in Transition,* adroitly traces the genesis of American values to the moral and intellectual traditions of Puritan settlers, the application of biological Darwinism to economic and social achievement (the fittest will survive and prosper), and to historical conditions such as the settlement of the American frontier, where rugged individualism and initiative really paid off.

In more recent years, central business values are shifting in response to factors such as the increasingly closer connection of nations in the global economy—there is no longer an open frontier in the global economy—and concern for environmental protection.[8]

Global interconnection incites a set of related business values:

- Global market share rather than domestic market share becomes the objective of strategy.

- Economies of scope (worldwide brand recognition) become as important as economies of scale (large production facilities, for example).

- Creating tomorrow's competitive advantages faster than competitors can mimic the ones you possess today.

As we shall see in more detail in the chapters on technology and politics, the economic development model has been seriously questioned in many countries. Poor countries do not perceive a single golden road to modernity. Most new countries that gained independence after World War II, for example, value some combination of capitalism and socialism in their economy. In a foreign setting, an international manager should not expect to find an enlightened elite committed to the values we have just listed and attempting to inculcate the masses with them. The ideas have been communicated abroad; some of them have become policy and some have been rejected.

Effective Values and Cultural Style

Finally, an international manager must learn to distinguish between the effective values deeply held by foreign counterparts—some of which are indeed those identified by Myrdal and Michael—and the very different cultural style that may mask their presence. Indian firms may or may not give the appearance of punctuality, diligence, and honesty. Behind the appearance, however, may lurk very familiar values. For example, any foreign firm considering a joint venture with the Birla firm will find that Birla has done its homework and will produce an extremely sophisticated financial forecast as part of the plan. Similar misleading appearances have been noted in Japan:

> Bunny Cramer, a partner in the Tokyo corporate communications firm of Witan Associates, says the Japanese negotiating styles can seem vague at first, but only until you learn to read the signals. "If they won't talk about the bottom line, they're indicating that they haven't made a decision to go ahead yet," she explains. "If they are ready, they'll talk about the bottom line harder than anyone you've ever met."[9]

As you can see, international managers must be cautious about assuming that traditional American business values are accepted as the best way to prioritize goals and activities. It is essential to learn the effective priorities—not just the appearances—of values among business and government counterparts in foreign settings.

Our discussion now turns to several values that deserve attention in order to develop intercultural communications skills that facilitate international business operations: values toward time; values toward work, wealth, and achievement; and values toward change.

VALUES TOWARD TIME

The clock, not the steam engine, is the key machine of the modern industrial age.

Lewis Mumford

For Mexican peasants, the distance of a trip is converted to time. A trip is measured in days, not in miles. A trip takes its time. You don't worry about getting there sooner. When people begin to travel they say that time no longer exists. And when they arrive, they say that time exists once again.

Joseph Spielberg

Attitudes toward time vary from culture to culture and even within a culture. The terms *hora American* and *hora Mexicana* or *mong Amelikan* and *mong Lao* indicate cultural differences in the importance of punctuality in business or social appointments. A clock *runs* in English but *walks* in Spanish and French. The midpoint between hours is half-past the earlier hour in many languages but half-before the next hour (6:30 is *half zeven*) in Dutch.

American and European managers frequently experience culture shock from differences in the treatment of time. They wonder why foreigners are so late for business appointments or so slow in getting down to business. Cutting through the diversity of cultural definitions of time, we can distinguish between traditional and modern values toward time—or to put it more accurately, between older, concrete orientations toward time and newer, abstract orientations toward time.

Older, Concrete, Traditional Values Toward Time

An old orientation to time reflects alternations and cycles observable in nature. In preindustrial societies, alternations such as day and night and annual seasonal cycles provide the model for productive and ritual activities. This orientation to time is more concrete than that employed in industrial societies.

In the traditional view, time is perceived as a circle. The natural events that measure time—the movement of the sun, the phases of the moon, the tides, the seasons of the year—all recur, suggesting a circular pattern. Most Asian religions have developed notions of time involving vast cosmic cycles during which all creatures undergo a series of rebirths. Existence itself is a cycle in which being and nonbeing alternate. In northern Sri Lanka, children play a game similar to hopscotch, in which four squares are labeled being, nonbeing, being and nonbeing, and neither being nor nonbeing.

Preindustrial societies differ widely in the precision of time reckoning. In some societies, periods of the day that accord with light and heat versus dark and coolness are classified as times to work and times to refrain from working. In Indian astrology, the day is divided into 60 periods (nalikai) of 24 minutes each. An astrological chart is calculated according to the nalikai of birth; important events, such as puberty, wedding, and funeral ceremonies, are scheduled accordingly.

It is a mistake to think that activities are leisurely because they are timed by natural events. Anyone who has watched peasants get down to work to harvest before the rains come and spoil the crops knows that their work is very intense. It is more precise to say that periods of leisure alternate with periods of intense activity: both are timed by natural events.[10]

This older version of time still exists not only in less-developed countries of the world, but also in subcultures of developed ones. In Brazil there is a great difference between the Sao Paulo industrialist and the farmer living in the interior. Even in the United States, there are vestiges of a more concrete orientation to time: One beer advertiser tells the public that after work, *it's Miller Time!* Another company suggests that *the night belongs to Michelob!*

Gross measurement of time by natural events will not work in industry, which follows the artificial, abstract but precise rhythm of the machine. In industry, everything must proceed like clockwork. This applies not only to the operation of an assembly line, but also to the punctuality, orderliness, and regularity of the worker in the factory. The alternation of periods of inactivity and periods of intense activity will not work on an assembly line.

An example from the Hopi Indians illustrates how a traditional view of time can bring trouble to nonagricultural work projects.

> For the Hopi, time is not fixed or measurable as we think of it. It is what happens as the corn matures or a sheep grows up—a characteristic sequence of events. There is a different natural time for everything. Hopi houses were often in the process of being built for years and years. The Indians had no idea that a house should be built in a given time span, as a house had no natural time system such as the corn and sheep had. This way of looking at time cost the government untold thousands of dollars on construction projects because the Hopi could not conceive of a fixed time in which a dam or a road should be built.[11]

Another aspect of the traditional view of time is the emphasis on the present versus the long-run future. Industrialization and economic development are difficult to achieve without long-range planning. An Argentinian discusses what the emphasis on the present has meant for Argentina:

> Argentines emphasize Present Time. This attachment to the Present and the emphasis on immediate goals have been accentuated in recent decades. The writings and works of the nineteenth-century men who shaped the union of the provinces and the political framework of modern Argentina show that they were leaders with some sense of future, long-run objectives.
> Early immigrants were people mainly driven by their pioneer spirit who were prepared to make sacrifices so that their descendants might have a degree of well-being not available to them. Recent immigrants are impelled by the hope of immediate gains. They emigrate primarily for their own sake, not for the sake of their descendants.
> The social and economic implications for a society whose members emphasize Present Time are obvious. Such an emphasis is inimical to planning

for the future; to long-run, political, economic, or social commitments; to the emergence of a collective sense of duty—especially of the sense of duty to do productive work; or to furthering the interest of a group, an organization, or a community.[12]

Abstract, Lineal Values Toward Time

A contrasting orientation to time is a more abstract, lineal version of time. This concept is held to be modern. In fact, the idea has been around for thousands of years. Early Christian theology was quite radical in its day, for it defined a unique, nonrepetitive history with a beginning (Creation) and an end (Apocalypse) to all things. In this orientation, time is measured less by recurring natural events than by the artificial but precise movements of the clock.

Monasteries and the Development of Mechanical Time

The mechanical concept of time arose in part out of the routine and the goals of the monastery. Within the monastic walls, order and learning reigned; outside was irregularity, caprice, and striving for power. In the seventh century, Pope Sabinianus decreed that the bells of the monastery be rung seven times in the twenty-four hours. Striped candles were an early means of keeping track of these canonical hours and assuring their regular repetition. Although the mechanical clock did not appear until the thirteenth century, the habit of order and the earnest regulation of time sequences had become part of monastic routine.

Some historians regard the Benedictines, the great working order (at one time there were 40,000 monasteries under Benedictine rule), as contributors to the rise of modern industry and capitalism. Lewis Mumford suggests that the monasteries helped give human enterprise the regular collective beat and rhythm of the machine, for the clock is not merely a means of keeping track of the hours, but of synchronizing the actions of people. The clock was essential to a well-articulated system of production and transportation.[13] The clock dissociated time from natural events and helped create the perception of time as an independent world of mathematically measured sequences.

Punctuality and Time Pressure

Especially after the Industrial Revolution, abstract time became the medium of existence. Industrialists enlisted contemporary religion and taught workers that punctuality was a virtue. When one thinks of time not as a sequence of experiences but as a collection of hours, minutes, and seconds, time becomes a commodity. Time is to be well used, to be saved, not wasted. Even modernizing Communists in Russia shared Ben Franklin's idea that time is money. In 1923, the Soviet Time League was obliged to report every waste of time encountered. They distributed leaflets bearing this message:

Measure your time, control it!
Do everything on time! Exactly to the minute!
Save time, make time count, work fast!
Divide your time correctly, for work and for leisure![14]

This orientation toward time, then, promotes a sense of urgency that is related to the productivity of industry. In Ben Franklin's day, 90 percent of Americans worked the land, and the rhythm of life was shaped by the natural cycles of agriculture. As the nation industrialized, the artificial time of the clock and of the assembly line came to regulate the rhythm of life. Frederick W. Taylor's time-and-motion studies were important steps in the development of scientific management. According to studies cited by McClelland, this sense of urgency is especially strong among individuals with a high need for achievement. Such individuals are acutely aware of the rapid passage of time.[15]

Whether on the societal or on the individual level, productivity is bought at the expense of leisure. Anthropologists have calculated that hunters, pastoralists, and even slash-and-burn agriculturalists attain their desired level of affluence by working, on the average, no more than 800 hours a year.[16] High achievers in industrial society work several thousand hours a year. See Table 5-1.

TABLE 5-1

AVERAGE ANNUAL WORKLOAD
IN MAJOR INDUSTRIAL COUNTRIES

	Working Days	*Working Hours*	*Paid Vacation Days*	*Weekends & Holidays*
Japan	253	2,102	9	103
United States	231	1,924	19	115
Europe		1,600		
Britain	230		23	112
France	228		26	111
West Germany	221		29	115

Sources: Japanese Ministry of Labor, reported in *The Economist* (January 7, 1989); *Business Week* (September 28, 1987).

Future Orientation

The linear conception of time also stresses the long-run situation as well as the present. Hall notes that "the American never questions the fact that time should be planned and future events fitted into a schedule. He thinks that people should look toward the future and not dwell too much on the past."[17]

A long-run perspective is important for modern industrial society. In *Future Shock,* Toffler suggests that the perspective needs to be even longer for post-industrial society.

It is worth noting individual as well as cultural differences in time perspective. McClelland cites studies showing that individuals with a high need for achievement have a longer time perspective than those with lower need for achievement. They also use more anticipatory tenses. He suggests that "the longer forward time perspective of individuals with high achievement may be in part the explanation for their superior ability to delay gratification."[18]

With the following statements in mind, one may question whether American business values are modern or traditional.

- In financial theory, rational investors are supposed to consider the long-term growth of earnings of a company in deciding how much to pay for its stocks. In practice, the orientation is often to the present.

- Brilliant entrepreneurs in high-technology growth industries such as computer software are tempted to go public to reap immediate profits. Afterwards, they find they no longer have the liberty to develop products at their previous pace but must be concerned with the quarterly scrutiny of their financial records.

- Leveraged buy-outs increase wealth for individuals but sometimes impose on the company a massive debt that can impair its long-term business prospects.

In conclusion, the international manager who was socialized with the abstract, linear, pressured, and future orientation to time must be willing to relax these constraints when dealing with foreign counterparts. Many stories could be recounted to bring home this theme. The basic lesson is that parochial managers from industrial countries (whether American or European) lose valuable contracts because they misinterpret delays in getting down to business. The foreign counterpart's orientation may be to spend time getting acquainted with the person before approaching contractual details; he or she may want to entertain visiting executives and introduce them to relevant local executives or government officials. In the foreign setting, an executive should often revise the saying "time is money" into "spend time so that I do not lose money!"

VALUES TOWARD WORK, WEALTH, AND ACHIEVEMENT

I've been poor and I've been rich. Believe me, rich is better.

Pearl Bailey

Use it up. Wear it out. Make it do. Do without.

Old Connecticut Saying

What accounts for the rise in civilization? Not external resources, but the entrepreneurial spirit which exploits these resources.

David McClelland

Values toward work, accumulation of wealth, and achievement may be the values that most critically affect a society's economic performance. We must define these terms. *Work* is human activity that is organized to achieve socially productive ends. A society's definition of work is strongly conditioned by the limits posed by that society's natural endowments. A society's priority on the *accumulation of wealth* and its definition of *achievement,* on the other hand, are more strongly conditioned by the society's cultural systems of power, rank, and religion.

Said again, definitions of wealth and achievement are culture bound. For example, the title of Adam Smith's book, *Wealth of Nations,* suggests that attitudes toward wealth and material gain are crucial in economics. Economics assumes a certain human nature. The economic person is a rational maximizer—one who believes that more is better, who is frugal, and who maximizes material returns. Smith's assumptions reflect the culture of the author and are not universally valid.

Westerners too often unquestioningly assume that others have—or ought to have—the same economic values that they have. Anthropological studies from many cultures have shown that *all humans are rational maximizers: they are willing to work hard for what they consider worth maximizing.*

Humans in different cultures, of course, differ in what they consider worth the effort. Traditional values, including those toward wealth, material gain, and achievement, differ from region to region and from culture to culture. The values of the population may differ from the values of national planners and developmental economists. The case of Turkish enterprise (cited on page 110)—which does not implement the intent of national planners—shows that actions may be a response to modern bureaucratic rules as opposed to traditional values. International managers should study the societies in which they operate to determine the particular situation and plan accordingly.

In summary, societies in similar natural environments with similar technological adaptations have some similarities in the organization of work. Among these societies, however, the definition of wealth and achievement may differ. These statements will be expanded as our discussion continues.

Technological Adaptation, Work, and Accumulation

A society's definition of work is conditioned by the technological adaptations that are possible in a given environment.

First, the natural endowments of the ecosystem condition the kinds of technology that can be used there. Desert and arctic areas (in the absence of massive investment to create an artificial climate) allow only the hunting and gathering technology. Steppelands allow herding as well as hunting and gathering. In temperate areas, industrial technology and agriculture can be added to the list. The greater the natural endowments, the greater the technological options. In anthropology, this connection between environmental differences and technological adaptations is called *environmental possibilism.*

Second, the chosen technology influences the organization of human work. A given technology calls for a work schedule, a given intensity of effort, a specified size of work group to be mobilized in coordinated activity, and a division of labor within a work group.

Less abundant environments allow simpler technologies with smaller work groups and less division of labor. In such a situation, achievement in the sense of storage or accumulation of goods or wealth is not rational; it is rational to work only several hours a day. Sahlins has noted that hunting and gathering bands work an optimal four to five hours a day. Lacking means to preserve food, and having to travel lightly, there is no sense in working and acquiring more food than will last about a week. These bands, however, are not living on the edge of survival. The Kalahari tribe, which inhabits an arid area in South Africa, for example, has resisted governmental efforts to settle them as agriculturalists. They gain a livelihood, in their opinion, with less effort. "Why should we farm when there are so many mongongo nuts in the world?"[19]

More abundant environments permit more complex technologies, which in turn allow a greater division of labor and larger coordinated work groups. It is possible to appropriate from the environment more than is currently consumed. Current consumption can be delayed; the storage of many items and the accumulation of wealth are possible.

Social Rank and Accumulation of Wealth

Within the limits of what is possible, societies differ greatly in their definition of what is socially desirable concerning the accumulation of goods or the acquisition of wealth. Values on achievement differ, depending on how acceptable is social stratification.

In South Asian societies, social ranking is acceptable. Even though caste memberships places barriers on social mobility, there is no barrier on an individual's acquisition of wealth.

By contrast, in Mexican peasant society, there are social mechanisms that resist the accumulation of wealth and maintain the stratification of people. A fortunate farmer who has several successful farming seasons in a row is appointed to an honorific position in the fiesta season. He becomes a sponsor of the fiesta. By contributing vast sums to the fiesta, he gains social honor but is put back on a par with other villagers in terms of wealth. Strong social sanctions support this practice. Anyone who resists is subject to charges of *envidia* (witchcraft, antisociality) and is socially dishonored. In this situation, values and practices do not favor capital accumulation.

Differing Kinds, Sources, and Uses of Wealth

Again, within the limits of what is possible, societies differ widely in their values toward the appropriate sources of income. Some ways of earning an income are considered more desirable and respectable than others. Indeed, source of income is one criterion used by sociologists in determining social status. As the following scale shows, business incomes rate high.

Status Level	Source of Most of Income
1	Inherited wealth
2	Investments and savings gained by earner
3	Business profits and professional fees
4	Salary or commissions on sales
5	Hourly wages
6	Private assistance
7	Public relief or nonrespectable sources[20]

The American pattern is not the norm. Business—especially commercial—activities often rate rather low as a way of earning a living. Groups defined as outsiders (even if they have been resident in the society for a long period) are allowed to take over the business and commercial activities. Groups such as the Jews in Europe, the Indians in East Africa, and the Chinese in Southeast Asia have been successful and eventually have suffered from the envy and resentment of nationals. In some cases they have been expelled by the nationals, who have taken over the businesses without necessarily having the requisite business skills.

In many societies that are technologically less complex than industrial societies, it is fair to say that wealth is more accurately measured by the number of personal allies a person has than by the quantity of material possessions. In a number of societies, objects of value are temporarily acquired by a powerful person and then redistributed to the followers. Melanesian "big men" gain the ability to organize social and religious activities by this largesse. This practice is stated in French as *noblesse oblige,* meaning that a person of rank has obligations. When Marie Antoinette said "The people ask for bread. Let them eat cake!" she ignored this principle and paid for it. The practice of philanthropic endowments by industrialists in the United States is a less-direct and less-personal version of the redistribution of wealth.

Objects of value differ greatly. In general, real objects are favored as objects of wealth. In some countries, gold is the principal accepted form of wealth. Even peasants accumulate wealth in this form. In Latin America, land and real estate have been the most popular forms of wealth. In some African countries, cattle are the favored form of wealth. The Masai will not work for wages, since tending cattle is the valued occupation and cattle themselves are the highest good.[21] Only in relatively limited parts of the world are securities (stocks and bonds) an accepted or desired form of wealth.

Differing values toward the appropriate form of wealth have significant impacts on how people direct their economic activities. They can affect the supply of funds for saving and productive investment. When hyperinflation rapidly erodes the value of cruzieros or pesos, the appropriate form of wealth is dollars-in-Miami. In general, finding capital to finance the development of business and industry is very difficult where cattle, gold, land, or other real property is the accepted form of wealth. This statement is not automatically true, however. On one hand, Dube mentions the Indian penchant for "seeking security in the ownership of gold rather than making possibly risky investments in productive pursuits."[22] On the other hand, among Sri Lankan peasant agriculturalists and fishermen, a principal form of dowry is a heavy gold chain. Peasant women may have to pawn this jewelry at the beginning of a productive season to finance productive operations and redeem it after the harvest, when they wear it during the temple festival season.[23] In the Japanese case, investment is more direct: "The early Meiji entrepreneurs were achievement oriented and frugal. They invested their capital in productive enterprises rather than in jewels, expensive clothes or conspicuous consumption."[24]

Wealth, of course, is obtained by two processes: (1) acquiring it and (2) by forgoing current consumption, holding on to it. Cultures differ in their values toward both of these processes. For example, the United States is more consumption-oriented than Western European countries. Americans more often take advantage of present opportunities to earn income by moonlighting or by having dual-career households. A higher percentage of American wives hold jobs than do European wives. Germans are more critical of wives' employment than people in any other large Western country. On the other hand, Americans are not so strongly oriented as are Germans to holding on to what they have earned. Americans use installment debt freely, whereas its use in Germany is very low. The German word for debt, *schuld,* is the same as the word for guilt.[25]

Achievement

Obtaining and accumulating wealth is a particular case of achievement. McClelland suggests that a society's values toward achievement are a major determinant of its economic performance.

One of the major early studies presented in support of his hypothesis was a comparative study, a measurement of the achievement drive of managers in four countries— Italy, Poland, Turkey, and the United States. The countries were chosen to represent different levels of economic development and different political systems. The American managers had the highest achievement score, followed by the Polish, Italians, and Turks. Although Poland had a slightly lower per-capita income than Italy, it also suffered more extensive war damage and had a higher growth rate than Italy up to the time of the tests (1960). In general, the results showed a rather close correlation between the achievement drive of the managers and the level of economic development.

Another major study was historical, going back to pre-Incan Peru, and covering Greece, Spain, and England during their centuries of prominence. The level of achievement drive was determined from the drawings on vases and pottery and from the literature, especially folk tales and stories for children. There was consistent support for the idea that achievement drive is a predictor of a society's performance. In other words, a high level of achievement orientation in one period means a high level of performance in the following period. Normally, a high (or low) concern for achievement was followed some 50 years later by a high (or low) rate of economic growth.[26]

Managerial Implications

Various economic implications of values toward work, wealth, consumption, and achievement have been suggested. Here we shall review briefly. Economic development is not just a question of making use of natural endowments, learning skills, and acquiring technology. Certain values are important for the mobilization of human effort with commitment. The American value on money mobilizes effort. In America, because money is valued not only for itself but also as a symbol of achievement and power, executives who earn more money than they can spend are still concerned about their total wealth and annual income.

> Mary Wells Lawrence earns $385,000 a year heading an advertising agency. She said, "The money isn't really what I work for. For one thing, I don't have the time to spend it."[27]

Many nonfinancial incentives such as occupancy of corner suites on the top floor of the office building are also important as signs of relative power and achievement.

International managers must learn the priority system in the country in which they are operating in order to manage the incentive system. They cannot simply export their country's incentives. For example, the backward-bending supply curve for labor reflects Western cultural assumptions. In economic theory, supply curves always slope upward to the right—that is, more will be supplied if the price is higher.

A frequent observation in less-developed countries is that the amount of labor supplied decreases with higher wages. The Western assumption that more money is always better does not always hold. Where other priorities are present, workers will quit as soon as they have reached their threshold of sufficiency. Sufficiency may mean enough capital to buy a plot of land large enough to support the family and pay for one's daughters' dowries.

Some companies attack this problem by providing incentive goods so that as one aspiration level is satisfied—say, a bicycle—another good can be made available—for example, a motorbike or metal roofing. This tactic assumes that aspirations are constantly rising, an assumption rooted in Western cultures. Incentives that closely follow indigenous priorities may be more effective. For example, the Indian Tata Company had some success in retaining workers by introducing a tenure system that resembled the traditional rural social relationships. Any worker who stayed on the job for over 10 years could name a relative or friend as a successor to the job.

VALUES TOWARD CHANGE

Values toward change are another basic variable in economic performance. By change, we refer to both goods and processes. New or different goods may be adopted with no change in process: for example, using a different seed but planting and harvesting in the old manner. Conversely, new processes may be adopted without a change in goods: for example, using the old seeds but adopting crop rotation. At heart, change is a transformation of ideas and priorities, a change in value orientations that is then, if possible, implemented in action.

Societies differ widely in the degree to which change is favorably perceived. At one extreme, new products or processes may be considered as undesirable disruption—or even evil. Among Marxist-Leninist academics and politicians, it is a serious charge to be labelled a revisionist of the Marxist-Leninist vision of society. Similarly, fundamentalist preachers revile human action that is held to contradict the norms prescribed in the gospel. "All innovation is the work of the devil" is attributed to Mohammed.[28] At the other extreme, change is held to be identical with positive progress. American advertisers frequently use this attitude by printing NEW! IMPROVED! in large letters on boxes of consumer products.

One definition of a traditional society is a society in which many aspects of social life are closely interrelated. In such a situation, a change in one element will affect many others.

> To the Chinese, the introduction of power machinery meant that he had to throw over not only habits of work but a whole ideology; for dissatisfaction with the ways of his fathers in one particular meant doubt of the fathers' way of life in all its aspects. If the old loom must be discarded, then 100 other things must be discarded with it, for there are somehow no adequate substitutes.[29]

A reduction in the interconnection of details of social life precedes an increase in the rate of change. American society was largely a traditional society until World War II, when geographical mobility of nuclear families reduced a strongly supported system of morality. The explosion of a variety of life-styles followed.

Risk Perception

Willingness to accept change depends on the amount of risk the potential adopter perceives in the change. Schein, discussing organizational change, notes that it is easier to implement change in organizations where the environment is perceived as nonthreatening than in organizations where the environment is perceived as threatening. In the latter, people want to hold on to what they have, even if it is unpleasant, rather than to risk a move to an unfamiliar and uncertain structure.[30]

Cultures define limits of change beyond which the innovator is at risk. This is true in low-technology societies where an innovator may risk social ostracism, or even death, by violating a taboo. It is also true in American society. When Valichovsky proposed that the Great Flood was caused by the planet Venus nearly hitting the earth, he was totally ostracized by the community of physicists. Reformers in Muslim societies may face assassination.

> The complete integration of religion, political system, and way of life make it extremely difficult to alter the institutions of Muslim countries unless the priests, or ulema, who interpret the Koran are favorable to proposed changes. If they oppose change, they may resort to fanatical opposition, up to and including the assassination of would-be reformers, as has happened in the case of the Muslim Brotherhood in Iran and Egypt.[31]

In such circumstances, change is an extremely high-risk proposition, and traditional behavior is likely to be maintained.

In America, there are fewer social risks in innovation because of the society's favorable image of newness. After 60 British executives spent a year in the United States, they reported that the success of American business was due partially to an attitude toward change and risk: "A belief whereby a successful experiment is not allowed to be crystallized into accepted custom, whereas an unsuccessful experiment is accepted as an occupational risk and is set against the experience that is gained."[32] In other words, American innovators are encouraged by the commonsense notion that you can't win them all.

It must be emphasized that this personal and social risk is in addition to the normal risk of innovation—that is, that the innovation might be unsuccessful. For example, in poor agricultural societies, small farmers may be slow to adopt a highly touted agricultural change. They realize that if the innovation is not successful, they could lose their whole crop, a disaster greater than they could afford. Such conservatism is often justified. Innovations developed elsewhere by well-meaning experts have not succeeded in a specific area because the laboratory tests did not take into account features of the local environment and culture. A strain of beans developed in a laboratory to repel a certain insect in Central America produced no beans in the fields because the new strain could not stand several hundred additional feet of altitude. Numerous examples of such failure are given by Arensberg and Niehoff in their book, *Introducing Social Change.*

View of Scientific Method

Various authors contrast the pessimistic fatalism of traditional societies with the more optimistic attitude toward change wrought by science and technology in Western industrial countries. Both of these contrasting orientations are to some degree a matter of belief. For example, fatalism in Muslim countries is held to stem from the Koranic teaching that everything is foreordained and recorded on the Preserved Tablet. Sayigh, an Arab economist, complains about the "slowness of Arab societies to change from a fatalistic attitude toward events to acceptance of technical and economic causality."[33] Similarly, Gillin writes of the sense of fatalism, a feeling of resignation, and a lack of hope for positive change in many Latin American societies.

> In public life, there is a tendency to shirk the seeking of constructive solutions to problems. In politics it has induced a general paralysis of action. In public health, one of the principal problems has been the ingrained belief that some amount of sickness and death is inevitable.[34]

Countries like the United States and Japan, by contrast, have a more optimistic attitude toward the ability of science and technology to solve major problems, an attitude that is tantamount to a belief in the efficacy of science. Americans are pleased but not astonished by the technological success of the space program. This attitude is reflected concretely in the planning activities and research and development expenditures in industry.

There is a third orientation to the use of the scientific method. Many authors do not deny that individual problems can be solved by the use of the scientific method.

They add, however, that the overall effect of a series of individual rational decisions, each decision based on a scientific approach, can result in systemic consequences that are unintended and not necessarily beneficial.[35] The owners of smokestack industrial plants in the northern United States and southern Canada have each made rational, optimizing decisions concerning the allocation of resources to deal with effluent material. The collective result of these decisions, acid rain, is not beneficial. International managers may want to temper optimizing solutions to a productive process located abroad with a consideration of the social and environmental impacts on the host country.

Political Influences

A society's openness to change can be further influenced by political factors. As we will describe more fully in Chapter 6, in the less-developed countries that were once colonies, many social, political, and technical changes were introduced by the colonial power. These changes were accepted by the host country populace because of the relative power of the colonials. For several decades after independence, there was a partial revulsion toward the colonial legacy. In practice, this meant a reluctance to accept innovations from the industrialized world when those innovations were seen as a form of neoimperialism. This trend, as we shall see, is now reversing as countries move to establish equitable relations with foreign companies.

Implications and Conclusions

Introducing change can be difficult and occasionally impossible in societies that have negative orientations toward change. When the ruling elites in such countries want to industrialize, there are important value judgments to be made concerning the necessity or desirability of change. Ideally, general agreement is better than having change imposed by a ruling group. That this agreement is often missing is evidenced by the common demands of planners and development economists for a change in priorities by the mass of the people. In some societies, the discrepancy in orientation is settled by revolution. This method has its costs. Most other ways of implementing innovation and change are slower. Some guidelines are available for slow, steady change.

First, one should *identify the deterrents to the proposed change.* Which traditions, values, and practices are related to the proposed change? Obtaining this information requires a detailed market-research type of study. In anthropology, the study is called a social and environmental impact analysis.

A second step is to *determine which cultural obstacles to the proposed change can be neutralized and which require modification of the proposed change.* If change in value orientation is a difficult and lengthy process, then adaptation is necessary. King Saud of Saudi Arabia was successful in modifying previous orientations:

Religious elders are reputed to have objected to the introduction of telephones in Saudi Arabia on the premise that they were instruments of the devil because they were not mentioned in the Koran. It is said that King Saud had a passage of the Koran transmitted over the telephone and won acceptance of the new technology with the argument that the devil would not permit an instrument of his to be employed for such a purpose.[36]

A third guideline for introducing change is that *the innovation must be tested and evaluated in terms of the host culture.* Too often planners or other agents of change assume that an idea, product, or process developed from a foreign planning office or laboratory will be suitable in a new environment. Indeed, many development projects fail not because people are unwilling to adopt an innovation, but because the innovation is contrary to their value orientations.

A fourth guideline is that *an innovation will be accepted more quickly if its effectiveness has been demonstrated locally.* Earlier we noted that people are unwilling to test an innovation if the risk of failure is too high. Small farmers may be unwilling to test a new fertilizer, for example, because the loss of an entire crop is a disaster. Wealthier farmers in the same village, however, might be persuaded to devote one of their fields to the experiment. If they are successful, other farmers may try it the following season.

A fifth guideline relates to the *nature of the innovation; technical change will be accepted more quickly and easily than social or political change.* Transistor radios, cars, and Coca-Cola have been more widely accepted than have Western educational methods, medical practices, or democratic political structures. Even technological changes, however, must be studied for possible social or political impacts.

Wealthy fish merchants in northern Sri Lanka (who employed hundreds of poor fishermen in beach seine fishing) violently resisted the introduction of nylon nets and motor launches. They anticipated, quite accurately, that these items would reduce the dependency of poorer fishermen. The latter indeed began to invest in these items and work for themselves.[37]

A final guideline is to *seek out in the existing culture those values that might be used to support the proposed innovation.* This has the advantage of going with the grain of the culture rather than fighting against it. A good example of this is the illustration of the Meiji Restoration.

Japan's relentless march towards modernization began with the Meiji Period in 1868. Before then, Japan was a feudal society (the Tokugawa Period). In less than a century, Japan became a modern industrial and military power. A major reason for the success of this government-induced development was the mobilization of traditional values.

The leaders of the Meiji period sought—within the traditional Japanese value system—those values which could serve both as motivation for modernization and as sanctions for the necessary social changes and sacrifices. The values used for this purpose were the emperor system and the family system—loyalty and filial piety. Both were Confucian values that had been modified by Shinto beliefs and the interpretation of Tokugawa scholars.

The Japanese were familiar and comfortable with the values of loyalty to the emperor and filial piety. Further, motivation to work for and accept change was provided by the value of loyalty to the emperor. Obedience to government directives was encouraged by both loyalty and filial piety. Even the Zaibatsu (the giant industrial combines) fit into this centralized hierarchy of authority, between the emperor and the family. This continuity with traditional values lessened the shock of the many changes which occurred in the Meiji period.[38]

For more detailed guidelines, a book such as Arensberg and Niehoff's *Introducing Social Change* is useful. The most important point for the potential change agent is to be aware of how the proposed innovation fits with the host culture. One must educate oneself before seeking to change others.

QUESTIONS

1. Attitudes toward time include ideas about lateness or promptness.
   a. What do you feel is the appropriate time to arrive for the following events? (Specify exact time or range.)
      (1) A class that begins at 10:10
      (2) A 2:00 P.M. committee meeting
      (3) A play scheduled to begin at 8:30 P.M.
      (4) A date for "around 8"
      (5) A plane departure scheduled for 4:13
      (6) Your job, which runs from 8:00 A.M. to 5:00 P.M.
      (7) A dinner party at 8:00 P.M.
   b. Do you feel that Europeans or Africans would specify times similar to yours?
   c. For each of the preceding events, how late could you be without being uncomfortable or feeling that you have to apologize?
   d. Do your answers differ from those of your classmates? Would people in other countries answer differently?

2. You are on your first business trip to Latin America. You have heard that appointments with officials or executives may not be held promptly and that you could be kept waiting for an hour or even more. How would you prepare for this—or how would you react to this different idea of promptness?

3. Myrdal reported that Asian economic development required various modernizing ideals, including punctuality. What, if anything, does punctuality have to do with economic development?

4. According to Kusum Nair, "A community's attitude toward work can be a more decisive determinant for raising productivity in Indian agriculture than material resources, or for that matter even technology."
   a. Do you agree with Nair? If she is correct, what should the Indian government do?
   b. How can the Indian government change these attitudes?
   c. Does the government have the moral right to change these attitudes?

5. a. Would local attitudes toward achievement and work be important for a firm setting up a factory in a foreign country? How might production operations be affected by unfavorable attitudes toward achievement and work?

    b. From the firm's point of view, a good attitude toward work would be reflected in what kind of worker behavior? Characterize this behavior.

    c. Should the firm avoid investments in countries where there are unfavorable attitudes?

7. Myrdal's modernizing attitudes and ideals include efficiency, diligence, and energetic enterprise. Are these related to attitudes toward achievement and work? How do you define the three terms? How might a Japanese manager define them?

8. Orientations to achievement and work are not ascertained as easily as economic or demographic data. How might a firm go about getting some information on these orientations?

9. Incentive goods are those that one is willing to work longer and harder to acquire. What goods or services might qualify as incentives in the American economy? in a less-developed economy?

10. There is said to be a "revolution of rising expectations" in the less-developed world. In the wake of the global economic changes due to OPEC, do you think this is true? What impacts might changes in expectations have on people living in less-developed countries?

11. In countries where the high-status occupations are the civil service, law, and politics, do you believe that high salaries are sufficient to draw competent people into business management?

12. In countries where the acquisitive motivation is relatively low, how should American consumer goods companies advertise their products? How can firms motivate their workers in the same countries?

13. Traditional societies are not amenable to rapid change. Russia and China achieved relatively rapid change by revolutionary means.

    a. Does this suggest that revolution is the best route to change?

    b. Are there examples of other countries that experienced relatively rapid economic advancement without a revolution?

14. Is newer always better? Cite several examples to support your answer.

15. Religious institutions are known to be both obstacles and aids to change (the Church in Latin America, monks in Southeast Asia, the Islamic sermon, etc.). Consider the following:

    a. Can governments use the religious institutions to promote their programs of social change? How?

    b. Should governments use the religious institutions in this way?

    c. Can business firms work with the religious institutions to accomplish their innovations? Should they?

16. When American marketers visited mainland China in 1984, they were first asked whether American advertising falsely portrayed the products. The marketers responded that the government strictly regulates truth in advertising. The Chinese delegation then asked, "Even if products are truly portrayed, how can you assert that your product is better than other products without causing the other products to lose face?" How would you respond?

ENDNOTES

1. Adapted from *Discover* (December 1985): 70.
2. Adapted from Robert J. Brown, "Swatch vs. the Sundial: A study in different attitudes towards time," *International Management* (December 1987): 80.
3. Kusum Nair, *Blossoms in the Dust, The Human Factor in Indian Development* (New York: Praeger, 1962), 190.
4. Gunnar Myrdal, *Asian Drama, An Inquiry into the Poverty of Nations* (New York: Twentieth Century Fund, 1968), 103–104.
5. Ibid., 61–62.
6. Donald N. Michael, "Technology and the Management of Change in a Culture Context" (Paper given at Conference on the Problems of Modernization in Asia, Honolulu, 1970).
7. Osman A. Atac, Aydin Muderrisoglu, and Nizam Aydin, "A Critique of the Theories of Marketing and Economic Development," unpublished manuscript.
8. Gerald F. Cavanagh, *American Business Values in Transition* (Englewood Cliffs, NJ: Prentice-Hall, 1976).
9. Madeline Pober, "Tokyo Woes: Orienting Yourself to Japan," *Savvy* (April 1984): 82.
10. Marshall Sahlins, "The Original Affluent Society," in *Stone Age Economics* (London: Tavistock, 1974), 55ff.
11. Edward T. Hall, *The Silent Language* (New York: Doubleday, 1959), 133.
12. Excerpt from Thomas Fillol, *Social Factors in Economic Development, The Argentine Case* (Cambridge, MA: M.I.T. Press, 1961), 13–14.
13. Lewis Mumford, *Technics and Civilization* (New York: Harcourt, Brace, 1934), 12–18.
14. Ross A. Webber, *Culture and Management, Text and Readings in Comparative Management* (Homewood, IL: Irwin, 1969), 14.
15. David McClelland, *The Achieving Society* (New York: Irvington, 1961), 326–327.
16. Sahlins, op. cit.
17. Edward T. Hall, *The Silent Language* (New York: Doubleday, 1959), 134.
18. McClelland, op. cit., 327–329.
19. Sahlins, op. cit.
20. Vance Packard, *The Status Seekers* (New York: Pocket Books, 1961), 218, 219.
21. Ross A. Webber, op. cit., 189.
22. Robert N. Bellah, ed., *Religion and Progress in Southeast Asia* (New York: Free Press, 1965), 54.
23. Kenneth David, field research in Sri Lanka.
24. Bellah, op. cit., 143.
25. George Katona, Burkhard Strumpel, and Earnest Zahn, *Aspirations and Affluence, Comparative Studies in the United States and Western Europe* (New York: McGraw-Hill, 1971), passim.
26. David McClelland, op. cit., passim.
27. *Time* (June 18, 1973): 69.
28. Bellah, op. cit., 74.
29. Webber, op. cit., 186.
30. Edgar G. Schein, "Is Organizational Change Possible?" (Paper presented at the 1981 meetings of the American Management Association).

31. Vera Micheles Dean, *The Nature of the Non-Western World* (New York: Mentor Books, 1956), 59–60.

32. Richard N. Farmer and Barry M. Richman, *Comparative Management and Economic Progress* (Homewood, IL: Irwin, 1965), 110.

33. Bellah, op. cit., 66.

34. John P. Gillin, *Social Change in Latin America Today* (New York: Vintage Books, 1961), 45–46.

35. Maurice Godelier, *Rationality and Irrationality in Economics* (New York: Monthly Review Press, 1972).

36. Farmer and Richman, op. cit., 218.

37. Kenneth David, field research, Jaffna, Sri Lanka.

38. Drawn from Josefa M. Saniel in Bellah, op. cit., 124–149.

PART III

The Social Organization of Human Behavior

THE SOCIAL NEED FOR COORDINATED, PREDICTABLE BEHAVIOR

Although the elaborate human brain has many advantages, it also has a limitation: humans cannot live with much disorder. A need for order in human social behavior means that people must be able to predict—within reasonable limits—what others will do in specific circumstances.

What is the basis of the problem? First, societies define socially approved goals that are appropriate to different circumstances. Classroom goals differ from soccer-field goals. Goals are achieved when there is coordinated, predictable behavior between individuals, among members of a group, and among groups. Second, coordinated, predictable behavior is only rarely (as in the game called "tug-of-war") a matter of everyone doing the same thing at the same time. Most frequently, public goals are achieved by the interaction of persons who have different but overlapping sets of information and skills and perform related tasks. In short, a social division of labor means a division of information, skills, and behavior. Third, the problem is complicated because participants differ in their motivations, practical interests, and in the available resources.

THE SOCIAL METHOD OF COORDINATING BEHAVIOR

How do societies deal with this problem? The social method of coordinating behavior is to define social reality—matching up social goals, contexts, and roles. Societies construct classification systems for social contexts and social positions and establish systems of norms for behavior among persons in relevant social positions.

Social Contexts

Each society devises a system of social contexts wherein some goals and behavior are appropriate and others are not. People in a society know verbal and nonverbal cues for distinguishing what is appropriate. If you show up at a party wearing blue jeans and a sweater and the host introduces you to someone as "Dr. George Smith," you receive a cue that the party is more formal (or the host more stuffy) that if the introduction had been, "This is George Smith. He's a doctor." In either case, information is transmitted not only about the person's name and profession, but also about nuances in the social context.

Classification of Social Positions

A society also devises systems of classification for social positions (also called social identities or social statuses). People attain social positions either by fitting into them (one becomes a child, then an adult, then an elderly person) or by achieving them (one passes an admissions test). Social positions are maintained by following proper rules for behavior in relation to persons in relevant other social positions in specified social contexts.

Role Relationships

The notion of relevant other social positions implies that social positions do not exist by themselves. There are role relationships only with relevance to other social positions. For example, there are roles (predictable behavior) between the social position of doctor and such relevant social positions as patient, nurse, or hospital administrator. The social position of doctor does not have a role relationship with the social positions of woman or man.

Norms

For each relevant role relationship, there is a defined set of rights and obligations called social norms, or codes for conduct. Norms are the guides of predictable, coordinated behavior in society. Norms allow persons to expect, recognize, and evaluate actual behavior.

In short, societies set limits on humanly acceptable behavior in specific social contexts. To express approval or discontent, one can shout almost anything at a football game, but only a few carefully timed words are appropriate in a theater. Proper behavior is defined in terms of recognized social positions. Thus, even though societies differ dramatically in what they consider right and proper, there is a general social method for limiting behavior to make it predictable and coordinated.

CONTENT OF PART III

Various cultural systems organize human behavior:

- *Technological systems* are a pattern of energy-extracting and processing techniques, appropriate to the society's ecological system, that obtain an adequate supply of products to fill socially defined needs.

- *Demographic systems* are the arrangement in space of socially relevant persons, plants, and animals (as well as all that is made by humans). This arrangement deploys these units in the ecosystem in a way that enables them to obtain livelihood from the ecosystem and to defend their means of producing that livelihood against human foes and natural disasters.

- *Kinship systems* define social positions and social duties on the basis of each culture's definition of natural bodily substance. The kinship system deals with problems of regulating sexuality, child rearing, and relationships among families and among wider groupings of kin. In many societies, the kinship system remains an overall guide to social relationships. Many traditional societies did not have distinct economic, political, and legal systems but embedded these functions in kinship relations.

- *Economic systems* regulate human control of the means of producing a livelihood, the intensity with which natural resources are appropriated for human use, the division of labor in production, and the sharing and exchanging of what has been produced.

- *Political systems* deal with problems of opposition, conflict, and change that stem from inequalities of distribution of material resources, human resources, and information. Political systems generally legitimize power into a system of authority. Legitimized authority facilitates solving these problems and thus regulates decision making and the implementation of public goals.

- *Legal systems* control social relationships by adding sanctions to enforce social codes for conduct.

These various cultural systems differ from the point of view of the cultural operations discussed in the introductory chapter: classifying, coding, prioritizing, and justifying reality.

Technological and demographic systems classify and code human interactions with nature. Kinship is (globally) the most widespread cultural method of classifying and coding human social relationships for a variety of social purposes. Economic systems classify and code human relationships regarding production and exchange.

Political and legal systems operate on other activities as guidance systems: they prioritize activities. These systems maintain other systems within viable operating limits, or under changing conditions can drastically revise other cultural systems. From Part II, we recall that the combined effect of the systems of education, values, and religion is to motivate human commitment to all of these cultural systems by justifying them with reference to a more-than-human order of existence.[1]

In the three chapters in Part III, we deal with most of these cultural systems for organizing human behavior.

ENDNOTE

1. For a more detailed introduction to these systems, see Marc Swartz and David Jordan, *Culture: The Anthropological Perspective* (New York: Wiley, 1980). For a more detailed account of the relationships between material determinants of human activity and the symbolic construction of human activity, see Kenneth David, "Epilogue," in *The New Wind: Changing Identities in South Asia,* in the series World Anthropology: Proceedings of the Ninth International Congress of Anthropological and Ethnological Sciences (The Hague: Mouton, 1977).

CHAPTER SIX
Technology

It seems strange that the human race took so long to make a serious effort to develop its science and technology, The technology of the most advanced parts of the world in the early 18th century was closer to the neolithic age than it is to us. Even in the 19th century, with the Industrial Revolution fairly started, the speed and extent of the transformation of the world that a concentrated effort at technology would make was still beyond the most far out imaginations.

Northrop Frye[1]

If one reviews major trends in the course of human history—the development of complex social organization, the patterns of uneven global economic development, and the shifts from local to national to international trade to multinational enterprise—the role of changing technology is evident in every trend. Yet Frye's statement is accurate.

After neolithic times, when humans began to partially control their environment through the technologies of plant and animal domestication, pottery making, glassmaking, and metalworking, a gap of nearly 2,000 years elapsed before further substantial changes were made—that is, technological changes that affected the lives of the masses. Only in the late eighteenth century were basic tools (windmills, waterwheels) replaced by advanced means of harnessing mechanical energy (internal combustion engines). Only during the twentieth century have truly global organizations (United Nations, World Bank, General Agreement on Tariffs and Trade, and multinational corporations) appeared and the practice of bilateral trade shifted to multinational operations.

In short, the neolithic shifts were the first steps in the human technological harnessing of animate and inanimate energy. The Industrial Revolution shifts of the eighteenth century were an advance in the technological harnessing of mechanical energy. The most recent shifts correlate with human technological control over the processing of information. *The history of human development can be summarized as (1) an increased control over energy and (2) an increased control over information.* This point should be remembered when we discuss international differences in technology.

The current international diffusion of technology is closely related to multinational enterprise. Perhaps the multinational enterprise is the single most important agent in the generation, application, and global transfer of technology. It is not surprising that the transfer of technology is a global political issue. For host governments, transfer of technology appropriate to development is a critical issue. The following focus cases show that newly industrialized countries have critical tasks of stemming the brain drain and developing advanced technological capabilities. For multinational firms, proprietary knowledge is a key factor in maintaining both competitive advantage over other firms in the marketplace and bargaining power with host governments. The topic of technology deserves close attention.

FOCUS CASES:
Technology in Newly Industrialized Nations

THE LOW COST OF ENGINEERS IN NEWLY INDUSTRIALIZED ASIAN NATIONS

While small economies have trouble providing competitively priced jobs for all their educated personnel, the situation has reversed in the Asian NICs (newly industrialized countries) of South Korea, Taiwan, Hong Kong, and Singapore and is now a source of competitive advantage.

Government officials once expected that as many as 80 percent of the students who received training abroad, principally in the United States, would not return to the home country; in recent years, the rate of loss has been closer to 20 percent. This is important because NIC industries had boomed during the 1970s due to cheap factory labor. More recently, other countries in the region, particularly China, attract industries that require the most labor-intensive work.

Instead, these countries are now competing with cheap labor of a different kind: low-cost engineers and technicians. These engineers lift ideas from products already on the market, modify them, draw up the designs, and oversee the manufacturing process. "Korea definitely has an advantage [over the United States or Japan] in terms of cost of engineers" said an executive from Gold Star, one of South Korea's three major electronics companies. At current rates, Korea and Taiwan hire two engineers for the price of one engineer hired in Japan, four engineers for the price of a single engineer working in the United States.

ACQUIRING TECHNOLOGY

There are several options for acquiring needed technology. A firm can develop the know-how by itself (research and development). A firm can buy the use of the technology from another firm (through licenses, patent fees, or royalties). A firm can combine the previous two tactics by licensing current technology and making modifications for its own use, either by upscaling the technology (the usual Japanese case) or downscaling it (a common practice when multinational corporations from newly industrialized countries are operating in less-developing countries). Downscaling is necessary, for example, in order to (1) accommodate the skill level of LDC workers or (2) adapt the machinery to use raw materials that are available within the less-developed host country but for which the machinery was not originally designed.

Japan has a long history of investing in new technology by buying it. Japan's annual payments for licensing technology rose from around $50 million in the early 1950s to $2.7 billion in 1970 to $3 billion in 1985 at constant prices. But by the 1980s, Japanese firms were earning large sums by selling technology: annual receipts of around $2 million in the early 1950s grew to $373 million in 1970 and $898 million in 1985. In relative terms, receipts rose far more than payments.[2]

Firms from newly industrialized countries are becoming more sophisticated in the technology transfer process. Over the past decade, South Korean firms have increased the technical sophistication of the kinds of international construction jobs they do. Starting as subcontractors to major Western firms, they began winning major contracts as prime contractor on the simpler types of projects such as building huge wharves and road systems (civil construction projects). Later, they began licensing technology in order to do more advanced installations. In 1982, the construction division of Hyundai—a firm best known for its subcompact car—took a novel approach to acquiring needed technology. They won the contract for an offshore oil rig installation. They had the know-how to complete the first stage. Hyundai subcontracted the second stage to an American engineering construction firm and sent over 100 of their engineers to the construction site to observe the designs and installation procedures the subcontractor used. Thus Hyundai acquired the technology.[3]

The primary objective of this chapter is to explore the policy implications of technology-related interactions between multinational firms and their host countries. After defining technology, we will discuss how international differences in technology relate to the several contrasting visions of global economic development, an issue that is highly charged politically. Then we focus on policy implications: strategies of companies and of countries regarding the international transfer and use of technology.

DEFINITION OF TECHNOLOGY

In the broad anthropological sense, technology is a cultural system concerned with the relationships between humans and their natural environment. A society is well adapted to its environment when its technological system is

1. *environmentally feasible* in that it produces a livelihood for the inhabitants without depleting the natural resources;

2. *stable* in that it can respond to temporary natural disturbances such as droughts, storms, and epidemics;

3. *resilient* in that it can return to a normal state of operations after a natural disturbance; and

4. *open to revision* when a natural disturbance reveals its inherent shortcomings.

A culture's technology defines what are natural resources and what are useful means of appropriating natural resources and transforming them into needed products. In the early days of natural gas production in Pennsylvania, for example, petroleum was defined not as a useful product but as a by-product that presented disposal problems.

Our definition of technology focuses on technology as a system of ideas as opposed to *material culture,* the physical objects (whether digging sticks or John Deere tractors, clay pots or oil refineries, quill pens or mainframe computers) that physically embody the culture's technology.

To aid the following discussions, we will define several terms associated with technology: A *science* is a body of concepts organized in theoretical frameworks that help explain observed phenomena. *Basic research* has two objectives: to explain phenomena and to improve the theoretical frameworks—the intellectual tool kit—for such explanation. When the term *research* is used in the phrase *research and development,* then *research* means a study done to improve the quality of existing products (or services) or to create new products (or services); *development* means activities to improve the technology for fabricating products or providing services.

New developments are invention and an innovation. An *invention* is the bringing together of previously unrelated ideas or physical objects. *Innovation* is the process of social communication of an invention. Innovation is a particularly important process in the international transfer of technology. Using the analogy of international technology as a communication event, a message (technological knowledge) is transmitted by a sender (the transferor of technology) to a receiver (the technology recipient).

Here are two problem areas. One occurs when the sender and the receiver differ in culture and business culture, or (within a country) corporate culture; the communication may be distorted. The other occurs when there are multiple receivers. If a transfer is made to a private company but permission must be granted by the host-country government, for example, both the private firm and the government agency are receivers of the message and evaluate it according to their own criteria. In other words, the social, economic, and political impacts of technology can never be ignored.

Determinants of Technology

Every social science discipline wrestles with the relative importance of three major determinants of human activity: the cultural, the material, and the motivational. Following the works of Weber, Marx, and Freud, who respectively stress cultural, material, and motivational determinants, many social scientists take one as the ultimate starting point of causality for all human activity. We shall not do so; we prefer to consider all three as necessary conditions in the explanation of human activity.

This point can be illustrated with a discrete example of rural agricultural productive activity in Jaffna, Sri Lanka.[4] An observable human activity (four men irrigating a rice field by means of a well sweep) is jointly determined by all three factors.

Jaffna is a dry northern area that would be infeasible for irrigated agriculture were it not for a limestone subsoil that holds pools of water 10–100 feet below the surface. Thus the ecosystem constrains inhabitants to use some form of water-drawing technology if they want to farm. A second ecological feature, rather crumbly soil, prohibits the use of such heavy tools as the Persian wheel. The well sweep is feasible with both ecological constraints.

As depicted in Figure 6-1, a well sweep is a long log. One end of the log is weighted; this end is attached by an axle to a base that rests on the ground. The other end holds the line (10–100 feet long) and bucket. Crosspieces are attached to the log so that two men, by walking forward and back, lower and raise the bucket. A third man tips the bucket into the main irrigation ditch, and a fourth shifts the small dykes in the earthen walls to water the various fields. Well-sweep technology requires four strong persons to operate it.

Up to this point, our account has focused on aspects of the observable activity that are materially (ecologically and technologically) determined.

As soon as we inquire who does which job, we turn to the cultural specification of the activity. The South Asian Hindu ideology of purity and impurity dictates that during the irrigation process, only clean caste males are allowed to touch the water and the earth on the field that will produce food to be consumed by upper caste Hindus. Because women of all castes are periodically impure due to menstruation and lower caste males are defined as impure from their parentage, neither women nor lower caste males may touch water or earth during irrigation. So while clean or unclean caste Hindus can walk the log, the more arduous job, only clean caste Hindus can tip the bucket and shift the irrigation ditches. The actual division of labor, then, is not determined by material (technological and ecological) conditions but is culturally specified.

The four workers are motivated to perform their jobs by a feudal reward system in which servants have not only quasi-kin obligations, but also rights to a livelihood. The reward system covers many fringe benefits, such as contributions from the landlord to all life cycle rituals and care during illnesses. Motivation is reinforced by a religious system described in Chapter 4: the religious logic of beings of unequal natural substances is tied to the secular division of labor in the Jaffna agricultural village.

The point of this discussion is to dispel any notion that human activity is determined exclusively either by the techno-environmental system or by culture.

1. The environment poses limits to what technologies can be employed. If they are willing to pay the costs, humans can dominate almost any environment. Domed cities can be built under the sea. Greenhouses can be built in a desert. Normally, the more abundant the environment, the wider the range of technologies that can be employed.

2. Further, the wider the range of technologies and the more energy appropriated from the environment, the more complex the human society that can exist there. Without great investment, only small bands normally inhabit an arid desert region. In a temperate region, bands, tribes, kingdoms, and industrial states can all be accommodated.

FIGURE 6-1

THE JAFFNA WELL SWEEP

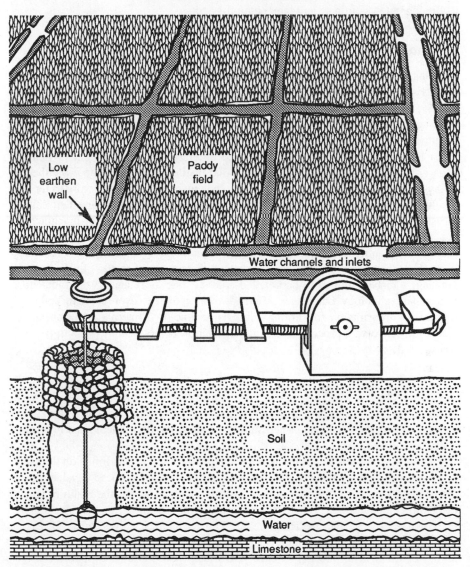

3. But it is culture—the social construction of reality—that specifies which form of social organization shall exist within the limits posed by the environment.

We shall now take a brief inventory of the mutual impacts of a society's technological system and its other cultural systems.

Technology and Language

Languages are rich and expressive in dealing with their traditional technology. Inuit (Eskimo) languages are typically rich in vocabulary describing varieties of snow and the appropriate technology for dealing with snow conditions. South Indian languages are precise in describing varieties of rice and dry grains, types of land where different species grow, and appropriate technologies for cultivation. Changing a language to accommodate modern technology is another matter. When the government of the state of Kerala (South India) instituted a program to avoid the use of the previous colonial language (English), they invented a Maliyali word to replace the English word *telephone* that roughly translates as "the machine that carries messages long distances by wire." Translating instruction manuals for machinery is not a straightforward task. Robert Pirsig, in *Zen and the Art of Motorcycle Maintenance,* quotes the opening line of a Japanese bicycle company's assembly manual: "Assembling Japanese bicycle requires great peace of mind."[5] In short, every language can be assumed to be detailed and accurate as relates to the indigenous traditional technology. Languages differ, however, in their ease of receiving and communicating information concerning industrial technology. International transfers of technology involve a process of cultural translation if the technology is to be fully transmitted.

Technology and Value Systems

Values were previously defined as priorities concerning social goals. Values guide choices of codes for behavior when various goals might be implemented in a given social situation.

Technology affects values because a society's technology sets limits on the range of social goals that are feasible. Mesthene said, "Technology can lead to value change either by: (1) bringing some previously unattainable goal within the realm of choice or (2) making some values easier to implement than heretofore, that is, by changing the costs associated with realizing them."[6] During the past two decades, for example, contraception technology allowed increased sexual activity. But the present inability of medical technology to cure AIDS has set limits on multipartner sexual activity.

Conversely, existing sets of priorities defining what is good, proper, desirable, or important in a society may set limits on the kinds of technology that can successfully be introduced therein. Production-line technology, for example, is not automatically alienating to workers. Japanese workers in quality circle groups valorize defect-free production. This priority can be understood in the context of Japanese management's valorization of the worker as a person, not just as a labor unit. The Ford Motor Company has taken steps in this direction.

Technology and Educational Systems

A society's technology deeply affects not only the initial education of children, but also the continuing education of adults. Programs such as "Sesame Street" and "The Electric Company" provide a common element in the socialization of children in many different social classes and ethnic groups, children who are otherwise socialized quite differently. India's satellite TV broadcasts educate isolated villagers in the basics of birth control and agricultural development. Awareness of geopolitical events is disseminated globally by the transistor radio. But technology can also further polarize the social distribution of knowledge: Computer technology is more widely available in affluent school districts than in poorer ones; in less-affluent communities, computer technology is available in the form of commercial video-game parlors.

Technology and Religious Systems

Because religious interpretations can either reaffirm or change the prevailing set of values in a society, they are in indirect relation to technology. Reacting to Indian dependency on England, Mahatma Gandhi justified his stand against technological industrialization with reference to the Hindu precept of nirvana, wantlessness.[7] On the other hand, Tamil fishermen of northern Sri Lanka studied by Kenneth David justified the technological shift from long lines of hooks to nylon gill nets on the basis of the Hindu notion of *ahimsa,* nonviolence, because the fish suffered less in the nets than on the hooks.

In summary, technology is a system of ordered information concerning the relationship of humans to the material environment from which they appropriate resources and transform them into socially desirable products. As a cultural system, technology is a system of understandings shared within a society. This system affects and is affected by other cultural systems, other systems of shared understandings in the culture.

INTERNATIONAL DIFFERENCES IN TECHNOLOGY

Understanding the technological gap between parties engaged in international technology transfer is vital to negotiations. According to Magee, a prime consideration in a firm's decision to engage in international business operations is the degree to which it can appropriate to itself profits from the technology in which it has invested.[8] The greater the gap, the greater the firm's bargaining power, the greater the degree of strategic latitude enjoyed by the firm, and the greater the appropriation. Conversely, the smaller the gap, then the greater the country's bargaining power, the more the firm will bargain in a nationally responsive manner, and the less the appropriations.

What follows is a tool kit for understanding relative differences in technology that we find more relevant than evolutionary schemes of development.[9]

Structure of Production and Employment by Sector

Table 6-1 indicates a correlation between national income and the national composition of productive sectors. As countries increase their national income, the movement is from primary (agricultural) to secondary (industrial, including manufacturing) to tertiary (service) sectors.

TABLE 6-1

SECTOR DEVELOPMENT AND EFFICIENCY OF WORK FORCE IN THAT SECTOR

	Number of countries	*Agriculture*	*Industry*	*Services*
China				
Production		31	46	23
Employment		74	14	12
India				
Production		32	29	39
Employment		70	13	17
Other low-income countries	(37)			
Production		38	20	41
Employment		71	10	19
Lower-middle-income countries	(34)			
Production		22	30	46
Employment		55	16	29
Upper-middle-income countries	(24)			
Production		10	40	50
Employment		29	31	40
High-income oil exporters	(4)			
Production		5	65	30
Employment		35	21	44
Industrial market economies	(19)			
Production		3	35	61
Employment		7	35	58
Planned economies	(9)			
Production		no data on production is available		
Employment		22	39	39

Source: *World Development Report, 1988* (World Bank, 1988), 226, 227, 282, 283.

- Industrialized countries' agricultural sectors as a percent of their GDPs (gross domestic products) are only one-thirteenth (3/38) of low-income countries' agricultural sectors as a percent of their GDPs.

- Industrialized countries' industrial sectors are about one and three-quarters times as large (35/20) as low-income countries' industrial sectors.

- Industrialized countries' service sectors are one and one-half times as large (61/41) as low-income countries' service sectors.

Said again, in lower-income countries, agriculture makes a larger contribution to the GDP than in higher-income countries; in higher-income countries, the industrial and service sectors make a larger contribution. In the global economy, progression beyond the industrial sector is essential. The high-income countries might better be labelled service countries or post-industrial countries, not industrialized countries.

The figures in Table 6-1 allow a rough prediction of the kinds of technology present in different nations: agricultural, industrial, and information-processing technologies.

Although the distribution of a country's labor force in the different sectors roughly correlates with the relative contribution of that sector to the gross domestic product, the figures can be analyzed to show the efficiency of the labor force. A high percentage (71 percent) of low-income countries' labor force produces only 38 percent of these countries' GDP; in industrialized countries, percentage of labor force correlates closely with sectoral contribution to GDP. In the former case, the situation is more labor intensive; in the latter case, the situation is more machine (capital) intensive.

Energy Production

Anthropologists of the ecological-evolutionary school study the relationship between the amount of energy harnessed by the technological system and the complexity of social organization. There are many measures, but a clear measure is called *techno-environmental advantage:* the ratio of calories produced per calorie expended in production. Table 6-2 illustrates this relationship.

TABLE 6-2

TECHNO-ENVIRONMENTAL ADVANTAGE AND SOCIOCULTURAL ORGANIZATION

Technology	Techno-Environmental Advantage	Level of Sociocultural Integration
Hunting and gathering	9.6	Band
Hoe agriculture	11.2	Tribe
Slash-and-burn agriculture	18.0	Tribe
Irrigation agriculture	53.5	Kingdom
Capital-intensive agriculture and industry	200.0	Nation-State

Source: Marvin Harris, *Culture, Man, and Nature* (New York: T. Y. Crowell, 1971), 203–217.

Higher techno-environmental advantage denotes lesser reliance on human or animal muscular power expended in producing energy and greater reliance on inanimate sources of power (fossil fuels, wind, water, steam, biomass, and mechanical devices). When more energy is produced, a society becomes more complex; the scope of territory integrated in its social system broadens, and the complexity of its role structure increases. Roles become inreasingly differentiated as more people are freed from direct involvement in producing a livelihood.

TABLE 6-3

TRANSPORTATION AND ENERGY CONSUMPTION

	Motor Vehicles in Use (1,000)	Merchant Shipping Fleets (1,000 Gross Tons)	Rail Traffic Freight-Ton-KMS	Energy Consumption per Capita (Kgs Coal Equivalent)
United States	135,155	16,188	1,206,366	11,374
Western Europe				
France	19,340	12,197	66,288	4,368
Germany	21,410	9,737	35,712	6,015
Italy	17,607	7,038	17,100	3,230
Spain	7,103	8,056	9,642	2,405
Sweden	3,043	6,508	14,782	5,954
United Kingdom	16,460	30,897	22,728	5,212
Latin America				
Argentina	2,907	2,001	11,567	1,873
Brazil	7,317	3,702	60,721	794
Colombia	558	272	1,215	700
Ecuador	129	201	46	505
Mexico	3,760	727	36,232	1,384
Peru	467	575	612	649
Asia				
India	1,496	5,759	144,030	176
Japan	31,379	39,182	41,317	3,825
Pakistan	288	442	8,677	172
Philippines	667	1,265	49	339
Sri Lanka	143	93	214	109
Thailand	533	335	2,505	327
Africa				
Egypt	347	456	2,201	463
Ghana	122	186	305	165
Ivory Coast	128	157	551	357
Nigeria	232	324	972	175
South Africa	2,985	661	69,330	NA
Zaire	161	110	2,203	69

Source: *Statistical Abstracts of the United States, 1980* (Washington, DC: Bureau of the Census, 1981), 920, 921.

Industrial Infrastructure

Another indication of the technological development of a nation is the infrastructure necessary for industrial activity. Tables 6-3 and 6-4 present data on energy consumption and on transportation facilities, both of which correlate closely with the industrialization and gross domestic product per capita in a country. The number of motor vehicles in use, the size of the merchant shipping fleet, and the volume of rail traffic (all per capita) are rough indicators of consumer mobility and the availability of transport for both sourcing of materials and distribution of the physical product. Energy consumption, in particular, correlates with the use of industrial goods in a country. The national differences recorded in these tables may be interpreted according to our earlier observation that the second major phase of human technological advance lies in the harnessing of mechanical energy (see p. 134).

TABLE 6-4

ENERGY CONSUMPTION PER CAPITA

		Energy Consumption per Capita in Kilograms of Oil Equivalents
India		208
China		532
Other low-income countries	(37)	86
Lower-middle-income countries	(34)	346
Upper-middle-income countries	(24)	1,527
High-income oil exporters	(4)	3,336
Centrally planned economies	(9)	4,552
Industrialized countries	(19)	4,952
Canada		8,847
United States		7,030
Sweden		5,821
Australia		4,811
West Germany		4,156
Japan		2,929

Source: *World Development Report, 1988* (Washington, DC: World Bank, 1988), 240, 241.

Communications Infrastructure

The third major phase in human technological advances lies in the processing and communication of information. Multinational corporations gain a competitive edge over local firms by the control of strategic information in every business function: international marketing intelligence, international siting of production in low-labor-cost areas, international logistics management of scattered site production, international financial management of cash flows in a system of headquarters and subsidiaries to optimize after-tax and after-tariff revenues and to minimize international currency risks, international promotional efforts based on experience in many countries, and so forth.

The extent to which a firm can implement the use of strategic information depends in part on the development of the communications and promotional infrastructures of the countries in which it is operating. Intracompany communications between subsidiaries or with headquarters will be equally dependent on local facilities. Table 6-5 shows the distribution and availability of several communications media in the major regions of the world.

TABLE 6-5

DISTRIBUTION OF COMMUNICATIONS MEDIA

	Telephones per 100 Pop.	Newspaper Copies per 1,000 Pop.	Radios per 1,000 Pop.	Television Sets per 1,000 Pop.
United States	76.0	268	2,101	798
Western Europe				
France	60.8	212	879	394
Germany	62.1	350	430	373
Italy	44.8	96	259	253
Spain	36.3	80	298	270
Sweden	89.0	521	868	390
United Kingdom	52.4	414	1,016	437
Latin America				
Argentina	10.4	NA	203	70
Brazil	8.4	57	391	184
Colombia	7.0	NA	139	96
Ecuador	3.6	64	293	64
Mexico	9.1	120	190	108
Peru	3.2	NA	175	97
Asia				
India	.5	21	66	5
Japan	55.5	562	787	580
Pakistan	.6	NA	90	13
Philippines	1.5	NA	175	97
Sri Lanka	.7	111	155	28
Thailand	1.5	NA	175	97
Africa				
Egypt	2.4	42	256	82
Ghana	.6	35	184	10
Madagascar	.4	5	213	8
Nigeria	.3	6	85	5
South Africa	14.3	NA	309	93
Zimbabwe	3.2	22	43	14

Source: *Statistical Abstracts of the United States, 1987* (Washington, DC: Bureau of the Census, 1987), 809.

In general, variations in communications infrastructure follow variations in the level of economic development. Thus Japan and the countries of Western Europe and North America are well supplied with all kinds of media. The developing countries in Africa, Asia, and Latin America are weak in all the media except for the radio. The table also illustrates the difficulties of gathering international comparative data. The developing countries are less effective at gathering statistics. A researcher may not find data available for the variables usually investigated in developing countries and must make creative use of proxy variables.

Research and Development

Analysts of competition within an industry commonly use share-of-market-captured as a sign of competitive edge over the long term. Investment in research and development might well be added to the methodological tool kit as a sign of future competitive edge. Table 6-6 gives comparative data on national expenditures on research and development. The figures must be viewed with caution for several reasons:

1. Data are unequally available from different countries.

2. Definitions of research and development differ among countries.

3. The term *research and development* usually denotes original research and development (R&D). The industrial development of Japan after World War II, however, was spurred by large investments in R&D via international purchase (licensing). And in newly industrialized countries, there is a mixture of investment in three categories of research and development: original R&D, international purchase (licensing) of R&D, and modification of the purchased R&D for application at home and abroad in less-developed countries.

4. Other measures would be helpful in getting a more accurate picture: patents per capita generated (not reregistered) in the country, number of Nobel Prize winners over time, number of scientific journals and conferences, and so forth.

With these reservations, the figures indicate national capabilities for global competitiveness: production of new products or services (research) and production of new industrial processes for making and delivering the products or services (development). Because the figures on R&D expenditures are expressed as percentages of gross national products, the differentials among countries are larger than they seem: industrial nations invest a larger portion of a much larger GNP.

Among the industrialized nations, some dynamic trends should be noted. While the United States is still a leader in some high-technology industries, its relative leadership has been declining due to a reduction in the federal government support for basic research in universities and in business. From 1964 to 1975, R&D in the United States declined from 3 percent to 2.5 percent of the GNP; numbers of persons employed in R&D declined from 63 to 59 per 10,000 persons in the population. During the same period, the United Kingdom, Japan, and Germany were increasing the numbers of persons employed in R&D toward the figure of 59 per 10,000. This enabled the

TABLE 6-6

HUMAN RESOURCES FOR RESEARCH AND DEVELOPMENT

	Personnel Engaged in R&D (Full-Time Equivalent)		
	Total	*Scientists & Engineers*	*Technicians*
United States	NA	702,000	NA
Western Europe			
France	230,766	72,899	157,877
Germany (F.R.)	243,680	128,162	115,518
Italy	81,445	52,060	29,385
Spain	9,623	6,006	3,617
Sweden	36,434	14,766	21,668
United Kingdom	163,100	86,500	76,600
Latin America			
Argentina	22,800	9,500	13,300
Brazil	NA	32,508	NA
Colombia	2,153	1,449	704
Cuba	14,793	6,834	7,959
Peru	8,794	6,525	2,269
Asia			
Indonesia	20,521	17,287	3,234
Japan	589,421	496,145	93,326
Philippines	7,474	5,146	2,328
Pakistan	11,620	5,144	6,476
Korea, Republic of	40,111	28,448	11,663
Africa			
Ghana	9,819	4,084	5,735
Nigeria	3,545	2,200	1,345
Sudan	7,077	3,806	3,271
Kenya	544	361	183

Source: *UNESCO Statistical Yearbook, 1984* (Paris: UNESCO Press, 1984), V-34, 35.

United Kingdom to maintain its R&D as a percentage of GNP, while Germany and Japan increased their R&D to 2.5 percent of GNP.

The 2.5 percent is apparently a threshold figure. In the U.S. emerging, high-technology industries such as computers, fiber optics, and aerospace, R&D as a percentage of sales is greater than 2.5 percent. These industries show a positive net trade for the United States. Conversely, in mature industries such as steel and auto, investment in R&D as a percentage of sales is less than 2.5 percent. These industries show a trend of negative net trade for the United States.[10]

Government plays an important role in a country's research. The U.S. government has waived antitrust restrictions for certain cases. Research collaboration among companies was permitted for the wartime Manhattan Project on the atomic bomb and the peacetime Apollo spacecraft project. More recently, after the Japanese technological invasion of American markets, the government permitted research collaboration in the computer industry, for example. But the United States is usually very restrictive about anticompetitive business activities.

> In the crucial emerging industry of robotics, for example, U.S. sanctions against corporate collaboration have served to diffuse the research effort among many agents: universities, users, major computer firms, fiber optics firms, and machine tool firms. Because robotics research in the United States has concentrated on robots for single tasks, much research is required on sensors for the recognition of patterns in order to identify the object about to be processed.[11]

Other countries permit extensive collaboration.

> In Japan, large-scale integrated projects were established by the Ministry of International Trade and Investment to produce a generic technology of robotics that can be used by various industries. The collaborative effort is directed towards producing a fully integrated system of robotics in which the location and orientation of the object being manufactured is always known. Thus the huge investment in sensors for pattern recognition is not necessary.

Summary: International Differences in Technology

After decades of developmental efforts by Third-World countries, large gaps remain between technological development and productivity in these countries and in the advanced industrial countries. Indeed, in the wake of the oil crises of the 1970s and the global recession of the early 1980s, the mood of international financial institutions such as the World Bank and the International Monetary Fund shifted from primary emphasis on development to emphasis on repaying debts and gaining some measure of solvency. Therefore it is predictable that a wide diversity of technological differences will continue. Both multinational companies and host countries will continue to bargain over such issues as the social and ecological impact of new technology and proper methods to effect international technology transfer. Next we will examine national and corporate strategies for dealing with these issues.

TECHNOLOGY-RELATED POLICY IMPLICATIONS FOR HOST COUNTRIES

Our discussion will focus mainly on policy issues for Third-World countries.

Technology Transfer and Developing Countries

The Technology Transfer Controversy

Following the series of technological changes known as the Industrial Revolution, the nineteenth century witnessed unbridled optimism about the impact of technology and a great expansion in its use. World opinion has come a long way since then. From the mid-twentieth century onward, multinational corporations faced increasing hostility from Third-World host countries. Multinationals were accused of furthering the underdevelopment of the host countries through their choice of capital-intensive technology that benefited the companies but not the countries. Host countries adopted the policy of import substitution—that is, restricting the inflow of foreign products and investments in favor of their own technological development and production. At the same time, host countries began demanding "appropriate" technology: technology suited to their industrial infrastructure and to the pressing need to employ more of their population. On other occasions, host countries pressed companies to transfer the most advanced technology available, apparently so that they might appear as showcases of development to neighboring countries.

Since the mid-1980s, the controversy has taken several new turns. It can no longer be said that all Third-World host countries are unsophisticated. Even less-developed countries can and do employ major consulting firms to develop strategies for technological development and for dealing with multinational corporations. Newly industrialized countries such as Singapore, South Korea, Taiwan, and Hong Kong (and in some industries, India) are no longer merely importers of technology. Besides importing and modifying technology, they also develop their own technology and export it in foreign operations.

Recent Shifts

Further, the attitude toward incoming technology may be shifting. Taking a more measured stance, governments now appear less averse to the presence of multinational corporations (and their advanced technology) in their countries, but they still are concerned with regulating incoming technology in order to fit it into national industrial policy.

A sign of shifting attitudes is the evolution of Arghiri Emmanuel's thinking on technology transfer. In 1969, Emmanuel wrote of the inequality of development of different countries, inequality fostered by prevailing patterns of technology transfer.[12] In 1982, Emmanuel took a new stance on the controversy with a book entitled *Appropriate or Underdeveloped Technology?*[13] His later premise can be summarized in three points. First, capital-intensive technology improves the social welfare of an underdeveloped country by maximizing the quantity of products made available. Second, arguments in favor of "appropriate" (labor-intensive) technology are invalid because transfer of modern technology cuts short the import-substitution path to development taken by many Third-World countries, a path that perpetuates underdevelopment. Third, multinational corporations, as the prime developers of advanced technology, are a favored means for abbreviating the development path of Third-World countries.

There are three issues here: distribution of wealth in Third-World countries, the level of technology (labor-intensive or capital-intensive) to be employed in Third-World countries, and the agency of transferring technology to Third-World countries. Perhaps it is folly to imagine that there exists a singular technology policy to handle all three issues.

Distribution of Wealth

Regarding choice of technology, distribution of wealth, and social welfare in Third-World countries, there are certainly implications for the type of technology chosen. Kumar writes of the favored class of workers employed by multinational corporations as opposed to workers employed by local companies.[14] Maldistribution of wealth, however, can be handled by other classes of government policy: taxation and transfer payments.

Agency of Transfer

Regarding the agency of transfer of technology, it should be noted first that multinational corporations are not prone to share core technologies soon after they have invested large sums to develop them. Third-World countries can, however, invest in processes of acquiring usable though older forms of technology. A radio manufacturing firm from the People's Republic of China, for example, has recently entered into a joint venture with Sanyo of Japan. The operation is currently not profitable because there is a high rate of rejection by quality-conscious Sanyo. The PRC firm is, however, going to school with a leading company. Current losses are regarded as an investment in technology transfer.

Second, multinational corporations from the First World are not the sole repository of technology nor the sole transferors of technology to underdeveloped countries. Multinational corporations from newly industrialized countries such as Hong Kong, Korea, Singapore, Taiwan, from borderline newly industrialized countries such as India, and from several Second-World (socialist) countries such as Czechoslovakia and Yugoslavia arc all part of the picture. Underdeveloped countries, then, have multiple sources of various levels of technology. With a more competitive international market for technology developing, it is likely that the demands set forth by UNCTAD in *The New International Economic Order,* demands for freer transfer of technology at better terms and with less restriction by patents, will eventually come to pass.

Level of Technology

Regarding the level of technology to be adopted, it appears first that it is unwise to define a technology as "appropriate" only in terms of utilization of locally available labor and materials. When a business firm formulates its competitive strategy, the firm must make three choices: technological process, product, and target market. A labor-intensive technological process that results in a relatively high-cost-per-unit product is appropriate only if the country market is protected and thus relatively uncompetitive. When they have attempted to export this business strategy in international joint ventures in countries with more competitive markets, Indian firms have found the technological choice was not appropriate.[15]

Second, countries are not faced with a simple choice between labor-intensive and capital-intensive technologies. Michel A. Amsalem studied 19 textile facilities and 14 pulp-and-paper facilities in Colombia, Brazil, the Philippines, and Indonesia. For each industry, he found that a limited set of alternative technologies (alternative mixes of labor and capital) could be employed. For each processing step of each firm studied, the cost of production that would have been obtained through the use of each of the alternative technologies was estimated on the basis of the cost of the factors of production to the firm as well as the social cost of these factors to the country in which the production facility was located. Amsalem then analyzed social and market optimum technologies. He found that the market and social optima differed in only half the cases studied—generally in the direction of choosing technologies more capital-intensive than the optimum. Reasons for this direction of choice are nonavailability of information, mimimization of risks due to human error in operating or maintaining the machinery, competitive pressures, and government policies.[16]

Third, countries are not faced with an inert, unchanging set of factor endowments for which a level of technology should be chosen. Rather, countries have resources that remain latent factors until mobilized by government policies and allocations for changing the industrial, educational, and communications infrastructures. Differences in the international competitiveness of Indian and Korean firms in the overseas construction industry and in the computer software programming industry, industries targeted as service export industries by both governments, are partially explicable by the pattern of policies that mobilizes or inhibits the mobilization of resources into factors of competitive advantage.[17] Human resources have recently been mobilized by the advent of the Responsibility System in the People's Republic of China and market incentives for agriculturalists in the USSR.

Technology Transfer and Industrialized Nations

While the last example indicates a shift from socialist regime in the direction of a market economy, the reverse is also occurring. The technology gap issue is also of concern to firms in advanced industrial nations, firms faced with increasing global competition in many industries.

No country has an overwhelming technological edge in every industry. Japanese chemical firms, for example, respect Dow Chemical's technical processes much as American automobile manufacturers regard Toyota or Honda. In response to increasing global competition, both firms and governments in the First World are revising policy away from open competition toward greater collaboration. To collaborate on shared technology, many international joint ventures have been established among firms from Organization of Economic Cooperation and Development (OECD) countries. U.S. computer firms have established a jointly owned R&D operation to produce generic technology. This sort of venture is still alien to American business culture. The chief executive of the R&D firm remarked that his previous experience as an admiral will help him in the job of compartmentalizing information—that is, doling out information selectively to the various partners in this venture. It is striking that the U.S. government, in line with the growing recognition that national industrial policy and the targeting of industries for global competition may be necessary to cope with global competition, has not forbidden this venture as violating antitrust law.

POLICY IMPLICATIONS FOR MULTINATIONAL CORPORATIONS

Whenever a multinational corporation plans to locate manufacturing operations in a country with technology less developed than its own, it faces the issue of adapting its technology to meet host-country conditions.

The issue is not a simple one. Transferring technology is a communication event with several audiences: the host-country government, international financial markets, and international regulatory bodies such as the World Bank and UNCTAD that may advise the host-country government. These agents have somewhat divergent criteria for evaluating projects. Transferring the latest technology to reduce costs of production may suit international bankers but not a host-country government that wishes to employ more of its population. Transferring older technology may have the opposite impact, for if the firm adapts exactly to the country level, it will be competing with local firms that do not have the added costs of doing business at a distance.

International agencies may evaluate the project in terms of its impact on the social relationships of persons in the country or in terms of its environmental impact. Fortunately, as we saw in the discussion of Amsalem's work, the choice is not all (latest capital-intensive technology) or nothing (older labor-intensive technology); different industries have different degrees of freedom—that is, larger or smaller sets of alternative intermediate technologies. Thus the following discussion will concentrate on contingencies that should enter the firm's planning process when it is deciding how much to adapt to host-country conditions.

Host-Country Reactions

When planning how far to adapt, a firm must assess the reactions of the host-country government. A firm should distinguish between the host country's rhetoric concerning appropriate technology (rhetoric that may be directed at the audience of countries in the region) and its practice. Some countries tend to demand state-of-the-art technology as a matter of national pride; they want to develop showcase industries. Some countries distinguish between production planned for export—in which case incoming firms are allowed greater freedom of choice because the external trade will improve the country's balance of payments—and production planned for domestic distribution—in which case firms are placed under greater pressure to comply with notions of appropriate technology. As a rule of thumb, a firm can start with the assumption that many countries will tend to approve a level of technology that is not the most labor intensive if the product has some priority to the country, if the technology is proven in efficiency, and if the technology is within the range of worker skills (with some training).

A second point to remember is that both companies and countries have much to lose by conflict stemming from the perception that inappropriate technology is being transferred. If a company is deported, it may lose both sales within the country in question and a link in its system of subsidiaries. On the other hand, host countries have a range of options short of deportation with which to chastise a firm considered to be acting contrary to national interest. Countries are constrained from implementing more severe options by the impacts on tax revenues, balance of payments, local employment, and potential multinational corporation investors. When a major company is told to depart, other companies revise their estimate of the political risk of investing in that country. India, for example, had some definite reasons for deporting IBM. The image of difficulties of investing in India, however, has been negatively influenced by this episode. It has taken years for the image of India's investment climate to improve.

Training Needs

A firm must evaluate the training needs for the technology to be employed. The firm may have to train both expatriate engineers and local engineers and workers. If the firm chooses technology it employed ten years ago, its home-country staff will probably know how to operate it without much training; a more severe adaptation to a technology employed forty years ago would require training of home-country staff. Conversely, the older the technology, the less the firm will have to train host-country engineers and workers. It is possible to combine both backward training of expatriates and forward training of host-country staff in one operation. Phillips has a plant in the Netherlands where they try to make all the products in a labor-intensive manner; they bring trainees from the Third World to assist in the process.

Stereotypes about the availability of skilled staff must be avoided. A Japanese firm located a plant in Singapore. When they sought staff, they found that suitable persons were not available in the industry because they were trained and co-opted for government service. After bringing in Japanese staff at great cost, the firm concluded that establishing a training center in Singapore would have been less costly. Current policy is to assess the staff situation and plan for training of staff as part of the logistics of locating operations abroad. Some countries recognize and respond to this need: Singapore now offers tax credits to incoming multinational corporations from developed nations who educate Singaporean suppliers to the multinational corporations.

Managing the Transfer Process

Depending on the type of international business relationship, the firm may have to revise its procedures for selecting, training, and monitoring personnel engaged in international technology transfer. International technology transfer is a communication event more difficult than the communication event that occurs in selling, for example, a consumer good. Technological information, of course, is both intangible and ambiguous. The difficulty of transferring technological information is greater when the transfer is international and thus intercultural. As we emphasized in the early part of this text, persons in business firms are triply socialized: in their national culture, their business culture, and their corporate (or organizational) culture. A transferor of technology needs intercultural communication skills as well as technical skills.

Selection and training of personnel for the task of intercultural communication involved in international technology transfer pose a relatively simple task if the technology is transferred within a firm from headquarters to a subsidiary. In this situation, corporate headquarters controls the organizational culture of the recipient unit. That is, headquarters can institute a training program to ensure that the senders of the message—the technology transferors—share understandings and expectations with the receivers of the message—the recipients of the technology.

The situation is entirely different if the technology is being transferred to an independent foreign firm, as in a licensing agreement, or being transferred as part of an international joint venture. In these situations, the transferor does not have the option of controlling the organizational culture of the recipient firm. A transferor cannot require the recipient to enter a training program and be socialized in the transferor's organizational culture. Rather, the transferor may have to institute selection and training procedures to ensure that the project team charged with the technology transfer is adept at responding to the organizational culture of its foreign licensee or joint venture partner. Describing such a regime exceeds the scope of this work, but let us touch momentarily on its aim: In these situations, technology is not skillfully transferred unless the sender and the receiver take the trouble to negotiate an adequate degree of shared understanding as they begin to negotiate the transfer of technological information.

Social and Environmental Impacts of Technology Transfer

A firm must attend to social and environmental impacts of the technology being transferred. Robock, Simmonds, and Zwick recommend as part of project evaluation the use of an economic cost-benefit analysis from the host country's point of view. This format attends both to benefits (for example, increment to GNP and to numbers of workers employed in the economy) and to opportunity costs (for example, allocation of funds from the domestic financial market) of the intended projects.[18] Economic impacts are only part of the social impacts of a project.

Social impact analysis includes pre-impact, post-impact, and decision-making processes. Pre-impact assessments attempt to forecast the outcomes of a project on a designated community. Such forecasting allows social benefits and costs to be weighed when considering whether or how to implement a project. The procedure requires (1) knowledge of the social characteristics of the community and of the social activities linked with the project, and (2) formulation of models of processes by which the community's social characteristics may change.

Post-impact assessments, studies done after the project is in operation, not only allow a comparison of projected and actual impacts, but are useful as guides for evaluating similar projects that are still in the planning stage. For example, the social impact of a reservoir project now in operation may be used in the pre-impact study modeling of potential impacts of a hydroelectric dam project. Decision-making processes are choices of inclusion of relevant publics as well as the initiators of the project in decisions concerning the project.[19]

The James Bay Hydroelectric Project

The James Bay Hydroelectric Project of the Ungava Peninsula in northern Québec Province, Canada, will serve to illustrate the differences between economic and social impact analyses. This massive project intends to dam seven rivers, create reservoirs, and build hydroelectric plants that are estimated to generate 10,040,000 kilowatts of electricity per year at a project cost of about 10 billion dollars.

Temporary economic impacts are the creation of about 125,000 construction jobs for the native Canadian (mainly Cree) population and for prison inmates; the long-term economic impacts are energy sufficiency in electricity for the province and revenue from sales of electricity to the United States (mainly New York State).

Social impacts are more complicated. The Parti Québecois views the project as a cornerstone of provincial economic independence that should further their objective of separatism from Canada. To the native Cree, much land previously used for hunting and trapping, the center of the traditional Cree economy, is being lost. The Cree must now either leave the area or rely on the national welfare system. There are also noneconomic social impacts for the Cree: the calendar of yearly productive activities, the division of labor by age and by gender, and other symbolic orientations are disrupted. Rates of juvenile delinquency, stress diseases, alcoholism, prostitution, homicide, and suicide have all increased for the Cree.[20]

The Amazon Jungle

Environmental impact analysis may uncover significant unintended consequences of a project. The traditional economy of various groups in the jungles of Brazil and Venezuela is a combination of hunting and slash-and-burn horticulture. Slash-and-burn horticulture, as the name suggests, is the technique of cutting down the vegetation in a plot to be worked, burning what cannot be cut, using the plot for a season, and letting the plot lie fallow for 10 or more years. The next season, a new plot is worked. Each plot regenerates. This technology is appropriate for the environment because it does not deplete the ecosystem.

As part of the economic developmental miracle of Brazil, several new technologies have been imported into the region: large-scale agriculture, herding, and timber cutting. These industries have been practiced in the jungle area near the Amazon River. It was assumed that the interior jungle, like the jungle near the Amazon River, was quite hardy. This assumption was wrong. Land near the Amazon was built up, like the Mississippi Delta, by effluent from the river. The interior jungle has only a thin crust of lateritic soil. The soil is regenerated by the continual droppings from the trees. The canopy in this tropical rain forest prevents the heavy rains from washing away the soil. When farmers, herders, or timber companies cut down the first growth of trees over a large area (as compared with a small plot in the slash-and-burn technology), the capacity of the jungle to regenerate itself is lost. Second-growth forest is comprised of hardier trees that no longer provide a protective canopy. The crust of usable soil is washed away. Clay remains. The new technologies are depleting the environment.[21]

Environmental impacts differ in the scope of region affected. Acid rain caused by sulphur-dioxide smoke emissions from factories in the Saint Lawrence basin and the Great Lakes region affects only that region of the world. In the South American case, the environmental impact is global. The tropical rain forest of the Amazon region produces one-third of the oxygen for our planet. Were the entire jungle destroyed, animal life on our planet would not continue as we know it.

When planning technology transfers to the Third World, multinational firms may have less immediate stimulus to invest in social and environmental impact analysis than they have with the level-of-technology issue. The reason is that developing nations may be more concerned with economic issues (increasing productivity, employing the unemployed, paying off foreign debts) than with avoiding unintended negative social or environmental impacts. If so, they are less likely to sanction incoming multinational investors on these grounds. If firms fail to develop decision criteria—that is, project evaluation criteria and managerial evaluation criteria—to attend to these problems, the problems are likely to continue.

QUESTIONS

1. Explain this statement: ''A culture's technology defines what are natural resources.''

2. Explain the interrelationships between technology and education.

3. Using up to five quantitative indicators, create a technology index that you feel would best indicate the overall level of technological sophistication of a nation. Justify your selection of indicators. Calculate the value of the index for 10 countries.

4. ''Economic development involves moving from an agricultural economy through an industrial economy to a post-industrial or service economy.'' Discuss.

5. Identify a good mixture of R&D investment for a developing nation from the following options: make it yourself, buy it, buy and modify it.

6. Ajax, Ltd., is a major, U.K.-based multinational manufacturer. Ajax is planning a new plant in a foreign country. The production process can range from a very labor-intensive to a very capital-intensive, automated process. How should Ajax go about selecting the exact process design to be used in the proposed plant? What factors should it consider? What information should it have to make the decision? How different are the answers if the plant is to be built in an industrialized country? a developing country? How do the answers vary between industries: for example, a food-processing plant versus a chemical plant?

7. Select one relatively new major technological innovation (interactive cable television, personal computers, or some other) and develop a list of the innovation's short-term and longer-range impacts on both society and the environment.

Organize your list of possible consequences under five headings: ecological, social, economic, political, and psychological.

8. Your firm is planning a new 800-kilometer natural gas pipeline that will run, if approved, through Canada. Your boss has just learned that a statement of environmental impact must be submitted to the government before the project is approved. You have been asked to quickly draft an outline of the major topics to be included in the statement. Your boss mentioned that the government interprets the word *environment* very broadly. What should the impact statement include?

9. Fearing a loss of jobs, organized labor in the United States wants to restrict the international transfer of technology by American firms. They suggest that technology be diffused to foreign countries at a slower rate. Evaluate these statements from the point of view of a corporate strategist, a U.S. Commerce Department official (who is concerned with trade balances), and a U.S. State Department official (who is concerned with demands by less-developed countries that technology be transferred).

10. What are the potential gains and costs to be expected by a host developing country with regard to the transfer of (a) state-of-the-art technology, (b) older, well-proven technology, and (c) outdated but labor-intensive technology?

11. Numerous observers see a need for a code of conduct to govern international technology transactions. Such a code would take into account the legitimate rights of the developers of the technology and the needs of developing-nation technology buyers, and presumably would be enforced by host-country governments. What should be the major objectives of such a code of conduct for technology transfer?

ENDNOTES

1. Comment in *Science* (April 1981): 128.
2. "Who are the copy cats now?" *The Economist* (May 20, 1989): 91.
3. Kenneth David, "International Competitiveness in Construction and Computer Software: The Case of South Korea and India," in W. Chan Kim and Philip K. Y. Young, eds., *The Pacific Challenge in International Business* (Ann Arbor: UMI Research Press, 1987), 289–330.
4. This area was the location of Kenneth David's intensive anthropological field research.
5. Robert M. Pirsig, *Zen and the Art of Motorcycle Maintenance* (New York: Bantam Books, 1974), 158.
6. Emmanuel G. Mesthene, "Symposium: The Role of Technology in Society—Some General Implications of the Research of the Harvard University Program on Technology and Society," *Technology and Culture* 10, no. 4 (October 1969): 500.
7. D. P. Mukerji, "Mahatma Gandhi's Views on Machines and Technology," *International Social Science Bulletin* 6, no. 3 (1954): 441.
8. Stephen Magee, "Information and the Multinational Corporation: The Appropriability Theory of Foreign Direct Investment," in Donald Lessard, ed., *International Financial Management,* (Boston: Warren, Gorham, and Lamont, 1979).
9. Rostow's five stages of economic development constitute one well-known evolutionary scheme of development:

Stage One: The Traditional Society. A society with limited production functions, primarily agricultural. The level of productivity in manufacture as in agriculture is limited by the inaccessibility of modern science, its applications and its frame of mind.

Stage Two: The Preconditions for Takeoff. Societies in transition toward modernization. Some investment in infrastructure occurs, and there is a widening scope of internal and external commerce. Some modern manufacturing appears, but the society is still mainly characterized by the old social structure and values.

Stage Three: The Takeoff. Resistance to change lessens, and the forces for economic growth come to dominate the society. Industries expand rapidly, requiring new investment. New techniques spread in agriculture as well as industry.

Stage Four: The Drive to Maturity. Continuing growth extends modern technology over the whole range of economic activity. The makeup of the economy changes unceasingly as techniques improve; new industries grow, and older ones level off. The economy extends its range into more complex technologies.

Stage Five: The Age of High Mass Consumption. The leading sectors shift toward durable consumer goods and services. The structure of the working forces changes with more employed in offices or in skilled factory jobs. The extension of modern technology as an objective is joined with a desire to improve social welfare and security. W. W. Rostow, *The Stages of Economic Growth* 2d ed. (Cambridge, U.K.: University Press, 1971).

This scheme may provide a general orientation to the idea of national differences in technology, but more specific indicators are needed.

10. Jose de la Torre (Lecture at the University of Michigan, March 16, 1981).
11. Ibid.
12. Arghiri Emmanuel, *L' Échange Inégal* (London: NLB, 1969).
13. Arghiri Emmanuel, *Appropriate or Underdeveloped Technology?* (Chichester, UK: Wiley, 1982).
14. Krishna Kumar, "Social and Cultural Impacts of Transnational Corporations: An Overview," in Krishna Kumar, ed., *Transnational Enterprises: Their Impact on Third World Societies and Cultures* (Boulder, CO: Westview Press, 1980).
15. M. K. Raju and C. K. Prahalad, *The Emerging Multinationals—Indian Enterprise in the ASEAN Region* (Madras, India: M. K. Raju Consultants, 1980).
16. Michel A. Amsalem, *Technology Choice in Developing Countries: The Impact of Differences in Factor Costs* (Washington, DC: International Finance Corporation—The World Bank, 1983).
17. Kenneth David, "Home Government Policy and International Competitive Performance of Third World Corporations: A Study of Indian and Korean Service Industries," in Thomas L. Brewer, ed., *Political Risks in International Business* (New York: Praeger, 1984).
18. Stephan H. Robock and Kenneth Simmonds, *International Business and Multinational Enterprise* 3d ed. (Homewood, IL: Irwin, 1983), 230.
19. Richard Bowles, *Social Impact in Small Communities* (Toronto: University of Toronto Press, 1980); Edward Johnathon Soderstrom, *Social Impact Assessment* (New York: Praeger, 1981).
20. John Stone, "Canada, Quebec Nationals, Cree Indians, and the James Bay Hydroelectric Project" (Paper for Seminar, Environments of International Business, Michigan State University, June 1983), passim.
21. Shelton H. Davis, *Victims of the Miracle* (Cambridge, U.K.: Cambridge University Press, 1977); Eugene Linden, "Playing with Fire," *Time* (September 18, 1989).

CHAPTER SEVEN
Social Organization

No firm can conduct foreign business without involvement in foreign social relationships. Foreign customers are oriented to their indigenous social organizations, which must be studied for market segmentation and target marketing. Agents for export trade, partners in joint ventures, suppliers, managers and workers in subsidiaries, and customers or clients—all are accustomed to codes for behavior in social relationships that differ from those of the foreign manager. These people cannot be expected to leave their behaviorial codes outside the door of a foreign company located in their country.

To avoid alienating these people and to negotiate mutually acceptable codes for behavior, the expatriate manager must develop cultural awareness. In a domestic setting, managers are experienced at negotiating business contracts. In a foreign setting, they often find it necessary to negotiate social norms for behavior before they approach contract negotiation. We begin this chapter with a focus case of social impacts of foreign companies and then provide general guidelines for gaining an understanding of foreign social organization.

FOCUS CASE:
Social Impacts of Maquiladora Companies in Mexico

Maquiladora industry developed along the U.S.-Mexican border following the Bracero program. The Bracero Act of 1942 instituted a bilateral program to regulate the transfer of contracted migrant workers to the U.S. southwestern agricultural region. In its 22 years, this program attracted about 200,000 laborers to the border region and beyond. In 1964, the United States ended the program due to the rapid increase of undocumented migration. The frontier then faced a 50 percent unemployment rate because many displaced braceros settled there.[1]

To quell political unrest at that point, the Mexican government instituted a national border program (PRONAF: *Programa Nacional de la Frontera*). The objective was to beautify the region and promote both commercial and touristic development. To encourage foreign investment, the government offered free-trade and other fiscal incentives. As U.S. MNCs were steadily increasing assembly operations in the newly industrialized countries called the "four dragons" (Hong Kong, Singapore, South Korea, and Taiwan) as well as other Asian nations, the Mexican government promoted the region's low labor and transport costs as an alternative for Asian operations.[2] The border region is also advantageous for companies that wish to avoid the complications of exporting executives to manage foreign operations.

Officially, Article 321 of the Mexican Customs Code defines a *maquiladora* as an industrial enterprise that either (1) uses temporarily imported machinery and exports its total production or (2) uses a permanent industrial plant that formerly supplied domestic markets but now exports part or all of its product with direct manufacturing cost less than 40 percent of its export value.[3]

The resulting maquiladora industries (also known as offshore processing plants, in-bond plants, the twin-plant system, or runaway plants) are typically used for assembly of automotive and electronic equipment, coupon sorting, clothing and toy manufacture, and other labor-intensive work. Wages are low. At around $1 per hour for assembly labor, "The average wage rate for unskilled Mexican labor is now one-sixth that of Japan and a little more than half that of Asia's four dragons."[4] In the past two years, some companies have established traditional integrated manufacturing facilities paying close to the average Mexican manufacturing wage of $1.57 per hour.[5] The number of companies has grown steadily: a total of 680 in 1983, 740 in 1984, 760 in 1985, and 940 in 1986.[6] Currently there are about 1,000 plants, 84 percent of which are located in six cities: Tijuana, Mexicali, Ciudad Juarez, Matamoros, Nogales, and Nuevo Laredo.

The large population of unemployed migrants in the region provides a large selection of workers. The assembly plants attract a new labor sector: somewhere between 67 and 85 percent of assembly workers are young women between the ages of 16 and 25. Common selection criteria are that these women have six to nine years of education, are childless, were recommended by another worker, and had no previous work experience. Critics charge that these criteria ensure a docile work force with no preconceived ideas. In an attempt to justify substandard wages, firms rationalize that these women's earnings are a supplemental income to the family. In reality, the wage is often a household's primary source of income or provides at least half of the total; male unemployment remains very high in the region.

Coming now to the focus of this chapter, the interaction of a foreign company with host-country social organization, we note that the employment of women in maquiladora companies conflicts in some ways with traditional Mexican social organization of gender roles. Reports of the issues are ambiguous.

On one hand, these women have more independence than ever before. They are exposed to norms for behavior that may isolate them from their families and communities. One observer holds that they have less chance of marriage: Mexican men view these independent women in the same class as prostitutes because they are willing to jeopardize traditional norms of dependency on men. Maquiladora employment certainly does provide an economic alternative to early marriage, and it offers greater personal autonomy. What is verifiable is the development of a new market focused toward "maquila" women: urban discotheques and bars frequented by unescorted women have appeared in Mexican border towns. Some women workers are challenging parental authority.[7]

On the other hand, many women workers view themselves as conforming with older social norms. They view work as temporary and intend to marry after retiring. The average length of employment is about three years. Retirement decisions stem not only from marriage prospects but also from some physical duress in working conditions not regulated by the Occupational Safety and Health Association standards. Some women report that their male kin expect them to perform all normal household duties despite the fact that their income is the main support for the household.

Conflicting reports are not uncommon in situations of social change.

GENERAL GUIDELINES FOR APPROACHING AN UNFAMILIAR SOCIAL ORGANIZATION

Definition of Social Organization

Social events and human behavior can never be totally regimented. Events and behavior are unique and changing over time: you cannot step in the same river twice. Yet humans have a limited tolerance for chaos. To impose an acceptable degree of social order, human societies limit the randomness of behavior. Each society defines its social goals, its social times and places, its social persons and groups, and its codes for behavior. People learn that not everything goes. Different tasks are done by different people in different settings. It is this set of social definitions of reality that we call social organization. *To the extent that members of a society learn and share these understandings and use them to predict and evaluate the behavior of others as well as to shape their own behavior, coordinated and predictable behavior is possible.*

Problems in Dealing with Foreign Social Organization

The manager abroad is faced with a recurring dilemma: how much should the foreign firm adapt to local business practices? To what extent should the firm refuse to conform to local norms and instead introduce new ways of managing and doing business? Insensitivity to host-country customs may not only result in misinformed decisions, but also precipitate local resentment and recrimination. In addition to *macropolitical risk* (which we will discuss in Chapter 8), a manager abroad also faces a *cultural risk* of mismanaging interpersonal relations and communications. Yet in order to be successful and to make a contribution, the foreign firm must introduce some special advantage such as managerial skills, distribution techniques, or new technology not currently available to local firms. Without this advantage, a foreign firm is less competitive than local firms that do not have the cost of doing business at a distance.

Because an outsider has internalized his or her own social organization, the outsider either screens out perception of the foreign social organization or perceives it and becomes somewhat disoriented. When one experiences such culture shock, the first step is to remember a simple maxim: *What they are doing makes sense to them*. Every fan of the television series "Star Trek" knows that the crew of the starship *Enterprise* often encounters behavior that is initially confusing and disorienting. They solve the resulting problems usually not with force but with understanding. Solutions appear when crew members have understood the alternative common sense they have encountered.

The actions of persons in a foreign culture and social organization are not nonsense; those people are simply driven by an alternative common sense. Each human society evolves an organization of social activities: patterns of behavior that provide culturally unique solutions to the set of problems (acquisition of food, clothing, and shelter; distribution of power; and so forth) that all human societies must solve if they are to remain viable. Similarly, all societies have evolved an organization of business activities—patterns of behavior that manage all the business functions. Among urban Mexican entrepreneurial families, for example, functions of finance, marketing, and distribution are carried out in the context of a large kin network. This network of relationships is constantly reaffirmed. In such families, allocation of time to attend family ceremonies (marriages, births, communions, and funerals) should not be perceived only as personal behavior; it is also part of organizational behavior.[8]

Avoiding culture shock can be an objective of business policy. When firms first plan international operations, they tend to trade with or locate operations in countries where the cultural distance is not too great. Cultural compatibility is favored over geographical proximity. An inexperienced American firm, for example, is far more likely to commence foreign operations in England than in nearby Mexico.

Let us examine this policy objective. Cultural compatibility does not ensure greater profit. Although the expatriate managers may initially feel more comfortable in a country that is culturally similar, they may overlook the fact that a culturally dissimilar traditional society can be more predictable in the long run.

Why? Advanced industrial nations have a complex set of social relationships. A person in society has to negotiate what is proper behavior. A particular relationship can be guided by a variety of crosscutting principles of social organization (kinship, age, gender, ethnicity, class, region). The relationships become ambiguous when these principles provide alternative codes for behavior.

- Natives of various European countries as well as the United States are not certain exactly how far removed a cousin must be (first cousin? second cousin? further?) before he or she is considered a legitimate sexual partner or spouse.

- For natives of various European countries and the United States, employing domestic servants is not as common a practice as it once was. Numerous mechanical devices save work for the householder. Whereas marketers once targeted women as primary decision makers in the purchase of household appliances, now they target men as well.

Said again, social life is not always predictable, even for the native of the society. Faced with these social complexities, marketers in advanced industrial nations must use complex statistical techniques in order to segment the market and define target markets.

In technologically less-advanced societies, principles of social organization are less conflicting. Social relationships are less ambiguous. A person's kinship, age, and gender statuses will probably define categorically the behavior expected of the person.

- In many non-Western societies, all opposite-sex persons of the same generation are classified as either *sister*-type (nonmarriageable) or *cousin*-type (marriageable).

- In South American countries, firms that advertised household appliances on television encountered poor response. In most cases, anyone wealthy enough to own a television also employs servants. Their orientation is "either you have one or you are one!"—if you do not have a servant, then you are doing the work of a servant in your own home. Then the lady of the house is not impressed by North American-style advertisements that show householders proudly using their own appliances.

When foreign social relationships differ significantly from one's own, they are less accessible *initially*. Once known, however, foreign social events and behaviors may be significantly more predictable than those in the more familiar setting.

A similar lesson is learned from less-developed nations' definitions of social time and social space. Multinationals often limit their productive and marketing operations to large urban areas. Industrial facilities for transport and communications are better developed in these areas. A large labor pool is available. Customers are more easily reached. Rural areas are not the target markets. When the social definitions of rural time and space are studied, other opportunities may present themselves.

- Visitors to cathedral towns such as Salisbury in England note the array of market stalls of the same architectural style as the cathedral.

- In less-developed countries, whatever the religion, large temple towns are the sites of fairs and marketplaces. Worshipers go to these towns both to worship and to shop. It is easy to locate these rural temple-market towns. By studying the connections among the natural calendar of seasons, the productive calendar, and the ritual calendar, one can also determine when a large congregation will be there with enough money to spend. Many religions have the most elaborate festivals just after the main harvest periods.

- In northern Sri Lanka, thousands of worshipers can be counted on to attend post-harvest festivals. As local artisans can and do plan their output to meet these seasonal peaks, there is no reason why corporations cannot imitate their business sense.

In short, Third-World rural markets are held to be small, scattered, and unreachable only because they are unfamiliar to the foreigner.

Rejecting Preconceived Notions

To begin to understand a foreign sociobusiness organization, managers must reject any preconceived notion that the social institutions of the host country are similar to those of their home country. Humans have invented a marvelous diversity of institutions. For example, anthropologists debated for years a definition of *family*. Domestic units assume numerous social forms ranging from minimal units of mother and children with a series of males (the matrifocal family of the Caribbean); to units of parents and children (nuclear family); to units of siblings, their spouses, and their children (joint families); to units of three generations, including grandparents, parents, and children (extended families); and even units of multiple group marriage (the Hill Muria of India).

Nothing is universal in business organization. After an extensive survey of differing work-related value orientations among managers and workers in 50 countries, Geert Hofstede argues that supposedly universal theories of *motivation* (Maslow's hierarchy of needs), *leadership style* (participative management and management by objectives), and *organizational structure* (centrality and formalization of the firm's administrative structure) are all rooted in American culture and do not export well.[9]

The following suggests some general patterns of differences in motivation:

1. Motivation by personal, individual success—wealth, recognition, self-actualization (United States, Britain, and Canada).

2. Motivation by personal security (Japan and Germany).

3. Motivation by security and belonging or group affiliation (France, Spain, Portugal, and Latin America).

4. Motivation by success and belonging (Scandinavia and the Netherlands).

Regarding leadership style, American-style participative management is difficult to implement because it is not authoritarian enough for countries such as France and Germany and because it is too authoritarian for Scandinavian countries.

Management by objectives is based on the American value structure that assumes that the subordinate is sufficiently independent to negotiate with the boss, that both the boss and the subordinate are willing to take some risks, and that goals should be set by individuals. When exported to Japan, management by objectives has become management by group objectives. Originally exported to France as Direction par Objectifs, MBO became Participative Management by Objectives (Direction Participative par Objectifs). This program was considered a failure because the customary French administrative hierarchy protects against anxiety, but DPPO generates anxiety.

Understanding Foreign Social Organization

Instead of holding to preconceived notions, a manager engaged in intercultural business activities should undertake three tasks to facilitate intercultural relationships. The first is to analyze the specific environment to determine how sensitive a communications task is present. The second is to observe and organize knowledge about the norms for relevant social relationships. The third is to gauge the extent to which outside values and forms of organization can be successfully introduced into the host culture.

Analyzing the Need for Adaptation

Kenneth David has suggested a framework for analyzing the variable need for adaptation to a foreign environment.[10] A business plan is the combination of a business strategy (product or service, technology, and marketing strategy) and an organization to implement the business strategy.

A business plan may be likened to a message sent by a firm to its environment. In international business, the receivers of the message are, first, the host country government; second, foreign business collaborators (partners, managers and workers, suppliers, and distributors); and third, consumers or clients. Each category of business relationship should be analyzed to discern how much a firm should adapt and how much it can impose its own business practices.

First, the decision to adapt or impose business practices depends partially on the bargaining power between the firm and the host-country government. Bargaining power varies from industry to industry. In industries such as mining, with mature, appropriable technologies, a firm must be more responsive. In industries such as fiber optics or robotics, with renewing, emerging technologies, the firm has more leeway. Further, the country can tilt bargaining power further in its direction when the country intervenes in consumer choice and prohibits products the country considers contradevelopmental.

Second, the decision to adapt or impose business practices also depends partially on the type of business relationship. There are two questions here. How closely must the business collaborators understand one another? Can one party impose its culture and practices on the other? Communication is less critical between a firm and its foreign sales agent than with a joint venture partner or a foreign subsidiary. While corporate headquarters has the authority to impose its culture (via intensive training) on a foreign subsidiary, a firm cannot impose its corporate culture on a joint venture partner.

Third, the decision to adapt or impose business practices also depends partially on the nature of the product or service offered and the consequent relationship with consumers, industrial buyers, or clients. Products like Coca-Cola and services like mechanized fast food need little adaptation because they are standardized, tangible, and unambiguous. Communication with a buyer of heavy industrial equipment is more critical because the item is expensive and may be custom ordered. Communication is most intense when a service such as large-scale computer software programming is provided. Here, the service is unique, intangible, and ambiguous. The service-providing firm cannot impose business practices. To appear credible to the client, the service-providing firm must be very responsive in various ways, including responsiveness to the client's corporate culture.

In summary, the first step in understanding foreign social organization is to analyze the sensitivity of intercultural communication tasks necessary to implement the firm's business strategy. The more sensitive the situation, the more effort should be allocated to the remaining tasks.

Observation

The second step is observation. In order to discern the social organization, anthropologists engage in an intensive form of participant observation. They learn the local language and live in a foreign community for a year or more. They participate in and observe formal and informal behavior, rituals and disputes, overt and covert behavior. Then they conduct surveys to verify the observations. Managers can rarely afford to allocate time and effort to replicate this intensive process of observation. But they can read articles or ethnographic monographs about the society to which they are assigned. They can seek out and question people previously assigned to that society. Intercultural communications consultants are now available.

However the information is obtained, extensive study is necessary to gather more than a superficial understanding of other societies. Entrants to a new society, it is suggested, should seek answers to dozens of questions about the social group in its environment, about family, kin, and friendship relationships, about economic and other social ranking structures, and about political and government structures.

The Social Group in Its Environment. What factors led to the group's present location in the area? What historical factors led to migration or settlement there? What internal divisions exist within the group? What influence does the group have in its society? What difficulties has this group faced in the host country? What political, economic, or value conflicts exist between this group and other groups? How explosive is this conflict?

Family Relationships. What is the average size of families? Where does a married couple live after marriage? Does the household include grandparents or other relatives? What is the structure of decision making within the domestic group? Despite public images of upper generation and male supremacy, do younger generations and women have a strong covert role in decision making? When do younger people attain a greater role in overt processes of decision making? What kinds of property are jointly owned by a family?

Kin Relationships. What are the rules for approved marriages? Must one marry outside of a specific kin grouping (such as a lineage or clan) or within a specified circle of kin (such as a caste or an ethnic group)? How are these marriage patterns related to commercial and political networks? What qualities make a good husband, wife, daughter, or son? What are the limits of proper behavior toward a man's wife?

Friendship. Is friendship defined as a lack of hostility rather than a close, empathic relationship? Are networks of friends important in economic and political matters? How do people show friendship? What types of displays of affection are acceptable? Where do people go to meet their friends?

Class and Social Status and Ranking. What idiom is used to express class or social status and ranking—hereditary privilege, industrial power, old school ties, age, gender, or racial/ethnic ranking? How is social status shown in one's daily life—are there unequal patterns of giving but not taking, unequal forms of address? What are the rules for class mobility? Is economic mobility permitted but social inequality maintained among groups? What kinds of discrimination are practiced against minorities—is there unequal access to jobs, education, and such?

Government and Politics. Does the group have a political power base? Is social mobility expressed in political mobilization? Which arenas of power are relevant, and what prizes are contested in these arenas? What are the normal rules for expression of political dissent? Are there covert networks of information in repressive regimes? Are mass media censored? Do citizens have effective options in selecting officials? What is the balance of power between elected officials, bureaucrats, and the military?

Observation and empathy help to break down the ethnocentric mental set that an individual takes into a foreign country. The ethnocentric mental set must be replaced with a new orientation that deals with features of social relationships and organizations.

Understanding the Impact of Innovations

The third step in understanding a foreign social organization is that of analyzing how its elements cope with change and innovation. A manager abroad should realize that he or she is engaged not only in marketing a product or service, but also in international social marketing. In other words, the answer to the *adapt-or-innovate* problem depends in part on whether the innovation fits in with or disrupts the social organization of the host country society and in part on whether the innovation will prove useful for economic development. A study of the introduction of American-style supermarkets for food retailing abroad illustrates this point. In African or Asian countries where no large middle class has developed, the introduction of supermarkets would be outside the range of feasible innovations.

For centuries food marketing in less-developed countries was dominated by the characteristics of two groups: the impoverished masses who purchased the bulk of the food with primary emphasis on essentials and low prices, and the affluent upper class which consumed many types of food with little concern for prices.

The needs of these groups were served effectively by small merchants operating out of little stores or more commonly in large open markets with low overhead and minimal labor costs. The lower classes haggled directly with the merchants for their simple needs, and the upper classes sent their servants to shop around among the tradesmen. The small middle class fitted itself into this picture uncomfortably but adequately. The middle class housewife might be able to afford a servant to do her shopping, but often as not she would go out herself to find the best bargains in the open market, accepting the noise and dirt as part of life.[11]

The supermarket of Western Europe, in contrast, fitted in well with the needs of a large middle class that has found relative affluence in the postwar period. The French have even taken the American innovation one step further and created the *hypermarché*.

As this example suggests, a society is never a passive recipient of new ideas, skills, or organizations. A society's response to the impact of foreign business or other external intrusions depends on whether the innovation satisfies or does not satisfy a need within the society. Possible responses are these:

1. Acceptance resulting in assimilation. Certain products, such as Coca Cola, Levi's jeans, and the transistor radio, have been accepted without modification in many societies around the globe. Some managerial techniques, such as managerial cost accounting, raise few problems when put in place in foreign settings. These innovations are accepted and become part of the host culture.

2. Selection and modification. Other innovations are generally acceptable but include details that do not jibe with the host culture. The diffusion of world religions such as Christianity and political ideologies such as Socialism typically occurs with a blending of some details from the original doctrine with some details from the host culture. The managerial technique of management by objectives was modified in different cultural contexts to accord with the host culture. For example, in Japan, the technique became management by group objectives.

3. Rejection and counteraction. Some innovations may be accepted for a while and then rejected, sometimes vehemently. American and European clothing style and youth culture behaviors were accepted in Iran while the Shah was in power but became a target of Muslim fundamentalism under the late Ayatollah Khomeini.

Even if the innovation satisfies needs of some sectors of society, there may be unintended consequences that disrupt aspects of the social organization. Those who work for a multinational corporation located in a less-developed country have no problem in accepting a higher standard of living than that of workers for domestic companies. Several unintended consequences can occur. Wage differentials may be resented by workers in domestic companies. Further, the relatively advantageous position of a multinational's young, skilled workers can incite role conflicts between these people and traditional elderly authority figures and disrupt normal patterns of marriage and obligations to kinfolk. Another unintended consequence occurs in multiethnic societies. If, perhaps due to the influence of a local personnel manager, a multinational unwittingly hires most workers from that manager's ethnic group, surprising political action may result.

Summary

In summary, domestic business relationships are not totally predictable and manageable, but they are at least familiar because the parties to the relationship have been socialized in the same culture and business culture. International business relationships cannot be assumed to be guided by a shared set of understandings. We have suggested that managers learn not to react to these differences with preconceived notions. Rather, managers should assess the business situation to determine how sensitive are the communications. They should observe and research the principles underlying social relationships in the foreign context. Then they will be able to formulate a more appropriate cultural policy for managing human relationships in the context of a foreign culture and social organization.

IMPLICATIONS OF FOREIGN SOCIAL ORGANIZATION FOR THE MULTINATIONAL FIRM

In this section, we shall illustrate the principles set out in the previous section. Foreign social organization affects the business practices of multinationals to the extent that unfamiliar forms of social relationships obtain between the firm and those with whom it deals in the host country. The definition of what it is to be a social person and how to act in social situations is a vast topic and can only be introduced here. We shall survey the international variation and impacts on multinationals of several key areas: kinship and business relationships, nonkin social groups and organizational behavior, systems of rank and managerial elites, and labor unions.

Kinship and Business Relationships

Family

Even in America, the family unit now varies widely. Besides the nuclear family unit of parents and children, the single-parent family is a fact of life. In the middle class, the single-parent family is motivated by career independence of both males and females; in lower-income groups, this unit is motivated by the economics of welfare and by tax laws that until recently discriminated against married couples. Joint or extended families that include other relatives also exist. Indeed, during times of recession, nuclear families with insufficient incomes often are reabsorbed into the upper generation household. American business responds to the differences in consumer buying behavior of these different forms of families. Personnel departments are also adapting to new demands of families, such as finding a job for the trailing spouse when one person in a dual-career family is transferred to another location.

The composition of the family unit varies widely around the world in response to differing socioeconomic conditions. International marketers should attend to the composition of families. Care is needed. Censuses in foreign areas may give separate figures for nuclear families and extended families. Marketers may wrongly conclude that there is always collective buying behavior with the large family. Anthropologists have found, by contrast, that within large extended households, nuclear families may each have their own cooking place (hearth). The hearth-hold is often a locus of consumer decision making in daily purchasing decisions. The entire extended household may be the locus of such major decisions as buying or selling land.

International marketers should also attend to patterns of overt and covert power in decision making within the family. Foreigners are often taken aback by the apparent dominance of males in Third-World countries. American culture places priority on public dominance relative to covert influence. Other cultures have other views. Backstage behavior—the power behind the throne—may be accorded more respect and influence. In a study of peasant agriculturalists and fishermen in northern Sri Lanka, David found that wives of large landowners and boatowners collaborate with their husbands to present an image of male dominance and female subordination. On the other hand, crucial productive decisions were made as frequently by the wives as by the husbands.[12]

Family and Business Relationships

Firms in many countries operate with fewer and less formal contractual business relationships than do U.S. businesses. When people distrust legal contracts, continuity and reliability are assured by working largely with friends or relatives. Kin and business relationships often overlap, making it difficult for outsiders to compete even at a better price. Where such a situation exists, it is often advisable for the foreign investor to enter into a joint venture with a local business.

> One U.S. manufacturer of poultry feed established a facility in Spain on the basis of market studies indicating a substantial demand for feed. Only once the equipment and raw materials had been secured and the product rolled off the line did the firm discover that it was unable to sell to local poultry farmers. The problem, they learned, was that the Spanish poultry growers and feed producers had generations of personal and familial relationships and effectively barred newcomers from the market. The U.S. firm attempted to solve this problem by buying a series of chicken farms, only to discover that they had no customers for chickens! The last word from the firm was that it was busily buying restaurants in Spain.[13]

The Family Firm

In countries where loyalty to kin is strong, where professional management is not widely accepted, and where trust of strangers in business is weak, the family business is prevalent. In preindustrial societies and in nonindustrial sectors of contemporary non-Western societies, individuals have access to means of gaining a livelihood via their status as kin. Trading activities in preindustrial societies were typically organized via wider kin networks. The use of family and kin networks to organize commercial and industrial activities is an extension of the pervasive functions of the kinship grouping. Family members are not necessarily trusted without reserve, but they are familiar and observable. Further, the family firm is prevalent in countries that are moving along the development track.

> India is by no means a country with undeveloped social and economic institutions. India has its own multinational firms operating from the Middle East to Southeast Asia. Yet the family business is still important in India. A family member in such a firm defines the scope of responsibility as any activities that

help implement the family consensus and that also stay within regulatory guide-
ines. This definition of responsibility contrasts strongly with the American model
in which scope of responsibility and authority are defined and delegated to a
position on an organizational chart.

Growth strategies in India also relate to family structure. There, family objectives such as creating employment for family members are a strong impetus
for forming a business. Recently, an American businessman suggested to his
Indian joint venture partner that the latter use a standard market-portfolio model
(à la Boston Consulting Group) to plan his business expansion. His partner
refused to invest unequally in the five existing businesses because each business
was managed by a son. Unequal investment would cause family discord. Even
in firms where some of the board of directors are not family members, the
norm of family consensus can be very strong. Family owner-managers often
hold private council before submitting plans to the Board.

Is a manager abroad to feel totally locked out when dealing with family firms?
The following anecdote illustrates the major point made earlier that an outsider may
face initial culture shock but find highly predictable patterns of behavior in a foreign
setting. A foreigner armed with a standard flow chart for gaining commitment to
a plan (for example, a flow chart of a sequence of encounters with initiators of plans,
decision influencers and evaluators, and resource allocators) may learn that unexpected persons enter the sequence.

A problem arose between a U.S.-trained M.B.A. and his uncle, the managing director of a medium-sized firm in India. The nephew presented a business
plan. The family astrologer attended the meeting and vetoed the plan. Later,
the nephew persisted and asked the astrologer to reconsider the plan. The
astrologer recommended various ceremonies after which the astral signs would
probably bend toward the plan.

Astrological ploys are common in South Asia. A mother, who must publicly
defer to her husband, frequently "cannot find" her child's astrological chart until
a candidate of whom she approves is being considered. Once these ploys are
known, it is not difficult to include the astrologer in one's list of decision evaluators and allow time for this subprocess in the decision sequence. On the bright
side, astrological approval furthers commitment of the family to a project.[14]

The family business is also common in some industrial countries. In Italy, where
loyalty to kin groupings prevails, the structure of business management often coin-
cides with that of the family group and serves familial interests even at the expense
of industrial expansion or profitability. Paternalism is the predominant managerial
style and applies even to people who do not belong to the family. In small enterprises, the proprietor is also the general manager. By appointing family members
to key managerial positions, family control is ensured even in large-scale enterprises.
In Italy, as elsewhere, competitive pressures for rationalization and efficiency are
forcing the introduction of professional specialists. In many cases the family may
retain control of the firm's ownership and destiny, but avenues to top managerial positions on the basis of performance are being opened.

Nonkin Social Groups and Organizational Behavior

Every human society has purposeful group activity. What differs significantly is the qualitative style of interaction within groups and between groups. Some societies have an individualistic orientation, while others have a more collectivist orientation. Some societies temper competitive interaction with strong ideals of cooperative behavior within and between groups. Some societies are comfortable with more informal, participatory interaction, while others favor more formal, ranked interaction. There is wide variation in actual-versus-apparent centralization of authority in decision making. American managers abroad may have to adjust their managerial style because American style is typically individualistic, participatory, and competitive.

Individualist and Collectivist Orientations

Iwata's discussion of the varying definitions of responsibility in Western and Japanese organizations illustrates the difference between individualist and collectivist orientations.

> In Western societies, importance is attached to the functions each individual is to fulfill; there is a constant attempt to clearly demarcate each individual's duties and responsibilities.
>
> Predetermining and clearly indicating the scope of responsibilities is one of the prerequisites for the individual's participation in a business organization. For this reason, in Western societies, job description and scope of responsibility must be clearly spelled out before the person is hired.
>
> As a result, the basic unit of Western-style business organizations is the job to which a person is assigned and for which responsibility is expressly defined. With this as the basic unit, Western-type companies are designed in such a way that these jobs adequately fulfill the overall management goals.
>
> In contrast to this, with Japanese business organizations, the scope of the job assigned to each individual is not necessarily clearly defined. Work is not designed with the individual's job as the basic unit but is rather farmed out to each section, department, or other unit of the work force.
>
> As a result, under the Japanese system, priority is put on accomplishing the task assigned to the work force rather than on the individual employee who is performing the job. This structural mechanism is surprisingly consistent with characteristic features of the Japanese attitude towards responsibility, namely the vagueness of individual responsibility, the idea of joint group responsibility, and the strong sense of responsibility towards the small, close group.[15]

Competition and Cooperation

Competition in American Business Culture. Competition is a key feature of American business culture. Competitive attitudes are common in management-labor relationships, in intracompany executive behavior, and in relationships between competitive firms.

- The relationship between management and labor is traditionally adversarial. Events in the U.S. auto, airline, and steel industries in the early 1980s, in which labor voluntarily took wage cuts in return for greater job security and, in some cases, representation on the board of directors, may be seen as a trend toward greater cooperation. Such a trend would be more credible if it occurred in a prosperous period of the U.S. economy.

- Competitive attitudes are fostered in M.B.A. programs. A graduating M.B.A. from the University of Michigan gained points among his peers, for when a company interviewer asked him how he felt about competing with M.B.A.s from Harvard, Stanford, and Wharton, he replied, "I have two advantages. I'm as good as they are. And they don't know it." A similar attitude is reported in the *Handbook for Young Urban Professionals:* "What is deadwood in the company? Anyone senior to me."

- Competition is institutionalized among groups in companies such as Procter & Gamble, which markets several competitive brands of laundry detergent.

- Cooperation between firms is sometimes seen between firms from different industries who aid one another to avoid a forced acquisition by a third firm. Cooperation between firms in the same industry, except in a special situation such as cooperation in exporting goods, is frowned upon as illegal collusion.

Competition and Cooperation in Japanese Business Culture. By contrast, there is counterpoint between competition and cooperation at various levels of Japanese business practice.

- Japanese quality control circles, which are voluntary associations of workers in many Japanese companies, produce both work and suggestions. In the Toyota company, according to Eiji Ogawa, thousands of suggestions are submitted annually by quality control circles, not by individuals. Each suggestion receives a low monetary reward. Rather, there is an intangible reward, honor to the group. Then the quality control circles compete to produce suggestions. Unimaginative groups, by the way, are not permitted to lose face. Suggestions are sometimes fed to them by R&D personnel. On the other hand, there is cooperation among these same groups in the overall attempt to produce defect-free work by the company. The honor of the company is at stake in the national Deming competition for defect-free work.

- Japanese companies not only compete but also cooperate. Large companies incite strong competition among their suppliers to produce high-quality components at least cost and to deliver them just in time (*kanban*) for use on the assembly line. If a supplier has difficulties, technical and managerial advice is available. And if a particular supplier is forced out of business by more competitive suppliers, efforts are made to hire the supplier. The code of lifetime employment can operate toward suppliers and not just toward employees.

- Another instance of the counterpoint of competition and cooperation occurs among firms regarding research and development. As we noted in the chapter on technology, Japanese firms that otherwise compete have pooled their efforts in collaborative research in the development of integrated robotics systems.

Formality and Ranking

Although there is much regional variation among U.S. companies (in frontstage behavior, East Coast companies display more formal ranked interaction then West Coast counterparts; but backstage, the West Coast companies are often more strictly ranked), American companies tend to permit more informal and participatory interaction among individuals and groups than do firms in many nations. As the following anecdote illustrates, American firms operating in strongly formal or authoritarian societies may encounter problems if they attempt to employ informal management styles.

> The managers of one American firm tried to export the "company picnic" idea into their Spanish subsidiary. On the day of the picnic, the U.S. executives turned up dressed as cooks and proceeded to serve the food to their Spanish employees. Far from creating a relaxed atmosphere, this merely embarrassed the Spanish workers. Instead of socializing with their superiors, the employees clung together uneasily and whenever an executive approached their table, everyone stood up.[16]

Variations in Centralization of Authority

The patriarchal style of many managers in countries where the family business is predominant is difficult to change because of the dependency of employees on top management. This may be true of government as well as business. The bureaucratic delays of many government agencies in Asia, Africa, and Latin America result in part from an extreme unwillingness to delegate authority. Consider the following observation about firms:

> There is a strong tendency for the head of the family to maintain virtually complete authority on all major issues even when there are other well-educated and potentially effective family members in the managerial hierarchy. There is also typically a high degree of centralization accompanied by autocratic direction in the larger public enterprises, since they are staffed largely by managers with a civil service background who are accustomed to this type of administration.[17]

Some European countries, on the other hand, have institutionalized participative management, and in Yugoslavia workers consider they have the right and duty to decide directly on any problems of production and distribution.

Centralization of authority is not necessarily counterproductive. The role of management in many highly efficient Japanese firms is a paternalistic one, rooted in the social organization of the country. The authority system of Japanese industry closely resembles that of the Japanese family, the clan, and other local institutions. As in Japanese society, employee status is determined largely by educational attainment and seniority. Two groups are segregated: executives are college graduates, while manual and clerical workers and first-line supervisors have elementary and high school education. Although a new generation of graduates influenced by American practices is altering relationships, it would normally be unacceptable for a bright junior executive to take the initiative and push ahead of those with seniority. Rather, cohorts of managers who enter the firm the same year are evaluated together and slowly advance in the hierarchy. Some managers slowly advance farther than the rest but retain loyalty to the cohort.

The impact of centralization of authority is different in the context of this process of group evaluation and promotion of cohorts. Despite a formal centralization of authority, there is a decentralization of decision making that is institutionalized in the *ringi* system of a series of approvals. In this system, every relevant manager must place a stamp of approval (ringi) on the project.

Systems of Rank and Managerial Elites

When Americans talk about systems of rank, they frequently use the term *social stratification*. This term reflects a cultural bias. As defined in the United States, rank is mainly a matter of accomplishments in a competitive world. The fittest shall not only survive but rise to prominence. An ideology of Social Darwinism underlies the American idea of social ranking. In many parts of the world, there is a contrasting ideology of rank, a socioreligious ideology that rank is intrinsic and inherited biologically. This ideology is close to the eighteenth-century ideas of Lamarck that personal characteristics can be inherited biologically. The point of this contrasting ideology is that people who are innately superior will also perform in a superior manner.

Socioreligious Stratification

Both ideologies are present in all societies to different degrees. The United States retains images of the aristocratic ideology in such cultural categories as Boston Brahmins, First Families of Virginia, and the Black Aristocracy of New Orleans. The United Kingdom, still a bastion of class consciousness (an ideology of accomplishments or of exploitation, depending on your viewpoint), also retains the socioreligious aristocratic ideology. A hymn, now deleted from the Anglican hymnal, went, "The Lord is in his castle./The beggar at his gate./God made them great and lowly./And gave each his Estate." In this hymn, social inequality is held to be divinely created.

The keynote of socioreligious ideologies of rank is that different categories of humans are culturally defined as if consisting of different physical substances that have different worth and potential for performance. Whatever one's emotional reaction to such an ideology, it is necessary to recognize that such ideas are the basis of predictable social interactions in society.

Naipaul writes of how a black Jamaican baker profited from his understanding of the correlation between ethnicity (a social identity based on physical substance) and occupations in Jamaica.

Having been apprenticed to Chinese bakers and desiring to open his own business, the man knew that Jamaicans, even black Jamaicans, would buy bread only from Chinese bakers. He gave the shop a Chinese name, hired a Chinese counterman, and, as he said, laughed all the way to the bank.[18]

The most thorough socioreligious ideology is the Indian caste system. In traditional values, different castes were thought to be made of natural substances, as different as natural species of animals. The physical substances of castes are held to be separate and unequal in purity, spiritual power, and the propensity to learn and perform tasks. Upper caste farmers were incredulous at the results of a study by a foreign anthropologist showing that the most efficient farmer in the village was from the lowest caste, an Untouchable.

Faced with a system of socioreligious rank, a foreign manager does not have to adopt the local codes but simply learn how to deal with them. A foreign manager should learn the local ranking distinctions and the social rules for acceptable interaction. Ranking differences can be compartmentalized between work and nonwork situations. The manager should consult with the local managers of whatever rank in the office. After-hours socializing with a group of personnel of various social ranks may be acceptable in a bar, for example, but not at a dinner in the home.

Social Stratification

Social stratification refers to the hierarchy of classes within a society and to the relative power, income, privilege, and social priorities of these various layers of society. The close interrelationship between occupations and social status is a crucial part of the international business environment. Developed and less-developed countries tend to have different profiles of social inequality. Figure 7-1 illustrates the differences in very general terms. Note the bulge near the top of the less-developed country hierarchy. This bulge denotes that a very small percentage of consumers control much of the wealth.

In a class system in industrialized Western societies, each class has somewhat distinct tastes, political views, and—as marketers know and use in distinguishing target markets—consumption patterns. Class mobility is not forbidden. These features can be acquired within several generations. The high class mobility of an industrialized society is conducive to the development of an economically motivated middle class and a managerial elite. Mobility is facilitated to the extent that an educational system is open to all qualified candidates. By this criterion, educational mobility is quite high in socialist countries. Mobility is restricted when the quality of public education is low.

Geographical mobility is also important for managerial effectiveness. American companies doing business in Western Europe have found that residential mobility in Europe is lower than in the United States, where 19 percent of all families change their residence each year.[19]

Increased social mobility does not, however, always improve the climate for international business. Rapid change of any sort can be disruptive. The pace of industrial

FIGURE 7-1

CLASS STRUCTURE

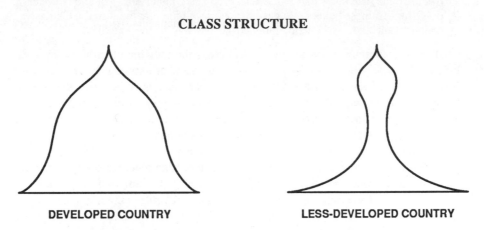

DEVELOPED COUNTRY　　　　　LESS-DEVELOPED COUNTRY

Source: Adapted from Richard N. Farmer, "Organizational Transfer and Class Structure," *Academy of Management Review* (September 1966): 204-276.

change often exceeds the pace of social mobility. Both the underprivileged and the privileged classes can incite social upheaval in order to gain or retain economic and political advantage. An international manager must look behind overt patterns of disruptive social mobilization for the underlying economic structure.

In Northern Ireland the overt pattern is the conflict between Irish Catholics and Irish Protestants. What is undercommunicated in the mass media is the economic structure of Northern Ireland. Northern Ireland was established as a conquest state when Scottish Presbyterians allied with the British for the conquest of Ireland. The Scots became the dominant landowners and, later, industrialists in the region. Both Irish Catholics and Protestants became the industrial working class. It is no coincidence that the Catholic-Protestant conflict started at the very time that workers of both religions began mobilizing as a common front against the Scottish management.

As a general rule, economic conflicts can be organized in terms of various emotionally charged social identities such as religion, language, territory, culture, or history.

Occupation and Social Status

Economic stratification, according to Karl Marx, determines the shape of social relationships, the culture, and the nature of social change in society. In most countries, a person's occupation is a key feature of social status. Especially in industrialized countries, there is impressive agreement across countries in the ranking of occupations.[20]

International executives are concerned with the availability and quality of managerial talent in host countries. This concern is greater in recent years because host countries want foreign companies to hire local managers. American companies have found that the scarcity of trained managers in many developing countries is due partially to the relatively low status of business people. In the Chinese civilization, scholars, public administrators, and large landowners far outranked people engaged in commerce or business. In the Indian civilization, priests and rulers outrank merchants. During the colonial period, local business managers became viewed with distrust as agents of the colonial power. Such attitudes die slowly, especially when new nations adopt a mixed socialist-capitalist economic system.

The managerial elite is sometimes tailored by the educational system. Typically, a select set of prestigious universities turn out a class of professionals who are assured of high-level careers in government or in industry.

> In Japan, the best students are called into government service. Tokyo University sends its best students to the Ministry of International Trade and Industry. Managing the country's industrial policy, it is thought, is more important than managing a company.
>
> Great Britain has a well-defined elite that directs British institutions, often called the "old boys clubs" class—a reference to the fact that many British managers are educated in a small group of well-known public schools.
>
> The French managerial elite is generally chosen from those having family ties by heritage, marriage, or a degree from one of the so-called grandes écoles. Graduates of these institutions frequently pass immediately into high-level government positions, whence they are eventually recruited into the ranks of a narrow class of industrial managers. It is hardly surprising to find that there is a sharp cleavage between the managers, primarily those professionally trained in the grandes écoles, and the managed, who may include middle management (cadres) recruited from lesser institutions.

Labor Unions Around the World

The class of social interest groups representing labor deserves a section of its own not only because workers are part of the business but also because unions have historically played a crucial role in many nations' polities and economies. Whenever a firm invests abroad, it must learn the local business culture of labor unionism.

Unionism in Europe, America, and Japan

While labor unions in America function primarily as interest groups to pose their collective bargaining power against the power of the company management, modern European labor unions were formed with the aim of a total social transformation. European unions still function in a much broader sphere than is suggested by the term "interest group." They are more properly called social movements, for their activities embrace many aspects of the workers' lives, such as recreation and education, in addition to political action. Historically, they sought and achieved major political goals such as the rejection of feudalism and the right to vote, European union members tend to have a much greater sense of worker solidarity than U.S. workers because suffrage and other rights were won by their collective action. European labor unions are closely identified with political parties and ideologies, particularly socialist ones.

The close association between unions and political parties means that they have substantial influence over government social policy when their party is in power. The British Trades Union Congress, for example, has a hand in drafting social legislation when the Labour Party is in power. Thus European unions have two routes to the enhancement of worker interests: collective bargaining and legislation. As a result, the scope of collective bargaining is less in Europe than in the United States. Many issues between labor and management that are negotiated in the United States are legislated in Europe. Another difference is the geographical scope of agreements. In America, collective agreements are limited usually to one firm or geographical region. The size of European nations, of course, resembles that of states of moderate size in America. In Europe, national bargaining and agreements between union federations and employers' associations are common.

> The differential impact of labor activity is clearly seen in basic accounting categories. In the United States, the category of variable costs (costs that vary according to quantity produced) includes not only materials used in production but also the cost of labor; the category of fixed costs includes items such as advertising, administrative overhead, and the salaries of executives. In northern European countries such as the Netherlands and West Germany, it would be highly uneconomic to hire and fire workers each time the quantity to be produced changed, for a company must pay a dismissed worker up to five years' salary. In these cases, the cost of labor is effectively a fixed, not a variable, cost.

American unionism has always been more pragmatic and concerned with the immediate needs and grievances of workers. Their collective action was not needed to overthrow a feudal system or gain the right to vote. Although modern U.S. unionism is concerned with such social issues as poverty, national medical care, and the environment, it started off as an effort to organize fragmented craft unions into national unions. The objective was to maintain a national level of wages that could not be undercut by a shift of plant location. In a general sense, American unions are usually identified with the Democratic party, which has traditionally forwarded their cause more than the Republican party. The ideological connection is not as central as in the European case. Union leaders try to line up votes behind the candidate who will best serve their interests. Without the strong identification with parties and their ideologies, American unions are more vulnerable to major structural changes in the economy. When changes in the pattern of global competition or technological change such as robotics affect an industry, labor unions find that their collective bargaining power declines.

The labor union system in Japan contrasts sharply from Western unions. It strongly reflects the Japanese familial system of social organization. Glowing reports of lifetime employment and other paternalistic benefits based on length of service and loyalty to the company are somewhat overemphasized. Lifetime employment, for example, is not universal, for many women and part-time employees are excluded. Nevertheless, compared with the more adversarial relation between Western workers and management, closer bonds are established between Japanese superiors and subordinates, both within and outside the workplace. Further, unions are limited to single firms and are only loosely federated into national industrial unions with limited authority. The industrial unions are in turn affiliated to four major labor centers, which, as in Europe, assume a highly political role in influencing government policies.

Labor Unions in the Developing Countries

In developing countries, labor unionism is even more of a critical force in the political and economic changes than in Western Europe. The international manager must understand that economic demands made by labor unions in such countries aim to bring about social and political change as well as an improved standard of living.

Why do political aims dominate labor unions in less-developed countries? In Europe and North America, political and economic modernization proceeded separately and over a long period. In less-developed countries, they are inseparable. The social transformation aims of unions in developing areas were more radical because of the colonial situation. In many African countries, unions were part of the preindependence struggle and are still headed by political leaders. Several union movements in Latin America sought to secure political rights for the illiterate mass of Indios. In most cases, unions became politicized and, after independence, became highly dependent on the government.

In the postcolonial era, there are several problems. First, ethnic conflict is sometimes reflected in unionism: in Sri Lanka, parallel trade unions exist in various industries for workers from the two major ethnic groups, the Tamils and the Sinhalese. Second, as nations moved away from the rejection of foreign companies and began to court them as part of country strategies for economic development, the objectives of the government and the unions diverged. The government may become intolerant of union action that impedes economic development. A poor country may court multinational companies at the expense of its workers. Multinationals are attracted to locations with low-paid, docile labor forces. When countries move into the advanced developing nation stage, the government has greater difficulty in maintaining this posture.

Finally, as with other business relationships, labor relations also benefit from knowledge of local norms of social relationships. When the Tata firm was operating a steel mill at Jamshedpur in India, it had difficulty retaining workers. The company found that skilled workers would not respond to monetary incentives. When they earned enough to buy land, they quit. The Tata management innovated a bonus system. Any worker who remained on the job at least ten years was allowed to name a successor. Tata promised to train and hire that individual. Workers responded well to this form of incentive because it resembled the traditional, paternalistic, jajmani system of relationships in Indian agricultural villages.

Labor Unions and Government

A general rule for the international manager to remember is that irrespective of the stage of development, the foreign business operation is in fact negotiating with the host country government as a third party to the bargaining process with labor unions.

> Spain is an example of a country whose labor movement plays a major role in political change and development. Spanish labor disputes involving foreign-owned enterprise became highly politicized as a result of labor's militancy in seeking social and political reforms during the Franco regime.
>
> Companies engaged in collective bargaining dealt not only with the *sindicatos,* the government-controlled unions, but also with *comisions obreras,* the underground unions that are active in virtually every large plant in Spain.
>
> The government, aiming to attract and retain foreign investment, kept the wage demands of the sindicatos to a minimum, but the comisions obreras demanded higher wages and employed less-orthodox methods of pressuring companies.[21]

When government objectives conflict with those of labor unions, the foreign firm may be caught between two fires.

MANAGING SOCIAL CHANGE

Political, ideological, social, and economic changes act on one another in complex ways. International business has encountered important opportunities and grave dangers in areas where these changes have occurred most rapidly. Earlier, we discussed the need for multinationals to consider intended and unintended impacts of their innovations in a foreign setting. Now we will concentrate on the following questions: What are the social consequences of industrialization and urbanization for countries? for international business?

Industrialization and Social Change

Industrialization causes social change and vice versa. Values and social relationships change because people want the standard of living that industrialization makes possible. People alter their social relationships to allow it. Usually, however, the causality runs the other way. Industrialization leads to social changes in the family, the role of women and the younger generation, mobility, life-styles, and urban migration. Let us take an inventory of the somewhat disruptive changes that have occurred.

Industrialization and Family Ties

Of the many social changes that accompany industrialization, some of the most severe strains occur within the family. What happens when women and younger members of traditional families seek and obtain an independent social and economic base?

- Industrialization demands relocation; the frequency and intimacy of contact among kin members decreases.

- A disparity of life-styles emerges between generations. Social mobility allows some kin members to move up rapidly, leaving others behind and making contact more difficult.

- The functions of large kinship groupings are appropriated by more specialized agencies and business firms in urban areas. Care of children can be bought in child-care centers. Children receive less preschool education from grandparents and more from "Sesame Street." The elderly can be sent to retirement homes. The family can be fed at fast-food restaurants.

- The tradition of helping family members find jobs breaks down. Occupations become more specialized and kinfolk are less likely to know of suitable positions or to have sufficient influence to help place a relative.

Impacts of Urbanization

About nine-tenths of all humans are crowded into a quarter of the land surface of the world. Apart from population increase, the growth of cities is largely the result of technological developments: the economies of a geographically concentrated industrial infrastructure; medical technology that enables high-density urban living; transportation technology that provides the necessary movement of persons, food, and goods; vastly improved communications; and the income disparity that has grown between industry and agriculture.

Although the developed countries are the most urbanized, the cities in less-developed countries have the highest growth rates. Table 7-1 indicates the correspondence between urbanization and GNP per capita. At lower levels of development, urbanization increases slowly. At intermediate levels, urban migration accelerates. At higher levels, the proportion of the population in cities begins to level off.

TABLE 7-1

URBANIZATION AND PER CAPITA INCOME

	Average per Capita Income in 1986 U.S. Dollars	Urbanization
China and India	300	23%
Other low-income countries (37)	200	22%
Lower-middle-income countries (34)	750	36%
Upper-middle-income countries (24)	1,890	65%
Centrally planned economies (9)	4,552	65%
High-income oil exporters (4)	6,740	73%
Industrialized countries (19)	12,960	75%

Source: *World Bank Development Report, 1988* (World Bank, 1988), 222, 223, 284, 285.

What the aggregate statistics do not show are the social problems that result from the unemployed poor jostling one another for housing, amenities, jobs, and services.

A remarkable—but not a typical—example is that of Djakarta, the capital of Indonesia. As many as 80 percent of its citizens are estimated to live outside the reach of basic public services. Only 15 percent have access to the water supply of the city. Eighty-five percent of Djakarta's five million inhabitants live in substandard housing. With the city growing at 5.6 percent a year, one governor of Djakarta declared that unemployed persons would not be permitted to migrate to the city.

Yet the decree is virtually unenforceable. Huge industrial development projects initiated by the Indonesian government cannot meet the demand for jobs by the incoming citizens. In fact, the more jobs created, the more attractive the city will appear to unemployed or underemployed rural peasants. They migrate to shantytowns to live with kinfolk. Foreign-owned and foreign-financed industries provide little relief because they tend to install capital-intensive technology.[22]

In order to avoid overburdening the cities' services, governments have taken to giving substantial subsidies, tax breaks, and other incentives to industry to locate in nonurban areas. Despite the attractiveness of locating near a center of industry and commerce, foreign companies have increasingly taken advantage of these incentives. Quite apart from the monetary value of the incentives, firms find that locating in development areas increases their value (and hence their security) in the host country and reduces the number of political confrontations that arise from city-based groups such as university students.

CONCLUSION

The record of governmental interference with Western-owned business operations in non-Western countries shows that many companies have, by default, chosen to ignore social and political forces. Other firms have acquired an understanding through experience. They establish a subsidiary in a foreign country with initially limited involvement and allow their managers abroad to immerse themselves in the foreign country. In these firms, the subsidiary may be allowed to operate autonomously as long as things go smoothly. Unfortunately, when things suddenly cease to go smoothly, the parent-company management may be able to discover neither the source of the problem nor whether it could have been averted.

Several companies have designed more sophisticated techniques for evaluating both the existing sociopolitical environment and the firm's probable impact on it.

One such company is DuPont, which has a group of researchers who have identified fifteen to twenty special interest groups per country, ranking from small landowners to influential bankers.

Each group is evaluated according to latent influence depending on its educational level, size, and ability to make its views felt. The DuPont researchers also consider group cohesiveness—in particular, the probability that the interest group will take a strong stand and mobilize its resources on issues that might affect operations abroad. These issues would include pollution, labor relations, and the ownership of local industry by foreigners. Measures of latent influence and group cohesiveness are quantified and multiplied together, and the resulting product is in turn multiplied by another figure, one that represents the government's receptivity to the group's influence. The final result (as well as the analysis that preceded it) helps the company to judge how it should react to social and political issues in a particular country. Even if the final figure is of little value in itself, the social-group examination has forced the company to think carefully about the peculiarities of social forces in each country.[23]

Many companies have neither the personnel nor the time to undertake such analyses of this depth. For general guidelines, management abroad should first take care to avoid common mistakes of the past, such as the following:

- Failure to place oneself in the other person's shoes.
- Insufficient understanding of different ways of thinking.
- Misunderstanding of different ethical standards.
- Insufficient attention to the social status and to saving face of the counterpart in negotiations.
- Lack of appreciation of the role of personal relations and personalities in decision making by firms and governments abroad.
- Inability to recognize the loci of decision making and influence.[24]

Second, recalling the guidelines discussed earlier in this chapter (see pages 166–167), a firm should analyze, for all those with whom it deals in the foreign setting, both how much bargaining power it has and how critical are the communications with the other parties.

Third, after analyzing the host country's sociocultural environment, how should the company react to it? What role should international business play? What should the company's cultural policy be: should Western management abroad try to adapt to the existing social order or should it try to innovate, regardless of the prevailing patterns of social relationships?

If the question is posed in this way, the usual answer is as follows: The foreign company has been invited to invest in the host country because it is different and can introduce valuable changes, both technological and organizational. The company should retain a primary long-run objective of achieving change that is useful for the economic welfare of the host country; conformity should be the strategy only when personal relations are crucial, when bargaining power is weak, or when change would be dysfunctional within the society.

A flexible cultural policy sounds rational. But perhaps this is not the best way to address the question, for the question assumes that the Western way to do things is the best way. This is a parochial view. Let us reexamine our principles.

Developmental economists have long stressed the fact that savings, capital, and industry alone cannot bring about self-sustained economic growth in a country.[25]

Another precondition, they argue, is the development of rational and impersonalized attitudes and social relationships as exist in Western cultures. Loyalty, intragroup harmony, and the family business must give way to individuality and emphasis on economic goals and performance. Farmer and Richman posit a utopia of productive efficiency, Islandia, where

> Islandians have a high regard for personal achievement. Persons gaining fame in any field, including management, are highly regarded, and well paid. It is commonly felt that any man can achieve much, if only he sets his sights high enough; and children are encouraged to plan their lives with maximum, rather than minimum achievement in mind.[26]

As we will see in Chapter 8, many of the economic assumptions of the developmental model have been challenged. In recent years, the human relations assumptions have also been questioned. Julius Nyerere of Tanzania has long advocated an African socialism in which village collectives, or Ujamaa, form the focus of economic development. A potent example is Japan, whose advances in industrialization and global competitiveness occurred without drastic changes from preindustrial Japanese relationships in the direction of the Western model. Indeed, after American companies began losing significant shares of their market to Japanese companies, there emerged a flood of writings on Japanese government-business relations, managerial style, labor relations, and business strategy. The main theme is that a restructuring of American industry may be facilitated by some revision of the rational model of human relations. There are lessons to learn from many countries.

If this stance has some validity, then the usual question—should the company adapt or innovate in a foreign setting?—is not the best question. A better question for thinking about cultural policy is this: How can the company learn from its foreign experience for (1) not only smooth operations in a particular host country but also (2) the improvement of sociobusiness relationships in other host countries and in the home country? This would be a geocentric cultural policy. Implementing such a policy would require investment in organizational features to collect information on cultural experience from foreign subsidiaries and use that information in future training programs as well as in formulating business strategy.

QUESTIONS

1. "The role of foreign investors is to innovate—to introduce modern business practices." Discuss.

2. What is the role (or roles) of the business manager in a traditional authoritarian culture?

3. "Economic development causes social change." Discuss.

4. What are the common characteristics of social groups?

5. Should business managers abroad be prepared, if necessary, to bribe government officials? If so, under what circumstances?

6. Select a country with a traditional, hierarchical social structure, and write an intracompany memo outlining how the social structure will affect your company's selection of personnel for a new plant in that country.

7. What special-interest groups are most important for the company considering an investment abroad?

8. Compare and contrast the role of labor unions in the United States, Western Europe, and less-developed countries.

9. Contrast traditional and modern family systems.

10. What are the causes of urbanization? Will urbanization continue at the present pace? Why or why not?

11. From the point of view of an American manager considering an investment in a Latin American country, show how you would analyze the potential of various social groups in the host country for generating conflict with foreign enterprise.

12. From the point of view of a local (host country) business firm, identify the ways in which foreign investors would affect your business adversely.

13. Quite opposite charges have been leveled at the relationship between a labor union and its management: On one hand, it is charged that the systemic antagonism between them results in lessened productivity. On the other hand, the top management of a labor union may be viewed as speaking the same language as management and conspiring with them: (As one worker said at a conference that included representatives of labor and the major U.S. auto makers, "You are speaking for the unions. And you three are speaking for the companies. But who is speaking for the working man!")

   Prepare a report on the Dutch system of industrial relations, which by law must conduct three-way negotiations: not only with representatives of labor and management, but also with a worker-elected unit called the Worker's Council (*Ondernemingsraad*). The worker's council has the right to veto various categories of decisions that directly affect them.

   Consider the feasibility of implementing such a system in the United States as opposed to modifying Japanese-style paternalistic practices for use in the United States.

14. In India, the Lall brothers own a family business, which they run with their sons. The Lalls live together with their children and grandchildren in a large house as a traditional joint family. Recently the Lalls entered into a joint venture with an American firm. The American firm sent an organizational specialist to help set up the venture.

   Disturbed by the loose organizational relationships in the Lall family business, the specialist decided to make an organizational chart with job descriptions for the Lall family managers and the two American staff members. One result was that the youngest Lall, who had an American M.B.A., was placed in a job slot above two of his older cousins, who lacked M.B.A.s.

Immediately a conflict arose among members of the two Lall families. The older sons were angry because their younger cousin had a business position that was not warranted by his age and position in the family. As the discord mounted, the family elders (the original Lall brothers) became worried. They both said, "What is the business good for if it breaks up the family?"[27]

a. How can this joint venture be saved?
b. How would you advise potential joint venture partners (both American firms and Indian firms) to avoid problems of this type?

ENDNOTES

1. Maria Patricia Fernandez-Kelly, *For We Are Sold, I and My People: Women and Industry in Mexico's Frontier* (Albany: State University of New York, 1983), 26.
2. Ibid.
3. Jorge Bustamante, "Maquiladoras: A New Face of International Capitalism in Mexico's Northern Frontier," in J. Nash and M.P.F. Kelly, *Women, Men, and the International Division of Labor* (Albany: State University of New York, 1983), 241.
4. Lynn Fleary, "Business makes a run for the border," *Fortune* (August 18, 1986).
5. Joseph Callahan,"Mexico's Hidden Treasure: The Magical Maquiladoras," *Automotive Industries* (June 1987): 87.
6. Susan Tiano, "Maquiladora, Women's Work, and Unemployment in Northern Mexico," Women in International Development working paper #43 (East Lansing: Michigan State University, 1984).
7. Ibid.
8. Larissa Lomnitz, "History of a Mexican Urban Family," *Journal of Family History* 3, no. 4 (1978): 391–409.
9. Geert Hofstede, "Do American Theories Apply Abroad," *Organizational Dynamics* 10, no. 1 (Summer 1981): 63–80.
10. Kenneth David, "Planning the Project," in Thomas L. Brewer, Kenneth David and Linda Lim, *Investing in Developing Nations: A Guide for Executives* (New York: Praeger; and Washington, DC: Overseas Private Investment Corporation, 1986), 30–50
11. John Fayerweather, *International Business Management, A Conceptual Framework* (New York: McGraw-Hill, 1969), 76–77.
12. Kenneth David, "Hidden Powers: Cultural and Socioeconomic Accounts of Jaffna Women," in Susan Wadley, ed., *The Powers of Tamil Women* (Syracuse: Syracuse University Press, 1979), 122.
13. "The Spanish-American Business Wars," *Worldwide P & I Planning* (May–June 1971): 30–40.
14. Kenneth David: field research.
15. Ryushi Iwata, *Japanese-Style Management: Its Foundations and Prospects* (Tokyo: Asian Productivity Organization, 1982), 5.
16. "The Spanish-American Business Wars."
17. Richard N. Farmer and Barry M. Richman, *Comparative Management and Economic Progress* (Homewood, IL: Irwin, 1965), 109.
18. V. S. Naipaul, *A Flag on the Island* (New York: Knopf, 1967), 135–146.
19. George Katona, Burkhard Strumpel, and Ernest Zahn, *Aspirations and Affluence: Comparative Studies in the United States and Western Europe* (New York: McGraw-Hill, 1971), 146–151.

20. Alex Inkeles and Peter H. Rossi, "National Comparisons of Occupational Prestige," *American Journal of Sociology* (January 1956); Robert W. Hodge et al., "A Comparative Study of Occupational Prestige," in Reinhard Bendix and Seymour M. Lipset, eds., *Social Stratification in Comparative Perspective* (New York: Free Press, 1966), 309–321.

21. "Spain: The Costly Passions of Labor and Politics," *Business Week* (November 23, 1974): 52–57.

22. Richard Critchfield, "The Plight of the Cities: Djakarta—the First to Close," *Columbia Journal of World Business* 6 (July–August, 1971): 89–93.

23. Christopher Tugendhat, *The Multinationals* (New York: Random House, 1972), 173–174.

24. These points are discussed in Ashok Kapoor, *Planning for International Business Negotiations* (Cambridge, MA: Ballinger, 1975), passim.

25. See, for example, Everett E. Hagen, *On the Theory of Social Change* (Homewood, IL: Dorsey Press, 1962).

26. Farmer and Richman, 356.

27. Incident adapted from Ashok Kapoor, "The Indian Manager Looks at the American Technician," in *Planning for International Business Negotiations* (Cambridge, MA: Ballinger, 1975).

CHAPTER EIGHT
Political Environment

In the contemporary age, when a petroleum boycott by militarily weak Arab states can upset the foreign policy of the world's most powerful nation and when private corporations possess assets far in excess of those of the vast majority of nation states. . .[we] can no longer afford to ignore the interaction of economics and politics.

Robert Gilpin [1]

INTRODUCTION: WHY WORRY ABOUT POLITICS?

Whether their operations are domestic or international, politics and the political environment are important to all business firms. For the international firm, the political environment is more complex and potentially more hostile. There are two fundamental differences.

First, for a domestic firm, especially one operating in an advanced industrial country, politics is generally viewed as a given. That is, managers have learned to manage the relatively predictable shifts in regimes and policies. For the international firm, the political environments are not only variable, but also diverse; the international firm operates in many, often conflicting, environments.

Second, to the extent that multinational corporations are not responsive to or controllable by any single nation-state, they do not fit into the world system of nation-states. Some writers, noting multinational corporations' size, store of knowledge, organizational capabilities, and command of resources (their global reach), have expressed concern that multinational corporations would someday overwhelm the system of nation-states and render them obsolete. These fears have proven exaggerated—or at least premature—but they do reflect the volatility of the political environment confronting international business.

We gratefully acknowledge the contribution of Dr. Stephen J. Kobrin to this chapter.

More to the point is the perception of host-country governments. Whatever their actual power or covert influence, multinational corporations are viewed as as significant political actors by host-country governments. Whether or not the perception is accurate, multinational firms are viewed as exercising power parallel to that exercised by national governments.

This perception complicates foreign operations. The image affects relations with various publics with whom the firm deals. People of various political persuasions have a monolithic vision of the implacable power of the multinational corporation. Subtleties such as the differences in relative bargaining power between multinational firms and host-country governments in different industries[2] frequently escape notice. Given these complexities, managing political relationships in multiple environments is a difficult task.

We will begin this chapter by exploring some basic concepts that will prove useful in analyzing the political environment. These concepts are drawn from the work of both political scientists and cultural anthropologists. Later, we will apply these concepts to gain a better understanding of the connection between international business and politics.

VANTAGE POINTS

We approach the political environment of international business from two vantage points. At the global level, attention focuses on the international political system as a whole: this is known as international politics, or international relations. At the country level, we are concerned with both the nature of the political environment within a country and the differences among national political environments.

In practice, these levels are intertwined.

- A multinational corporation must be concerned simultaneously with its relations with its home country, its relations with host countries, and the changing relationship between home and host countries. A home country's permission for its firms to operate in a host country is interpreted by the home and the host governments as a signal of foreign policy. Forbidding such operations is also foreign policy.

- A multinational corporation must be concerned with relationships among the host countries in which it operates. Due to the visibility of a large multinational corporation, actions and responses by multinational corporations and government agencies in one host country may well set precedents for dealings between companies and agencies in neighboring countries. One large multinational, for example, looks for signs of status competition among countries in a world region so that it can negotiate for favorable terms with host governments when bringing in a high-status technology.

GLOBAL-LEVEL CONCEPTS

The International Political System

The international system is markedly different from the formal lawmaking and law-enforcing authority of a domestic political system. The system is neither pure anarchy nor a set of formal and rigid authority-subordinate relationships. "Anarchy moderated or inhibited by a balance of power is a fairly accurate description of the rivalry between sovereign nation states."[3]

Although the international political system is a system in the general sense (changes within some units set off changes in other units in the system), it is not a tightly definable system in the specific sense of well-regulated operations among units. Rather, relationships of accommodation, negotiation, capitulation, deterrence, and threat exist among nations.

Shifting relations are communicated by a language of words and actions that is known and shared by diplomats. Ping-Pong diplomacy, in which table-tennis players from the People's Republic of China and the United States exchanged visits, was rightly interpreted as an action signal—that is, as a sign that more formal trade and diplomatic relations would be established between the two countries.

Actors in the International Political System

Various units can be considered actors in the international political system.

Nations continue to be the main source of international action. It is important, however, not to overrate the nation as an actor. In practice, international impact stems from the actions of particular agencies within nations. The nation's chief executive may or may not act quite in line with ministries. A nation's ministry of foreign affairs is frequently out of line with the ministry of commerce—whenever the dictates of alliances with other nations do not coincide with particular advantages of bilateral or multilateral trade.

Certainly, nations are not the only source of international action. Individuals and various domestic groups become known as international actors when there is adequate press coverage of behavior that transcends national boundaries. Various separatist movements (such as the Basque ETA, the Irish Republican Army, and the Palestine Liberation Organization) recognize that a combination of terrorist and more diplomatic activities keeps them in the international spotlight. Nonstate actors (whether ultra-violent groups such as the Iranian Jihad or determinedly nonviolent ones such as Greenpeace) have noted that they seek press coverage and photo opportunities just like standard politicians.

Besides nations, two other important actors in the system are international organizations and transnational political entitites.

International Organizations

International organizations certainly affect global politics. International governmental organizations (IGOs) differ from international nongovernmental organizations

(INGOs), depending on whether the international organization was established by an agreement among governments.[4] The United Nations and the European Economic Community are IGOs; the International Alliance of Women and the International Confederation of Free Trade Unions are INGOs.

Although both IGOs and INGOs play a vital role in international politics, IGOs are more important than INGOs. The difference stems from the fact that "states are the primary focal points of political activity in the modern world and IGOs derive their importance from the character of their associations with states."[5] INGOs must concentrate their efforts on persuading the governments of states to change their policies.

The effectiveness of some IGOs is limited by the voluntary participation of nations. The World Court in The Hague can try cases involving different nations, but the decision is binding only if all parties to the case agree to be bound. Usually, the process is nonbinding arbitration with pressure brought to bear by informal world opinion. Other IGOs have more clout—the United Nations, the International Monetary Fund, and the World Bank are arenas of international political action where groups of nations ally to affect policy.

Jacobson suggests it is possible that international organizations could gain greater authority in the future, but "for the moment they must be regarded as voluntary associations of states [or of private persons], largely dependent on the voluntary actions of these states for the implementation of their decisions."[6]

Transnational Actors

Other nongovernmental international organizations such as large labor unions and multinational firms are transnational political actors in their own right or are pressed into service by governments. American-incorporated petroleum firms paid royalties to an Angolan government that was opposed by the government of the United States. Multinational firms are frequently pressed into service to communicate foreign policy by home-country governments (as when the United States tells firms they may trade with the People's Republic of China but not with Libya) or by host-country governments (as when Arab countries announced they would cease trade with those companies that continued to trade with Israel). For example, in hopes of being recogized as nations, separatist social movements seek publicity through international news media. In such instances, both the social movements and the news media are transnational actors.

Such units are actors in international politics, or, more specifically, transnational actors. Typically, a transnational organization is functionally specific; it has a distinct interest, such as the maximization of profit or the welfare of its members. The transnational organization has a "broader-than-national perspective with respect to the pursuit of highly specialized objectives through a central optimizing strategy across national boundaries."[7] If we are to understand the international political environment, we must accept the presence of a relatively large number of transnational actors and understand their effects on the international system as a whole.

Political, Economic, and Technical Integration

Especially since the end of World War II, there have been many attempts at political integration and international cooperation. Major examples are the European Economic Community, the Andean Common Market, the International Monetary Fund, and, of course, the United Nations.

In a world of nation-states bent on preserving their sovereignty, however, the impact of political integration and international cooperation will be, at best, prudently slow. No nation is anxious to surrender its independence—no matter how desirable the goal.

Nations of the European Community have decided on and are now implementing a substantial economic integration: a free flow of workers and goods across their boundaries. Dozens of task forces have worked out ways to "harmonize" previous national differences. Harmonization does not happen quickly. For example, one task force has taken two years to find a way to establish a standardized European electrical plug and outlet. At the time of this writing, harmonization of national currencies into a European Currency Unit is being attempted and may soon be accomplished. Following the political movement to reunify West and East Germany, proposals are now being voiced to create a political union into a United States of Europe. It remains to be seen whether such unification would harmonize all systems or whether European nations will retain control of vital entities such as their social welfare systems (see below, page 204).

There are, by contrast, no such restraints on the pace of integration via communication and transportation technology. Innovations such as the radio, television, and satellite communications have continually reduced both the time and cost of international communications. Distance has seemed to shrink with each passing year. Routine business trips to any part of the globe are possible and economically feasible. Electronic transfer of information and teleconferencing are alternatives to the physical movement of executives.

These significant differences in the rates of political and technical-economic integration result in change and conflict. Decreasing distances (both geographically and, in some instances, culturally) and better communications capabilities have increased the importance of nongovernmental transnational actors relative to nation-states. Transnational actors, particularly multinational corporations, are both causes and effects of the rapid pace of technological and economic integration. By linking interest groups in various countries, increasing the interdependence of nations, and impinging on state politics, they both facilitate and take advantage of increased world integration.

The result is often conflict. International business rationality entails optimizing returns from worldwide operations. A subsidiary of a multinational corporation may be ordered to implement a business strategy that is not optimal from the point of view of the host country. The ability of a multinational firm to transfer capital within the corporation but across national boundaries (by a variety of means including transfer pricing, loans, royalties, etc.) is viewed by countries as an obstacle to the enforcement of fiscal and monetary policies.

In summary, any model of the international political system that describes inter-actions predominantly in terms of sovereign and independent nation-states no longer accurately depicts reality. Nongovernmental transnational actors—particularly multina-tional firms—have become increasingly important. Multinational firms are also part of the world political system.

Imperialism and Dependency

Both nation-states and multinational corporations are transnational actors that can be viewed with hostility for perceived imperialistic actions. While accusations of im-perialism may be partially factual and partially rhetorical, it is prudent to under-stand them.

Imperialism and dependency are historical phenomena even though we tend to think of them as modern conditions. One hears of economic imperialism, (political) neoimperialism, cultural imperialism, and information imperialism. From the point of view of the subordinates, the correlates are economic, political, and sociocultural dependencies. Whatever we call it, we are dealing with "a relationship of effective domination or control, political or economic [we would add 'or cultural'], direct or indirect, of one nation over another."[8] Imperialism and dependency are used so often to convey negative connotations that one suspects the terms are often simply attached to foreign policies or economic policies one disagrees with and to countries one is opposed to. There is no consensus. Rather, analysts have generally proceeded from one of several distinct viewpoints.

The Early Liberal Position

Hobson, an English economist who wrote at the turn of the century, saw economic motives for imperialism: the necessity to search out new markets as productive capacities exceeded demand in the more industrialized countries. To this position, imperialism is not a fundamental result of world capitalism. Rather, maladjustments in the system—primarily inequitable distribution of income—result in an excess of production over demand and an excess of available capital over investment oppor-tunities. These surpluses lead to a search for new markets and to the establishment of colonial relationships.[9]

The Marxist View

Radical economic theorists (Marx, Luxemberg, Lenin) reject this line of thought. Lenin's theory continues to be the most influential. While Hobson saw imperialism resulting from a maladjustment of the system, Lenin saw imperialism as the natural and necessary outgrowth of capitalism. Lenin defined imperialism as "the monop-oly stage of capitalism." He argued that the high concentration of capital that occurs in mature capitalist economies leads to the creation of monopolies within a country. Monopolists begin to export capital for foreign investments instead of just exporting commodities. Major capitalist economics, or "international capitalist combines," divide the world among themselves. He argues that the mature stage of capitalism would lead to the decadence of the imperialist nations as they transferred their capital and technology to the peripheral, less-developed nations. In Lenin's view, the periphery would develop dynamic economies, while the imperialistic powers would decline into "parasitism and decay."[10]

The Development Approach

So long as imperialism was viewed as synonymous with colonial expansion, there was little evaluation of the more subtle economic relationships between countries. However, following World War II, the colonial empires broke apart and a whole host of new nations was born. A new discipline of development studies was formed to provide coordination, support, and advice to these new nations on how to fulfill their potential for development.

This discipline followed a diffusionist model, which held several assumptions: (1) that "underdevelopment is an original state, characterized by backwardness or traditionalism";[11] (2) that "development means advancement toward certain well-defined general goals which correspond to the specific conditions of man and society to be found in the most developed countries of the modern world";[12] and (3) that "underdeveloped countries will progress towards this as soon as they have eliminated certain social, political, cultural, and institutional obstacles."[13]

From these assumptions, a path for development was charted. It was considered essential that capital diffuse from the developed capitalist countries into the periphery in the form of foreign investment or aid. It was also considered essential that there be a change from outwardly directed development toward inwardly directed development (that is, import substitution, consumption of locally produced goods instead of imported goods). A locally controlled economy that does not rely on foreign trade would then have the chance to develop, and a more developed economy would facilitate a mass-based, democratically oriented society that incorporated the traditional oligarchies and the rural population.[14]

This developmental model was followed by the less-developed countries in the postwar period. By 1960, however, it was recognized that the import substitution strategy had failed to turn LDCs into autonomous societies with dynamic economies. Rather, import substitution policies coupled with high trade barriers to protect the new industries often reduced the incentive for reduction of costs and prices and for improvement of quality of the goods produced. The gap between developed countries and less-developed countries had widened. This crisis led to a reexamination of previous assumptions, and the problem of development was approached from a different perspective.

The Dependency Approach

The dependency approach, a contemporary radical viewpoint, contradicts the developmental model. Writers such as Andre Gunder Frank see an inherently exploitative relationship between the developed capitalist countries and underdeveloped countries. As the system of world capitalism spread from Europe in the sixteenth century, some economies became developed while others became underdeveloped.

> ...most of our theory fails to explain the structure and development of the capitalist system as a whole and to account for its simultaneous generation of underdevelopment in some parts and development in others...historical research demonstrates that contemporary underdevelopment is in large part the historical product of past and continuing economic and other relations between the satellite underdeveloped and the now developed metropolitan countries.[15]

The dependency approach views underdevelopment as created by the developed countries. Since both development and underdevelopment evolved together, one could not have been a stage preceding the other as is suggested by the diffusionist and developmental models. Both result from the same process. As Frank points out,

> history shows that underdevelopment is not original nor traditional and that neither the past nor the present of the underdeveloped countries resembles in any respect the past of the now developed countries. The now developed countries were never underdeveloped, though they may have been undeveloped.[16]

Therefore the underdeveloped countries of today will not achieve development by passing through the same stages the now-developed nations went through. In addition, today's underdeveloped areas remain dependent because they have developed social forms structured towards dependency. The political and economic elites, the landowner and the exporting classes, profit from the pattern of dependency and are unlikely to change it.

The core idea of dependency theory, then, is the relationship between central, developed countries and peripheral, underdeveloped countries. These are joined in an international division of labor. Center countries are those with dynamic economies that grow and respond to their own internal needs and that benefit most from the world economic system. Peripheral countries are those that react to the center rather than to their own needs; they benefit least from the world market. The integration of the periphery into the global system meant that these societies were structured economically, politically, and socially to fulfill the needs of the central countries for raw materials or for markets for finished goods. This international division of labor drains the periphery.

Currently, the underdeveloped (often ex-colonial) countries are seen as the peripheral satellites whose resources are drained to ensure the continued enrichment of the metropolitan centers. Foreign-based multinational companies and foreign aid increase the dependency of peripheral LDCs. Hymer analyzes the hierarchical organizational structure of multinational companies as reflecting the hierarchical relations of exchange between nations.[17] That is, a corporate organizational chart reflects the geographical and power distribution. Corporate headquarters is located in a central country, while subsidiaries are located in peripheral countries. Decisions flow from the central to the peripheral countries. Furthermore, free market exchanges perpetuate this system of unequal exchange—that is, stagnation and poverty in the less-developed satellites of the system.

Summary

In summary, the dependency approach rejects the central analysis of the diffusionary, developmental approaches. Whereas *diffusion* sees development as historical and universal, *dependency* sees it as historically conditioned and holds that each country's situation must be analyzed as a unique case study. Whereas diffusion holds that underdevelopment is caused by premodern ideas and cultural norms, dependency sees those norms as enlisted to enforce the dependency situation. The diffusion model argues that less-developed countries were left out of the world capitalist system, while dependency sees less-developed countries as fully integrated and views this integration as the cause of underdevelopment. While the diffusion model sees the middle classes as the leaders of democracy and the force for new ideas and values, dependency sees them as tied to the traditional oligarchies and dependent on foreign control. Finally, while diffusion sees aid and foreign investment as the solution to the problem of underdevelopment, dependency views them as deepening dependency and draining surplus value from the periphery.

We have seen that multinational corporations can be viewed with hostility because they are perceived as agents of postcolonial imperialism. Because many Third-World countries accept dependency theory as part of their political ideology, it is important for those involved in international business operations in the Third World to understand this theory.

COUNTRY-LEVEL CONCEPTS

To approach the question of national political environments and international differences in political environments, we must first define some basic terms: *control, power,* and *the political system.* As a framework for comparing political systems, we will then distinguish nonlegitimate power (coercion) from types of power with an aura of legitimacy (authority and sovereignty).

Control, Power, and the Political System

The role of politics in the organization of social life is to deal with problems that arise from unequal control. Different persons, categories of persons, or groups of persons in society have unequal control of certain tangibles and intangibles:

1. Material resources: wealth and access to different positions in the system of production of goods and services
2. Human resources: followers and dependent persons
3. Information: strategic knowledge
4. Administration: access to processes that set and implement priorities for social action.

Whatever the source of control, relative control is power, which we define here as control over the environments of others (other persons and the behavior of these persons). Power differentials often result in opposition, conflict, and change. The political system manages these processes.

Nonlegitimized Power: Coercion

Power can be wielded in ways that are wasteful of society's resources. If a power holder relies on coercion to mobilize social action, some of the population will usually be uncommitted or rebellious. Repressive behavior to enforce commitment or to quell rebellion requires allocations of resources that could be more productively employed. Russian troops deployed in Lithuania produce only compliance rather than marketable goods or services that could reduce that country's foreign debts. Although a coercive regime can be effective in the short run in getting things done the way the power holder wants them done, the regime is neither efficient nor necessarily stable in the long run.

Legitimized Power

Power can be wielded in ways that are more efficient in the use of society's resources. Power wielding can be viewed as legitimate when the power wielder is defined as having authorized power or sovereign power. These legitimized powers require lesser allocation of society's resources to implement social objectives than does nonlegitimized, coercive power. While the latter rules peoples' external actions, authority and sovereignty can rule their thoughts and motivations.

Authority

Americans are accustomed to the authority mode of legitimacy, a political system in which power is distributed in formal organizations. In this mode, power and responsibility are delegated to formal, defined positions. Persons recruited to these positions have legitimate power to make decisions only within specified areas of action. Individuals exceed their authority when they wield overt or covert influence (as in influence peddling) beyond the scope of their activities. Legitimacy attaches to the position, not to the person. A soldier is taught to salute the uniform, not the man or woman. Legitimacy requires continuing social consent of those governed. The Supreme Court may decline cases if they are fairly certain that the judgment cannot be implemented (due to lack of social consent); too many instances of public disobedience would cast doubt on their aura of legitimate authority.

Sovereignty

With sovereignty, whether applied to a person (the Queen of England) or to a territorial unit (the Sovereign State of Pennsylvania), we are dealing with an older and more concrete image of legitimacy. Here the aura of legitimacy is embodied in the person or in the land. In the eighteenth century, Louis XIV could well say "L'état, c'est moi." Royalty in England is still felt to be made of finer stuff than other aristocrats or commoners. Monarchs still have sovereign rights, despite the fact that their legitimate authority has declined over the centuries.

Regarding sovereignty attaching to land, the Basques and the Kurds feel a connection with their territories and remain uncommitted to or even despise the abstract map lines dividing France and Spain, and the USSR and Iran. People's feeling of connection to their land can be deep seated and ferocious.

American soldiers interrogated a Vietcong infiltrator who had previously been their trusted, friendly barber. "Why did I join them? You built your command post over the rice field where my ancestors are buried. We are part of the land. The land is part of us."

This distinction between authority and sovereignty is important for understanding differences among national political systems. Europeans and Americans may well underemphasize the importance of sovereignty by projecting their authority-based system where it does not apply.

It is no coincidence (1) that Indira Gandhi followed the political footsteps of J. Nehru, her revered father; (2) that Rajiv Gandhi became the political leader of India after Indira's assassination; and (3) that Sanjay, Indira's son, was before his death considered a probable future leader of India despite protests about his activities that would probably have wrecked the political career of a Western politician.

It is no coincidence that Eva Peron and Sirimavo Bandaranaike, wives of charismatic political leaders in Argentina and Sri Lanka, succeeded their husbands. Even in the United States, Lurleen Wallace, wife of Alabama Governor George Wallace, won that office with no real opposition when state rules forbade her husband's reelection.

In general, humans may oppose intervention with their system of authority but can tolerate the imposition of a new, previously alien regime that they view as legitimate. If the system is in the sovereignty mode, the opposition to change is more fierce. Outsiders are foolish to tamper with such a system.

Further, international managers may find systems of sovereignty and authority coexisting in a foreign setting.

According to Lorissa Lomnitz, there are two elites in Mexico. Old, revered families control large industrial and commercial assets. Foreign firms typically ally with such families in order to meet Mexico's local ownership requirements. The government elite, by contrast, stem from a variety of social backgrounds but tend to speak a common language after their (socialist-leaning) education. Codes for behavior and motivations of Mexican nobility differ from those of socialist bureaucrats and politicians. Systems of sovereignty and authority exist side by side in Mexico.[18]

The Nation-State

What is the nation-state? We approach the answer from three directions: political-territorial, political-participation, and social viewpoints.

We may define the state in terms of political authority over territory as: "a political unit that recognizes no superior with all of its members falling under the political jurisdiction of the same government."[19] Here the state is a political unit with governmental agencies defining geographical boundaries, establishing requirements for citizenship, controlling trade in goods and the movement of people across its borders, settling disputes through control of a monopoly of force, and protecting the nation against outsiders.

To the political scientist, legal sovereignty is almost synonymous with the concept of the nation-state. In this sense, sovereignty entails ultimate control over territory and the persons who live there: it is the ultimate right to make and enforce laws. States are extremely wary of any potential infringement on this right. A state rejects the legitimacy of any external restraints on its behavior except those to which it has consented. We shall be concerned with infringements on sovereignty—in particular, conflicts between national sovereignty and transnational actors, whether multinational corporations or IGOs such as the World Bank.

Although all recognized states enjoy legal sovereignty, governments vary in their ability to implement policies within their nations. To preserve legal sovereignty, the government of a state must have sufficient power to protect autonomy and reject external restraints.[20] Further, all states are subject to a certain degree of influence from external forces, and small states are particularly vulnerable. When a state loses independence and is no longer able to control affairs within its territory (USSR occupies Afghanistan; North Vietnam takes charge of South Vietnam), it has lost sovereignty.

One can also view the nation as a social phenomenon in terms of participation in government. Based on the level of involvement of the subjects in governing the state, there are, according to Organski, three periods in the history of the nation-state. The nation-state is a relatively recent human invention.

- In the feudal period before 1500, the king or sovereign was in fact no more than a feudal lord with only very tenuous authority over his vassals, and with higher allegiance often owed to pope or emperor.

- In the dynastic period (1500–1815), the state was embodied in the person of the king and perhaps a few nobles. The nation-state began to emerge in sixteenth-century Europe and was built on the ruins of the feudal system. As the feudal system deteriorated, the monarchs submitted their nominal vassals to actual control, and Europe began to divide into distinct states whose rulers recognized no superior authority. The great mass of people could scarcely be considered part of the nation; rather, they were merely subjects to be taxed and ruled.

- As the commercial and industrial revolutions took hold, a new merchant middle class rose in power and influence. The notion of divine right legitimizing a monarch's rule was challenged by such eighteenth-century social-contract theorists as Hobbes and Locke. The French Revolution guillotined the notion in favor of liberty, equality, and fraternity. To Organski, by 1815, the state became synonymous with the middle class, or bourgeoisie, and the government was based on nineteenth-century liberal, pragmatic, and democratic philosophy. Involvement of the masses was still limited. Property determined participation.

Although some would point to modern political institutions such as lobbies and political action committees and say that this is still the case, Organski holds that the general populace became fully integrated into political process after World War I. With increased urban migration, with rising levels of education and income, and with increased media coverage of the demands and aspirations of special interest groups in recent times, it is fair to say that in Western industrialized countries, there is fuller participation in the state's political process than was previously the case.

Finally, one can also view a nation and nationality in a social context, in terms of people and their culture. The degree to which citizens of a country think and act together as a community is a function of the specific features of culture, history, political-economic structure, and geography. A nation, at least in theory, entails a community of individuals sharing a common ethnic or cultural identity. In theory, a culturally homogeneous nation would facilitate full participation of citizens in political processes of decision making affecting their fate.

Almost every country, by this definition, is heterogeneous, for almost every country has two or more distinct ethnic groups with dissimilar cultures within its boundaries. In some countries, such as Sweden and Holland, ethnic diversity does not seriously affect political process. In other countries, such as Canada, Ireland, and many Third-World countries, ethnic conflict can be seriously disruptive.

In fact, many of the new states' borders were fixed arbitrarily as lines on a colonial map in an attempt to assert political control over a territory that does not even begin to correspond to a nation as a community of individuals. Anthropologists have noted that many tribes and ethnic groups, especially in Africa and Asia, had no concept of tribe or ethnic group before colonial administrators reified a system of lineages or of clans into a larger unit as an administrative convenience. Many tribal names mean nothing more than "people" or "the folks" or other vague replies to a colonial administrator's persistent questioning as to whom these people were.[21] As we shall see, both tribes and ethnic groups became highly relevant and politically mobilized after independence from the colonial power.

In conclusion, the concepts of self-determination and even of the nation-state are rooted in the Western European experience. When we apply this conceptual framework to the non-Western world, the fit is often poor.

Nationalism

Nationalism is a relatively recent phenomenon that reflects the increasing involvement of the great mass of the population with the nation-state. It can focus the loyalty of citizens on a nation and can provide a basis for cohesion and legitimization of central authority. Nationalism can provide ideological commitment, the basis for individual and collective sacrifices necessary in times of national economic and military emergencies. In its Western European birthplace, then, nationalism developed in the context of nations that had existed for hundreds of years and functioned to legitimize the central political authority.

The darker side of nationalism is national machismo—that is, engaging in foreign military operations to distract the population from civil or economic discontent at home. This tactic was apparent in the fight over the Falkland Islands by Great Britain and Argentina. Argentine officials admitted this motive. Brazil, by contrast, uses less-destructive diversion techniques. When the population is discontent, the government schedules international soccer matches or rowdy carnivals.

National Interest and National Goals

Decisions are sometimes defended as being in the national interest. A news blackout is imposed "in the national interest." Regulations for control of foreign investment are waived "in the national interest." The concept of national interest is imprecise.

Lerche and Said propose a rather idealistic definition: The national interest ". . . may be considered as the general, long-term, and continuing purpose which the state, the nation, and the government all see themselves as serving. It is rooted in the social consciousness and cultural identity of a people."[22]

Gilpin is perhaps more realistic: To a degree, "the national interest of a given nation-state is, of course, what its political and economic elite determines it to be. . . . But the national interest comprehends more than this. More general influences, such as cultural values and considerations relevant to the security of the state itself, are of greater importance."[23]

The goals or objectives of nations flow from their perceived national interests. While one can conceive of a broad spectrum of goals for nations, there are several that are common to all:

1. Self-preservation. The prime goal of any entity, whether it be an individual, a tribe, or a state, is self-preservation. While absolute security is certainly unattainable in practice, states try to maximize their opportunity for continued existence and to minimize threats.

2. Social development. A nation attempts to improve the actual conditions of existence and the collective well-being of its citizens.

3. Prestige. Nations seek prestige both as a means to obtain further objectives and as an end in itself.

4. Promotion of an ideology. Nations often attempt to promote or protect an ideology. During the Cold War period, the United States was certainly interested in exporting capitalism and the Soviet Union socialism over and above that required in the interests of security.

5. Power. Nations want to increase their power relative to others.

Because business firms effectively have joint ventures with the governments in whose territories they operate, it is a challenge for them to mesh their objectives with those of a nation; the incentive to do so is to reduce political risk.[24]

Supranationalism and Subnationalism

While maintaining good relations with the nations in which they operate, international managers have the additional challenge of keeping track of political developments beyond and below the level of the nation. While these two kinds of social collectivities are more fluid in composition than nations and are generally less well reported in the international press, they can significantly affect business operations.

Regionalism

When countries form and maintain an effective economic alliance such as a free trade zone or a common market, the economic interdependency may also result in common political action.

In some cases, national differences have destroyed the attempted union.

- The East African Federation failed because, after independence, Kenya became a capitalist-oriented country that collaborated with multinationals, Tanzania chose a fairly strong form of socialist economy, and Uganda had Idi Amin.

- The Latin American Free Trade Association could not overcome the contradiction of two very large countries—Argentina and Brazil—allying with a set of small countries. The alliance ended with the small countries declaring they were replacing global dependencia with regional dependencia.

In other cases, opposition to a perceived common enemy in the region helped overcome opposition to reduction in the member's sovereignty.

- The European Economic Community formed with political motives—opposition to the Soviet Bloc countries—as well as economic interests. Similarly, the Association of Southeast Asian Nations formed in the context of Far-Eastern communist expansion activity.

- In 1990, with European tensions subsiding due to vastly increased trade between EEC and Comecon countries and the political/economic changes in the USSR under Gorbachev, the common opponent is Japanese industry.[25]

On some occasions, countries hold strongly to their own sovereignty and fight over internal matters.

- Despite the EEC integration planned for 1992, European countries steer away from reconciling differences among their social welfare systems. The reason is that northern countries such as the Netherlands and West Germany maintain a regime of high taxes and comprehensive social welfare services, whereas various southern countries tax less and provide fewer social welfare benefits.

Subnationalism

In much of the non-Western world, countries are not a product of long-term political growth but often of rather arbitrary geographic surgery by European colonial powers. In this context, nationalism attempts to unite diverse peoples (from different tribes, ethnic origins, languages, and religions) under a central government. Nationalism can serve as a means of reconciling a new nation's traditional past with demands for modernization, operating as an ideological basis for sacrifice needed for development or as a means of repudiating the recent colonial experience and strengthening a new national identity. In sum, nationalism in the Third World functions as an ideology for forming a nation from diverse and often conflicting elements rather than simply a means for legitimizing a central political authority.

In the Third World, nationalism does not as frequently have a darker side as it does in the First World; more frequently, nationalism is suppressed or nonexistent when sectional, tribal, or feudal loyalties predominate. Over 40 years have passed since colonial territories emerged as new nations. They are no longer new nations. And their record shows a greater history of communal conflict than of communities pulling together as a nation. Further, nationalism has limited relevance in the postcolonial era.[26] The constructive side of nationalism (uniting diverse peoples, calling for sacrifice to foster development) is an appeal to civil sentiments. More frequently, the reified tribes and ethnic groups became politically mobilized by electoral appeals to such primordial sentiments as race, language, territory, religion, or shared history and culture. Less-literate populations are more easily moved by primordial sentiments than by civil sentiments (it could be argued that all populations are).

The result is often the replacement of international subordination in the colonial situation by an intranational subordination of minorities to the dominant social grouping in the nation. Many Third-World nations, from the conflict between Ibos versus Hausas and Yorubas in Nigeria to the conflict between Tamils and Sinhalese in Sri Lanka, have witnessed domestic strife that is mobilized along these lines. A key indicator of potential strife is the presence of a well-educated, prosperous, minority group (such as the Ibos or the Tamils) that draws the wrath of a less well-endowed majority group.

Thus nationalism is a potent force that manifests itself in many ways. Its specific expression is a function of the political and socioeconomic context. Its form and content vary in different countries and at different times. It is, however, a factor that must be carefully reckoned in international business.

THE POLITICAL ENVIRONMENT AND THE MULTINATIONAL FIRM

Now that we have developed some concepts, it is time to analyze the political environment of international business. In the remainder of this chapter, we will explore the interaction of international business and the political environment: the complex of home-country/multinational-firm/host-country relationships.

Home-Country Relationships

The location of the home or parent country of a multinational firm is still important. Most companies start as domestic firms and then expand overseas. Few, if any, have reached the state of a total geocentric, or worldwide, orientation. Many firms—particularly American ones—still have their largest subsidiary, the largest concentration of assets, and their international headquarters in their country of origin. Further, the majority of their executives and owners typically live as residents of the parent country.

Sources of Home-Country Control

The parent government has greater control over a given multinational enterprise than any other government. Behrman points to three sources of home-country government control:

1. The headquarters company is under its legal jurisdiction. The company is incorporated under its laws, and the government "has the ability to compel certain actions affecting the entire multinational enterprise. It can alter the financial flows, change the trade patterns, alter the competitive relations, control the flow of technology, alter the pattern of intercompany pricing and restrict the movement of persons."

2. There may be close ties between the multinational's top managers, who also tend to be home-country nationals, and parent-country government officials. They are often members of the establishment, products of the same social and political cultures. There is often interchangeability, with executives doing a stint in government and government officials moving easily into industry.

3. Finally, the greatest concentration of the multinational's assets is usually found in the home country.[27]

Internal Problems: Impetus to Home-Country Control

Because a firm's international operations can directly affect the domestic economy, home-country governments often attempt to control their multinational corporations. Unions may press for higher tariffs to protect jobs, and the government may press for capital export controls to restore a balance of payments deficit. These controls can substantially affect the multinational corporation's worldwide operations.

A major issue between multinational corporations and their home countries arises over charges that multinational corporations are exporting jobs. It is argued that jobs are exported through direct investment in foreign operations, joint ventures, licensing, and particularly through the increasingly popular practice of sending semifinished goods abroad for assembly in low-labor-cost sites and then reimporting them for sale. Another major charge is that multinational corporations strengthen foreign competition by licensing advanced technology.

Home-country governments are increasingly concerned about these issues. Therefore they subject multinational corporations to controls that not only affect the multinational corporation itself but may also impinge on other countries' sovereignty.

Extraterritoriality

A host country views the subsidiary of a multinational that is incorporated under its laws as a citizen of its country totally subject to its lawmaking and law-enforcing authority. To the extent that the home-country government attempts to extend its authority over the same foreign subsidiaries, a potential for conflict arises. We shall explore examples of this situation of extraterritoriality: taxation, fiscal policy, the use of subsidiaries of U.S. multinationals to achieve the political objectives of the Export Administration Act (previously called the Trading with the Enemy Act), and the attempt at worldwide enforcement of U.S. antitrust regulations.

Taxation. The outreach of U.S. Internal Revenue Code over foreign subsidiaries is a complex issue. The Code holds that corporations are to be assigned nationality according to the place of incorporation. Thus a multinational corporation parent corporation is fully taxable, but the string of foreign subsidiaries is not. Enterprises can defer taxes—that is, postpone payment of U.S. tax—until the income returns to the United States. This privilege benefits the multinational corporation if foreign tax rates are lower than U.S. tax rates, a condition, however, that is less and less common in those countries where the bulk of American investment is to be found. In conversations with corporate counsel, "a general disdain [has been found] for elaborate tax planning in this vein on the ground that the margins are simply too small to matter."[28]

Efforts to eliminate the deferral privilege have generally resulted in immensely complex measures that attempt to distinguish abuses from normal operations. To avoid direct confrontation with foreign governments, the U.S. Treasury has been careful not to levy the special tax on the foreign corporation involved but rather upon the American controlling shareholders.

Capital Controls. Capital controls are a particularly volatile political issue because they involve the home government's regulation of foreign investment and repatriation of profits. "The regulations restrict the making of new investments abroad by multinational enterprises, put pressure on them to repatriate portions of their foreign investments, and influence them to borrow funds abroad to support their overseas expansion."[29] These regulations are justified by the notion that overseas investments will not generate enough earnings to offset the investment flows. This is a shortsighted strategy, however, since returns for outflows are often substantial.

Export Administration Act. The international principle of territoriality prohibits the prosecution of foreigners for acts committed outside the nation. The Export Administration Act (formerly the Trading with the Enemy Act), however, authorizes the U.S. president to regulate and control transactions with communist countries and to embargo trade with North Korea and North Vietnam (and previously with Cuba and the People's Republic of China). The act applies to U.S. citizens, to any persons employed by corporations organized under U.S. law, and to any partnership, association, corporation or other organization wherever organized or doing business if it is owned by persons so described.[30]

The multinational corporation is caught in the middle. A subsidiary organized under French law is a corporate citizen of France. If owned by a U.S. corporation, it is still subject to the Act. A transaction encouraged by France may render the parent company liable to criminal prosecution in the United States.

> Fruehauf France is a French corporation controlled by a U.S. parent company. The parent held a majority of its shares and controlled five of its eight directors. At a time before U.S.-Chinese trade relations improved, the subsidiary contracted to sell equipment to Berliet, another French corporation, for use in trucks to be sold to the People's Republic.
>
> The U.S. government then ordered the parent to suspend the contract under the provisions of the Act; the parent asked its subsidiary to terminate the contract. Berliet, however, refused to negotiate termination and threatened to sue. The three French directors of Fruehauf France then sued the American directors, asking for execution of the contract.
>
> The French courts granted their case, finding that refusal to execute the contract would have imperiled the very existence of the company and the jobs of its employees.[31]

The U.S. government's ability to enforce the Export Administration Act is deteriorating. An attempt to prevent shipment to Cuba of Ford and GM trucks manufactured in Argentina was thwarted when the Argentine government threatened to nationalize the subsidiaries' output and sell it to Cuba. The two U.S. multinational corporations were caught in the middle. The Argentine government held the matter as a strictly domestic case. Until it backed down, the U.S. government insisted the subsidiaries were under its jurisdiction.

The controversy over the Western European-Soviet gas pipeline had a similar outcome. The pipeline now supplies Soviet gas to Western Europe.

> A report released in November 1981 by the Office of Technology Assessment cast doubt on the ability of the U.S. to affect Soviet energy development by restrictions on technology and equipment transfers, particularly in absence of cooperation from West European countries and Japan.[32] Despite this report, the Reagan administration suspended the licenses granted to the Caterpillar Tractor Company and to the General Electric Company for the export of equipment to be used in building the pipeline. The ban was to include West European licensees of General Electric.
>
> As a result, Komatsu Japan won the Caterpillar contract. Western European governments defied the U.S. ban, and Western European subsidiaries and local companies fulfilled all contracts. The pipeline was, in fact, completed earlier than anticipated. From the point of view of companies, there is concern that they may no longer be considered as reliable suppliers. And there is chagrin at losing contracts to major global competitors. The worst "outcome of the export restrictions has been to inflict immeasurably greater economic and political damage on the Western alliance."[33]

The Antitrust Problem. The United States has relatively stringent antitrust laws compared with most of its trading partners. The U.S. cultural and legal environment favors free competition to a greater extent than do most European countries, where cartels are common and in the past were often legally and officially encouraged. Many Europeans fail to see the advantage of having many competitors fighting continually and prefer a more orderly, less-competitive market.

U.S. antitrust laws have been interpreted not only to prohibit anticompetitive activity within the United States, but also to prohibit any such activity worldwide that would affect the U.S. market. As an extreme example, even if they are not violating legal or ethical principles in their own country, European companies acting to fix prices on goods they export to New York could be charged for violating the law.

While enforcement of the law in this hypothetical example might be difficult, the problem is very real for many U.S. multinational corporations, who can be caught between the laws of the home and host countries. It may be impossible to be a good corporate citizen of both countries. Because the home country generally has more power over its multinational corporations than any other country, the multinational corporation is more strongly pulled in the direction of the laws and practices of the home country.

There are some recent ironic twists to the issue of antitrust regulation. When standards of industry concentration and market share are calculated on a national basis, as they are in the United States, the growing impact of global competition in many industries is entirely ignored—to the detriment of U.S.-based multinationals. On the other hand, an international joint venture between Toyota and General Motors to produce subcompact cars in America was not forbidden by the Reagan administration even though it was challenged by Chrysler as a violation of U.S. antitrust laws.

Thus the problem of extraterritoriality can severely complicate operations of multinational corporations and relations between home and host-country governments. The problems of enforcement of taxation, fiscal policy, the Export Administration Act, and antitrust regulation illustrate the overlapping of international business and politics. The firm's position as a transnational political actor complicates both its life and the lives of governments with which it interacts. Extraterritoriality raises questions that go to the heart of the issue of national sovereignty.

International Impacts of Business-Government Relations

A home-country government can impinge on other countries' sovereignty not only when it regulates, but also when it comes to the aid of a multinational corporation's foreign operations. The perception of such supportive actions by host-country governments can be skewed because of important cultural differences in business-government relationships concerning industrial policy and foreign policy.

In practice, despite statements by Milton Friedman on the evils of overregulation of business by government, the U.S. industrial policy regarding relationships between business and government should be described as comparatively adversarial—that is, a relationship with a low degree of control and a low degree of cooperation.

Let us compare other systems of industrial policy. In centrally planned economies, firms are units in a national bureaucracy. In North Korea (and in pre-*perestroika*

USSR), production is centralized to the point of a central computer. There, control is near absolute, and cooperation remains undefined because there are no separate entities to cooperate or not. By contrast, in industrialized countries such as Japan and in newly industrialized countries such as Korea or Singapore, governments maintain a degree of both cooperation and control greater than that found in the United States. Popular accounts stress the myth of Japan, Inc., as simple cooperation between the Ministry of International Trade and Industry, the Central Bank, and industry. In fact, much control is exercised in transferring resources from declining to rising industries and in weeding out the weaker competitors among the latter.

Cooperation and control can be analyzed not only for industrial policy but also for the relationships between governments and firms concerning the transmission of foreign policy. Is there a strictly arm's-length relationship with interaction limited to regulation, or are business and government intertwined? Does government use overseas subsidiaries to achieve political ends, and, quid pro quo, does it lend its power to help multinationals achieve their business objectives?

In the United States, government and business are viewed in principle as separate entities with an arm's-length relationship. The expectation is that their interaction will be limited to regulations that are consistent with a basically free enterprise economy.

To most observers, the actual relationship between the U.S. government and its multinational firms lies somewhere between the idealized arm's-length model and a full partnership.

> At the turn of the century, gunboat diplomacy in support of U.S. business was common. The U.S. Marines landed in Cuba in 1906 to protect sugar plantations; warships were sent to Honduras in 1907 and to Nicaragua in 1909. In 1912, the National Bank of Nicaragua (a U.S. company) asked for help, and 2,700 Marines promptly responded, occupying the country with a small force to ensure stability until 1933. (Note the first lines of the U.S. Marine Corps anthem: "From the Halls of Montezuma to the shores of Tripoli/ We shall fight our Country's battles/ In the air, on land and sea.")

While the era of overt gunboat diplomacy may be over, the question of nonmilitary and covert aid still lingers.

> In 1970, ITT feared that its extensive holdings in Chile would be nationalized if the Marxist candidate, Dr. Allende, was elected. The United States mounted an economic and political campaign in opposition to Dr. Allende. A member of the Board of ITT met with Dr. Henry Kissinger, the U.S. Special Assistant to the President for National Security Affairs, and a former director of the Central Intelligence Agency. ITT offered a million dollars to help undermine the new regime. The offer was reportedly refused. However, the U.S. government, for its own reasons, spent millions of dollars on numerous anti-Allende covert activities over several years before and after Allende was in power. Thus the objectives of the U.S. government and ITT converged. Whether the government and ITT actually colluded is not clear.

For societies where explicit or tacit cooperative business-government relationships are the norm, the notion of an arm's-length relationship between business and government may be inconceivable. Host-country observers will, in this case, assume that a local subsidiary of a U.S. corporation will have the U.S. government's power and influence behind it. Whether the relationship in fact exists is thus beside the point. The assumption that it does can create difficulties with citizens of the host country and with the host-country government.

Relations with Host-Country Governments

International business covers a wide range of endeavors from indirect export to full-blown manufacturing subsidiaries. In general, the greater the commitment of resources and the greater the scope of managerial activities on foreign soil, the more the firm must be concerned with relations with the host-country government. Managers typically are concerned with threats to foreign operations. What is overlooked is that relations with host governments can also be sources of business opportunities.

The concern for political risk analysis grew out of particular historical circumstances. Multinational corporations became concerned with reducing uncertainties and losses stemming from political upheavals in, and unfavorable policies of, their host countries. As foreign exposure is greatest when manufacturing firms invest abroad, attention was directed at this form of business venture. Firms from advanced industrial nations, whether or not the firm came from a previous colonial power, drew the greatest adverse attention from new nations in the postcolonial era.

Thus a restricted subset of international business relations has drawn the lion's share of attention by international business scholars. In practice, political risk analysis has mainly meant analyzing the likelihood of adverse relations between multinational firms from advanced, industrial nations and their host-country governments concerning direct foreign investments in manufacturing industries.[34] "Most political risk research has focussed on violence, government instability, and expropriation in developing countries."[35]

This trend has its limitations. First, managers should be concerned with foreign political opportunities as well as threats. In financial analysis, the term *risk* is neutral, implying both positive and negative variations from the mean. In business-policy analysis, environmental assessment includes assessment of both threats and opportunities for competitive strategy. In practice, then, analysis of the political environment need not be concerned only with negative consequences for overseas competitive behavior.[36]

Second, managers impose this restriction because political risk, as presently defined by managers, is a culture-bound definition. That is, conceptualization has followed commonsense assumptions of American business culture regarding the relationship between government and business. In other business cultures, such as those of India and Korea, the government-business relationship is not so adversarial as in the United States. With a relationship of greater control and greater cooperation between the government and firms in an industry, Indian and Korean firms look to their ministries not only as sources of hindrance but also as strategic resources.

As Shrikant documents in an account of two Indian industries, firms in an industry can mobilize in order to manage their relationship with relevant ministries and incite policies favorable to the accomplishment of crucial competitive tasks.[37] Then Indian and Korean firms are concerned with a particular kind of political risk—the state of the relationship between firms in an industry and relevant ministries, and power shifts among government ministries—as sources of business opportunities as well as business threats for both domestic and international operations. Foreign managers planning a joint venture with an Indian firm should be instructed to do the same.

In this section, then, we shall be concerned with the assessment of the political environment—relations between firms and host-country governments—for both threats and opportunities.

Goals of Companies and of Countries

The scope and objectives of the firm and the state differ. The sovereign nation-state strives for autonomy and control and resists external control. As Raymond Vernon observes:

> There are several unresolved conflicts. Sovereign states have legitimate goals toward which they direct the resources under their command. Any unit of a multinational enterprise, when operating in the territory of a sovereign state, responds not only to those goals but also to a flow of commands of other sovereigns. As long as the potential clash of interests remains unresolved, the constructive economic role of the enterprise will be accompanied by destructive political tensions.[38]

The multinational's interest lies in allocating and using resources to maximize its after-tax profits on a global basis. The firm is interested in maximizing returns to the system of headquarters and subsidiaries as a whole. The nation-state, on the other hand, formulates its goals in national macroeconomic terms: growth of output, reduction of unemployment, lowering of inflation. These goals overlap only partially. Discrepancy of goals yields a potential for conflict.

Sources of Conflict

Fayerweather notes specific areas of conflicts between foreign firms and host-country governments: outside control, outside threat, and cultural change.[39]

Autonomy Versus Control. The most basic conflict centers on issues of equity and control. By accepting a subsidiary of a foreign parent, the host country gives up some degree of control over its industrial and economic affairs. The problem may be exaggerated by the real or apparent domination of the local economy by foreign firms. In some smaller, less-developed nations, foreign subsidiaries may well control a sizable portion of local industry or even the local economy. Even in larger, more-advanced economies, foreigners may well dominate a specific industry. Given the technological or managerial advantages that help establish the foreign company in the first place, the industry is likely to be very visible.

Further, a multinational can indeed evade national controls easier than local firms. In times of tight credit, capital or short-term funds can be imported. If taxes are raised, intracompany but international transfer pricing, royalty payments, and fees can be used to reduce local profits. The multinational firm thus challenges the ability of the state to implement policies within its boundaries.

Outside Threat. If multinationals are viewed as taking unfair, or probably even fair advantage of nationals, they may be viewed as an outside threat. Certainly multinationals have no armies. Certainly a small oil state can expropriate the biggest oil company's refinery and no Marines will land to defend it. Yet unease remains. Why? Military force is but one aspect of power; the economic power of multinationals is a force to be reckoned with.

Michael Clapham identifies four fears that breed suspicion and create antagonism.[40] First, the image of a world monopoly of multinationals based on a combination of size and technology still lingers. In the past, for example, it was feared that IBM, a company with an enlightened corporate policy, would dominate the global market by sheer superiority in technology and size. This specific perceived threat has now passed as global competition has increased in the computer industry. Nevertheless, the recognition of global competition has led to a trend toward massive mergers and acquisitions in various industries. Thus industry concentration is increasing. Are governments wrong to be concerned about global oligopolies, if not monopolies?

Second, the regulation of multinationals by their home-country governments provides evidence for host-country fears of home governments using their multinationals as instruments of policy. Corporations are frequently expected to comply with government regulations in the following areas:

- Foreign policy—participation in nationally or internationally desirable development plans and in economic sanctions.
- Trade policy—supporting or curtailing trade in certain categories of goods, certain industries, or vis-à-vis certain countries.
- Balance of payments policies—participation in export promotion or import substitution policies to diminish a balance of payments deficit or, in some spectacular cases, to reduce a trade surplus.
- Monetary system policies—participation in compensation deals.

Third, the reverse of Clapham's second fear, the home government may become the instrument of company policy. It is feared that a multinational may grow so economically important to the home country that the government will act as its tool.

Fourth, particularly in developing countries, there is fear that large and wealthy multinationals will deliberately corrupt or undermine governments to further their own ends. The cases of the Lockheed bribery scandal in Japan and ITT's political intervention in Chile are not so quickly forgotten. On the other hand, it should be noted that large multinationals seeking to operate in many countries have a greater need to maintain clean reputations than do national companies.

Agents Inhibiting or Promoting Cultural Change. Conflict also arises because the multinational can have great impact on the host country as either inhibiting or promoting sociocultural change. Large multinational enterprises may well have negative effects, acting as inhibitors of change. Because firms favor stability and cooperation over uncertainty, they have supported unpopular and autocratic regimes. This support has enhanced the power of ruling elites and actually inhibited political development.

Multinationals also have the opposite impact. No matter how sensitive multinationals are to the local conditions, transmission of innovation is their *raison d'être*. They can be viewed as a threat to the established culture. Alternatively, the presence of Western enterprises may foster the development or intensification of nationalism. Their visibility makes them excellent targets for crystallizing socioeconomic discontent. They may become the designated enemies of the established government or determined social movements.

Western enterprise can also contribute to the process of political development in a positive sense by introducing management techniques that aid in administering a modern political system. By providing opportunities for training and by recruiting and promoting their personnel on the basis of achievement instead of status or connections, foreign firms may accelerate the development of an indigenous middle class in an otherwise polarized social structure.

In sum, the foreign firm can both inhibit or incite change, change with both positive and negative effects.

Host-Government Control

While the host government has less control over subsidiaries than it does over domestic corporations, it can still bring very substantial pressures to bear. The government is the ultimate lawmaking and law-enforcing authority. At the extreme, it can simply expropriate assets. Long before that point is reached, however, many alternatives are available:

1. Governments are increasingly screening foreign investments. Takeovers, as opposed to new investment, are viewed with a jaundiced eye. Further, certain sectors of the economy may be closed to foreigners, to protect domestic competition, to ensure national security, or to channel investment into areas where the government feels resources are most needed. Australia and Canada, for example, are closely screening takeover bids, and the Andean Pact countries prohibit investment in banking or insurance.

2. There are attempts to increase local participation. There may be requirements for a certain percentage of local ownership. Unless a specific exemption is granted, Mexican regulations limit foreign ownership to 49 percent.

In many countries, there is increasing pressure for joint venture participation in ownership and control. Many countries require that companies employ a certain percentage of their citizens, especially in technical or managerial positions. Finally, there are local content regulations. A certain percentage of the raw materials or the intermediate goods used in the final product must come from local sources.

Such localization requirements attempt to integrate the foreign enterprise into the national economy. On one hand, localization increases the foreign enterprise's contribution to national development. On the other hand, if a firm is acting as a good corporate citizen, it develops clout with the host government otherwise enjoyed by domestic firms. For example, Kimberly Clark established operations according to Mexican guidelines. Later, Kimberly Clark was able to move the Mexican government to establish prohibitive import tariffs against competitors from the United States. The implied threat was that Kimberly Clark would cease operations—at the cost of local sourcing of materials and local employment—if the tariffs were not posted.

3. Finally, expropriation or nationalization of foreign investment can proceed gradually as well as suddenly. Appropriation of assets or skills can be accomplished with a mutually agreed-on procedure such as a fade-out contract, where the firm agrees to sell ownership to nationals after a given number of years. Firms can calculate the time span of the technological advantage and agree to a fade out rather than invest in research and development necessary to maintain the technology gap. In less-cooperative situations, the expropriation may result from unilateral action by the host government. As justification for the unilateral action, the host government may claim either excess profits or unscrupulous deals with prior governments.

Host governments then have various options for asserting control over multinationals. Most host governments accept the need for foreign investment. They realize that they need the resources, technology, management skills, capital, and foreign exchange that foreign investment brings. But governments of both industrial and developing countries increasingly want foreign investment on terms that maximize contribution to national goals and minimize the threat to national sovereignty. Industrial countries have generally welcomed multinationals in their economies but oppose unchecked foreign investment.

Through the 1960s and 1970s, less-developed countries became quite aggressive in trying to control multinationals. Expropriations were common during this period. Such actions have a cost for the host country. Foreign investors rate such countries as politically risky and refrain from new or further investment. More recently, however, governments from less-developed countries have become increasingly sophisticated in dealing with multinationals. Government hire international consulting firms such as McKinsey and Arthur D. Little to plan country strategies for offering a package of benefits and responsibilities to firms, a package that will provide both a reasonable return to the investor and a degree of control over the enterprise that the government finds acceptable.

Some International Differences: Less-Developed Countries

While much of our discussion can be applied to developed and less-developed nations alike, the latter often present a special environment for international business. First, a poor country's macroeconomic goals are more likely to emphasize a catch-up rate of growth, industrialization, increases in employment, and repayment of heavy foreign debts. Second, the political system of a new nation may be less developed, and, in line with our earlier discussion of non-Western nationalism, still in need of legitimizing its central government in face of competing ethnic or religious groups. Third, less-developed countries are typically non-Western countries. Their historical past and cultural environment are likely to be very different from those of the multinational's home country. Last, many developing nations emerged from colonialism during the lifetime of current leaders. All these factors can affect both the quality and stability of political institutions and the view of multinational firms based in the industrialized and ex-colonial West.

The main mistake to avoid is prejudging the political environment. Many new nations espouse some degree of socialism as a reaction against capitalism, the economic system of the ex-colonials. Managers of foreign subsidiaries in such countries are well advised to inquire into the content of policies falling under the rubric of socialism rather than simply to react to a stereotypic hostile environment. In Sri Lanka, all political parties from right of center to radical declare themselves socialist. Socialism is not a monolithic structure; it accommodates to local cultures.

Perhaps the best advice is to attend to the policies and forget the labels. Nationalism should be of greater concern than socialism because nationalism, ironically, combines animosities toward foreign powers with intranational rivalries among competing ethnic groups. A frequent tactic is for one group to identify its rival group with a foreign firm and then to vilify both parties.

Western business often occupies a unique position in less-developed countries:

> The imperfections of the market mechanism in the typical less-developed country plus the small market size of many, render more industries natural monopolies in the sense of making them decreasing cost industries by reason of the restraint on output imposed by the small size of the relevant market. One upshot is that many less-developed countries have less faith in the capacity of private business to satisfy national objectives than do the more-developed countries.
>
> Other forces pushing resources into the public sector include: the historical disrepute of private business—because of the identification with either foreign interests or ethnic or religious minorities, coupled with the natural tendency towards monopoly in small, isolated markets; the greater importance of externalities where industry is combined with an important educational function and is viewed as a lever for long-term national or regional development; and the ineffectiveness of commercial law thereby rendering unlikely anything other than family-size corporations.[41]

In many developing countries, subsidiaries of multinationals are looked upon unfavorably. The very size and power of the parent corporation is often seen as cause for alarm. Further, the Western multinational often bears the brunt of the historical relationships between the First and the Third Worlds. Whether or not a particular firm was involved in exploitative activities during a colonial regime, as apparent legacies of a colonial past and agents of Western imperialism, subsidiaries are seen by some as not contributing to—in fact, even inhibiting—the achievement of national goals.

EVALUATING THE POLITICAL ENVIRONMENT

The political environment can be related to international business through the concept of political risk. Earlier, we discussed the point that the term *risk* is neutral, implying opportunities as well as threats in a foreign political environment. In this section, we comment further on the main concern of most firms—that is, avoiding adverse consequences. Political change can be difficult to anticipate and can certainly affect the ability of a firm to achieve its goals. The firm must be concerned with home- and host-country relationships and with their complex interactions. The lack of certainty in the political environment implies a risk to operations. Operations may be disrupted by internal conflict. Restrictions may be placed on repatriating profits. In the extreme case, a subsidiary may be expropriated.

Firms must learn to anticipate dire consequences but not to overreact. Not all changes in the political environment increase the risk of investments. If changes are gradual and evolutionary, if they can be predicted from past trends, the rise in risk is minimal. Contingency plans can be made. When there are abrupt discontinuities in the political environment, it is more difficult to predict and plan for contingencies. Even abrupt discontinuities do not always increase the risk to operations. A coup d'état, for example, may result only in a change of personnel without any change in attitudes toward foreign investors.[42]

It is important, then, to distinguish between risk and uncertainty. Risk is a situation where the exact outcome is not known. Risk does not represent a novelty. Probabilities can be calculated. Overall investment risk is low when probabilities can be assigned to both political events and their potential effects on foreign investors.

Uncertainty, on the other hand, implies that the outcome cannot be predicted because the situation is novel. The situation has not been previously observed and managed. Planning is extremely difficult under conditions of uncertainty. But some uncertainty is in the eyes of the observer; some events that are not so novel may appear novel due to the lack of understanding of the environment. Understanding the political environment—that is, the structure and functioning of political processes—can reduce the perception of novelty and uncertainty. When a firm can distinguish between disruptive and benign discontinuities that may occur, it can perceive business opportunities and not just business threats.

Environmental Analysis

As the orientation of this book is environmental rather than managerial, we will not review techniques for analyzing political risk in depth. We will, however, discuss one frequently encountered application: the investment decision. When a firm is planning to expand foreign investment, it should screen the political environment. In practice, the problem is complicated by the fact that often many countries must be screened. Further, political risk is not only country specific but also project specific. One would not expect a single analysis to apply to both the construction of a major dam and the installation of a factory to assemble high-quality automobiles.

Many techniques have been developed for screening investment climates. These range from simple go or no-go decisions based on superficial and subjective impressions, to sophisticated probability analyses using Baysian techniques, to return on investment analyses in which returns are discounted not only by the cost of capital but also by a political risk factor. Sophisticated quantitative analyses do not ensure a correct answer. But they force the analyst to question qualitative assumptions and not prejudge the situation.[43]

Responses by Multinationals to Home- and Host-Country Controls

The possibility of nationalistic responses to threats to sovereignty mitigates actions by multinationals that could cause conflict. The multinational is aware that it may generate strong nationalistic reactions that may force the government's hand. It is not uncommon, for example, to see foreign subsidiaries strictly adhering to tax laws in a culture where evasion is the norm. Management feels that actions acceptable for a national may well be unacceptable for a foreigner. The threat of reprisal acts as a countervailing force, offsetting some of the potential for conflict with national objectives. *The multinational firm must weigh (1) maximization of worldwide corporate returns with greater political risk against (2) suboptimization of returns and good corporate citizenship in its host countries.*

Recent research challenges the assumption that monolithic multinationals are always globally maximizing profits of a system of subsidiaries to the detriment of national macroeconomic goals. A more accurate picture is that some firms pursue a global integration (global maximizing) strategy while others pursue a national responsiveness strategy. Choice of strategy depends on the relative bargaining power of the firm and of the nation.[44]

- Sources of multinational firms' bargaining power are renewing technology, economy of scale operations, scattered sites for different stages of production, and control and coordination of international logistics, finances, and marketing activities of the system of subsidiaries.

- Country sources of bargaining power are the percent of government control as a buyer in the industry, mature expropriable technology that can be obtained from other firms or managed by its citizens, and the host-country government's refusal to let their consumers buy the multinational corporation's products because the products are considered luxurious.

Here lies the point mentioned earlier: the political environment can be assessed for business opportunities as well as threats. Bargaining from a position of relative power, a firm such as Boeing in Europe is concerned with avoiding the perception that it is a threat to the power of the national governments. When Boeing compromises its global integration strategy and suboptimizes on one or more parameters, they are paying costs of good corporate citizenship (as well as taxes) in order to avoid reprisals and thus reduce political risk. Bargaining from a position of relative weakness, a nationally responsive firm such as Honeywell Bull of France may indeed bargain for and receive host government subsidies and protection. When power is more evenly balanced between the firm and the country, adaptive responses and administrative flexibility are required.[45]

CONCLUSION

The multinational firm has emerged as an important and influential actor in the international political system. Because of its flexibility, its integrative abilities, and its far-reaching network of operations, it is perceived as posing a threat to the sovereignty and independence of nation-states. This is particularly so for less-developed countries that are politically and economically weak and whose governments attempt to maintain tight national controls. Because multinationals are responsible for the international movement of capital, technology, and personnel, they are agents of change in consumer tastes, skills, ideas, and even political and social systems. Many governments resent this power over the tastes and views of their populace.

On another front, we have noted that improved communications and transportation facilitate global markets. International business is gaining a greater role in the integration and interdependence among nation-states in the world economy. The number of multinationals will not diminish in the near future. Rather, it is increasing as globally competitive firms emerge from such advanced developing nations as Hong Kong, Korea, Singapore, and Taiwan. The scope of integration increases as socialist countries such as Hungary open their markets and permit foreign investment. Pressure for integration could lead to greater cooperation among countries but could also greatly exacerbate political and economic tensions by creating new dependencies and further undermining the ability of nation-states to implement policies of their own choice.

The issues for the future will be difficult to solve. Unless they are addressed, the potential global economic benefits from international business will not be achieved. Continuing attention to the political environment is essential to successful international business operations.

QUESTIONS

1. Identify two major international governmental organizations and suggest how they might affect the operations of multinational firms.

2. Identify some current political leaders. Do they have support from authority? sovereignty? both?

3. How do European and non-Western nationalism differ?

4. Contrast the views of classical economists and dependency theorists on the interrelationship of the international capitalist system, the global distribution of wealth and productive capabilities, and further prospects for the development of currently less-developed nations. Discuss the relevance of notions of dependency to Third-World politicians and bureaucrats. What would you say to a host-government official in a poor country who charges that companies like yours are continuing to extract wealth from poor nations?

5. How do home countries exert control over their multinational corporations?

6. What is meant by the extraterritorial application of national law?

7. Is conflict between multinational corporations and host countries inherent in the structure of multinational corporations? If so, how? How do multinational corporations from newly industrialized countries differ from multinational corporations from industrial countries in this respect?

8. What differences would you expect to find in the relationship between foreign investors and host countries in advanced and in poor countries?

9. What steps are host countries taking to increase control over foreign investors?

10. What are the major problems that nationalism poses for foreign investors?

11. What are some of the impacts that foreign investors have on the social and political environments of host countries?

12. What steps can multinational corporations take to resolve conflicting pressure from home and host countries?

13. What is political risk? What steps can investors take to minimize it?

ENDNOTES

1. Robert Gilpin, *U.S. Power and the Multinational Corporation* (New York: Basic Books, 1975), 3.
2. Yves L. Doz and C. K. Prahalad, "How Multinational Corporations Cope with Host Government Intervention," *Harvard Business Review* (March–April 1980): 149–157.
3. Roger D. Masters, "World Politics as a Primitive Political System," in James N. Rosenau, ed., *International Politics and Foreign Policy: A Reader in Research and Theory* (New York: Free Press, 1969), 104–118.

4. Harold K. Jacobson, *Networks of Interdependence: International Organizations and the Global Political System* (New York: Knopf, 1979), 5.

5. Ibid., 8.

6. Ibid., 9.

7. Samuel P. Huntington, "Transnational Organizations in World Politics," *World Politics* 25, no. 3 (April 1973): 340.

8. Benjamin J. Cohen, *The Question of Imperialism* (New York: Basic Books, 1973), 16.

9. See J. A. Hobson, "The Economic Taproot of Imperialism," in Kenneth Boulding and Tapan Mukerjee, eds., *Economic Imperialism: A Book of Readings* (Ann Arbor: University of Michigan Press, 1972), 1–17.

10. Cohen, op. cit., 46, 164.

11. James D. Cockroft, Andrè Gundar Frank, and Dale L. Johnson, *Dependence and Underdevelopment: Latin America's Political Economy* (New York: Anchor Books, 1972), xi.

12. Theotonio Dos Santos, "The Crisis of Development Theory and the Problems of Dependence in Latin America," in Henry Bernstein, ed. *Underdevelopment and Development in the Third World Today* (Baltimore: Penguin Books, 1972), 58.

13. Ibid.

14. Ibid.

15. Andre Gundar Frank, "The Development of Underdevelopment," in *Imperialism and Underdevelopment: A Reader* (New York: Monthly Review Press, 1970), 19.

16. Cockroft, Frank, and Johnson, op. cit., xi.

17. Stephen Hymer, "The Efficiency (Contradictions) of Multinational Corporations," in *Multinational Corporations: A Radical View* (Cambridge, MA: Harvard University Press, 1979), passim.

18. Larissa Lomnitz, "History of a Mexican Urban Family," *Journal of Family History* 3, no. 4 (1978): 391–409.

19. A. F. K. Organski, *World Politics* (New York: Knopf, 1964), 18.

20. For further discussion, see E. Raymond Platig, "International Relations as a Field of Inquiry," in James N. Rosenau, ed., *International Politics and Foreign Policy: A Reader in Research and Theory* (New York: Free Press, 1969).

21. Maurice Godelier, "The Concept of the 'Tribe': A Crisis Involving Merely a Concept or the Empirical Foundations of Anthropology Itself," in Jack Goody, ed., *Perspectives in Marxist Anthropology*, Vol. 18 of Cambridge Studies in Social Anthropology (Cambridge, UK: Cambridge University Press, 1977).

22. Charles O. Lerche and Abdul A. Said, *Concepts of International Polities* 2d ed. (Englewood Cliffs, NJ: Prentice Hall, 1970), 25.

23. Gilpin, op. cit., 39.

24. For further discussion, see Thomas W. Robinson, "National Interests," in James N. Rosenau, ed., *International Politics and Foreign Policy: A Reader in Research and Theory* (New York: Free Press, 1969), passim.

25. Bill Powell, "Battleground: Japan sees profits in Europe's single market but braces for trade disputes," *Newsweek* (October 2, 1989): 22–26

26. Clifford Geertz, "The Integrative Revolution: Primordial Sentiments and Civil Politics in the New States," in Clifford Geertz, ed., *Old Societies and New States: The Quest for Modernity in Asia and Africa* (New York: The Free Press, 1963). Kenneth David, "Epilogue: What Shall We Mean by Changing Identities," in Kenneth David, ed., *The New Wind: Changing Identities in South Asia* in the series World Anthropology, Proceedings of the IXth International Congress of Anthropological and Ethnological Sciences (The Hague: Mouton, 1977).

27. Jack N. Behrman, "The Multinational Enterprise and Nation States: The Shifting Balance of Power," in Ashok Kapoor and Philip D. Grub, eds., *The Multinational Enterprise in Transition* (Princeton: Darwin Press, 1972), 412.

28. H. R. Hahlo, J. G. Smith, and R. W. Wright, eds., *Nationalism and the Multinational Enterprise* (New York: Oceana Publications), 12.

29. Dos Santos, op. cit., 13–14.

30. William L. Craig, "Application of the Trading with the Enemy Act of Foreign Corporations Owned by Americans: Reflections on Fruehauf v. Massardy," *Harvard Law Review* 83 (January 1970): 585.
31. Ibid., 580.
32. Jonathan P. Stern, "Specters and Pipe Dreams," *Foreign Policy* (Winter 1982): 31.
33. Ibid.
34. Kenneth David, "Home Government Policy and International Competitive Performance of Third World Corporations: A Study of Indian and Korean Service Industries," in Thomas L. Brewer, ed., *Political Risks in International Business* (New York: Praeger, 1985).
35. Thomas Brewer, "Political Risk Assessment for Foreign Direct Investment Decisions: Better Methods for Better Results," *Columbia Journal of World Business* 16, no. 1 (1981): 6.
36. Kenneth David, "Home Government Policy and International Competitive Performance of Third World Corporations: A Study of Indian and Korean Service Industries."
37. Manesh Shrikant, "Management of the External Competitive Context" (Harvard D.B.A. thesis, 1979).
38. Raymond Vernon, "Foreign Trade and Investment: Hard Choices for Developing Countries," in *The Economic and Political Consequences of Multinational Enterprise: An Anthology* (Cambridge, MA: Harvard University Press, 1972), 24.
39. John Fayerweather, "Nationalism and the Multinational Firm," in Ashok Kapoor and Philip D. Grub, eds., *The Multinational Enterprise in Transition* (Princeton: Darwin Press, 1972), 347.
40. M. Clapham, *Multinational Enterprises and Nation States* (London: The Athlone Press, 1975), 28–29.
41. Richard D. Robinson, "The Developing Countries, Development, and the Multinational Corporation," *Annals of the American Academy of Political and Social Science,* 403 (September 1972): 39.
42. Stephen J. Kobrin, "The Environmental Determinants of Foreign Direct Investment: An Ex-Post Empirical Analysis," *Journal of International Business Studies* (Fall 1976): 29.
43. For a more detailed review of the analysis of investment climates, see Robert Stobaugh, Jr., "How to Analyze Foreign Investment Climates," *Harvard Business Review* (September–October 1969): 73.
44. Yves L. Doz and C. K. Prahalad, "How Multinational Corporations Cope with Host Government Intervention," *Harvard Business Review* (March–April 1980): 149–157.
45. Christopher A. Bartlett, "Multinational Organization: Where to after the Structural Stages?" (Paper presented at the 1981 Annual Meeting of the Academy of International Business, Montreal).

For additional information on this complex topic, we suggest the following readings:

George W. Ball, ed., *Global Companies, the Political Economy of World Business* (Englewood Cliffs, NJ: Prentice Hall, 1975).

Kenneth E. Boulding and Tapan Mukerjee, eds., *Economic Imperialism: A Book of Readings.* Ann Arbor: University of Michigan Press, 1972.

Thomas L. Brewer, ed., *Political Risks in International Business* (New York: Praeger, 1985).

Robert Gilpin, *U.S. Power and the Multinational Corporation* (New York: Basic Books, 1975).

Richard D. Robinson, *International Business Policy* (New York: Holt, Rinehart, and Winston, 1964).

Raymond Vernon, *Storm over the Multinationals* (Cambridge, MA: Harvard University Press, 1977).

For reviews of the literature on political risk, see

Robert T. Green, *Political Instability as a Determinant of U.S. Foreign Investment* (Austin: Bureau of Business Research, Univ. of Texas, 1972).

Stephen J. Kobrin, "Political Risk: A Review and Reconsideration," *Journal of International Business Studies* 10, no. 1 (Spring–Summer 1979): 67–80.

Jeffrey D. Simon, "Political Risk Assessment: Past Trends and Future Prospects," *Columbia Journal of World Business* 17, no. 3 (Fall 1982): 62–71.

EPILOGUE
Environments and Issues

MANAGERIAL AND ENVIRONMENTAL APPROACHES

Most international business textbooks are managerial. They provide the reader with specific techniques used by international managers to solve specific problems. We suggest that international managers need a wider orientation to the international business before they begin applying specific techniques. *The overall aim of this book is environmental: How should organizations orient themselves to respond to issues that stem from the differing logics and objectives of the foreign organizations with whom they are associated?*

ENVIRONMENTS OF A FIRM

All firms must respond to the opportunities and threats in their environment. To achieve superior economic performance while responding to the sociopolitical setting, firms must carefully define the environment and adjust their business strategy, their administrative structure, and their corporate culture to meet the demands imposed by the environment. Responding to the environment is more important in international business than it is for firms with solely domestic business operations.

The firm's environment is composed of forces extrinsic to the firm—that is, forces that are neither as controllable nor as predictable as the firm's corporate environment. Extrinsic forces can be classified into three sectors: the physical environment, the task environment, and the societal environment (see Figure E-1).

The Physical Environment

The physical environment is the ecosystem (climate, geography, plant and animal life, and natural resources). All human societies domesticate their physical environment; they modify their physical environment in the course of technological activities. Social definitions of the physical environment vary significantly. Currently, affluent nations are far more environmentally conscious than are poorer nations. As the steady destruction of the Amazon jungle illustrates, poorer nations are willing to sacrifice

FIGURE E-1

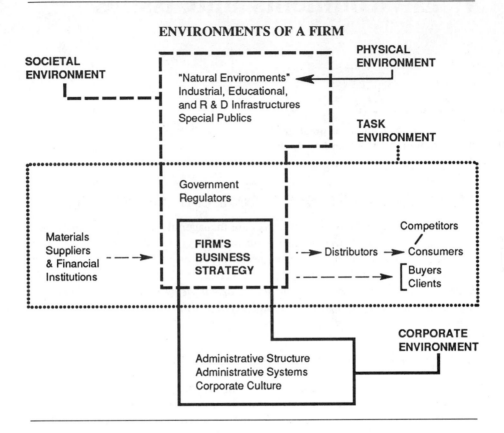

ENVIRONMENTS OF A FIRM

the natural environment for the sake of progress and debt repayment. We call this socially defined physical environment the "natural" environment and place it within the societal environment in Figure E-1.

Availability of natural resources poses constraints. Because no business operations can occur when the environment has been seriously damaged or depleted, environmental impact studies should be of concern to business managers. In Chapter 6, this issue was addressed under the topic of international technology transfers.

The Societal Environment

The societal environment also includes the wider patterns of social relationships and of cultural definitions of life in a society: language, social organization, law, and politics. Two sectors of this environment that particularly affect business operations are the infrastructure and regulatory systems.

- Infrastructure development. A country's technical, educational, and research infrastructure constrains business activity. The level of infrastructure development sets outer limits to the range of viable activity.

- Regulation. In different societies, government industrial regulatory policy can either facilitate or hinder business practice to varying degrees. The relation between governments and firms varies from a state-control mode, as in Eastern Bloc countries, to a partnership mode of cooperation and control, as in Japan, Korea, and Singapore, to an adversarial mode, as in the United States.

The Task Environment

The task environment includes the structures and sociobusiness relationships directly relevant to formulating and implementing a business strategy: the structures of the economy, technology, market, and competition in the industry; relationships with government agencies, suppliers, partners, distributors, customers, clients, and competitors. Because business cultures differ from society to society, home-culture perceptions of the task environment may be inappropriate when operations are located abroad.

The Corporate Environment

The corporate environment has three sectors, each of which contributes to helping organizational members understand "how things work around here": the firm's formal administrative structure, its administrative systems, and its corporate culture.

Formal administrative structures, as recorded in corporate organizational charts, represent the hierarchical distribution of authority, responsibility, and information within the firm. Administrative structure is the social structure of a firm. The larger the firm and the greater the complexity of its operations, the more complex the administrative structure. Units of the administrative structure are usually established according to criteria such as the following:

- Business functions (Accounting, Finance, Marketing, etc.)
- Geographical divisions (East Asia, North America)
- Product divisions (Electronics, Household Appliances)

Formal administrative systems, to some business theorists, are as important as administrative structures in implementing strategy. By adjusting formal systems of control of operations, evaluation, and reward of managers, upper management is held to incite, without immediate supervision, patterns of decision making that are necessary to implement the chosen business strategy.[1]

Corporate culture is a learned, relatively enduring, interdependent system of meanings that classify, code, prioritize, and justify activity both within the organization and toward the external environments it has defined as relevant. This system of symbols and meanings, which is imperfectly shared by interacting organizational members, allows them to explain, coordinate, and evaluate behavior and ascribe common meanings to stimuli encountered both in the organizational environment and in the external (task and societal) environments.

To summarize, a viable business strategy fits three conditions:

- Sociopolitical constraints of the *societal environment*
- Economic, technological, and market conditions of the *task environment*
- Organizational capabilities of the *corporate environment*

The conditions are relevant for both domestic and multinational corporations.

ADDITIONAL COMPLEXITIES FOR COMPANIES DUE TO INTERNATIONAL BUSINESS

Although the main body of the text has spelled out the details, we want to introduce three points as a guide to the additional complexities companies face when they engage in multinational business operations. Multinational corporations (1) engage in diverse business transactions, (2) operate in multiple and diverse environments, and (3) are subject to cultural risk and political imperatives as well as competitive requirements.

Diverse Business Transactions

Compared with domestic firms—even those that export to other countries—multinational corporations have a greater variety of business transactions. To clarify this point, we must first define several crucial terms.

A *multinational corporation* is a corporation that has a headquarters and a system of foreign subsidiaries. This corporation is legally incorporated and has production facilities in its *home* country as well as production and sales facilities in its *host* countries. *Foreign direct investment* is investment in a production plant abroad by a multinational corporation. A *subsidiary* is a unit of a multinational corporation located abroad and controlled by the parent company.

Various *transactions* occur within this system of headquarters and subsidiaries:

- Administration from headquarters to subsidiaries
- Trade flows—for example, parts shipped from one subsidiary to another
- Financial flows—payments for intrafirm trade, loans, royalty payments, repatriation of dividends, and so on.

Further, as illustrated in Figure E-2, a multinational corporation is engaged in a variety of business transactions—domestic and international—with both external and internal (intrafirm) customers.

What is the significance of this variety of transactions among the multinational's headquarters and set of foreign subsidiaries? Domestic firms' export operations are constrained by trade barriers at national boundaries. National boundaries often create

FIGURE E-2

PROFILE OF INTERNATIONAL BUSINESS AND MULTINATIONAL ACTIVITY

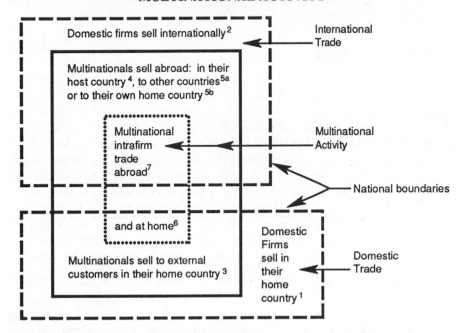

EXAMPLES FOR FIGURE E-2

DOMESTIC FIRMS SELL TO EXTERNAL CUSTOMERS
[1] Domestic firms sell in their home country:
   Quality Dairy sells you some milk
[2] Domestic firms sell internationally:
   Dutch farmers export eggs to Germany
MULTINATIONAL FIRMS SELL TO EXTERNAL CUSTOMERS
[3] Domestic trade in their own home country:
   A Dutch branch of Philips sell electric razors in Holland
[4] Domestic trade in a foreign country:
   A United States subsidiary of Philips sells electric razors
   to consumers in the United States
[5] International trade:
   A United States subsidiary of Philips exports electric razors
   (a) to consumers in Brazil
   (b) to consumers in Holland
MULTINATIONAL FIRMS ENGAGE IN INTRA-FIRM TRANSFERS (BETWEEN BRANCHES OR SUBSIDIARIES OF THE COMPANY)
[6] Domestic trade in their own home country:
   A Michigan branch of Dow Chemical sells chemicals to a Pennsylvania branch of Dow Chemical
[7] International trade:
   A Michigan branch of Dow Chemical exports chemicals to a Japanese subsidiary of Dow Chemical

market imperfections in the free flow of funds, information, proprietary technology, and so forth. The capability of multinationals to effect these various transactions internationally but within the firm results in a distinct advantage: they can enhance revenues or reduce costs. In practice, multinationals are far less restricted by national boundaries than are domestic firms.

Diverse Environments

Although a particular foreign environment may appear unusual (and sometimes problematic) to a manager living abroad, it is not unusual (though sometimes problematic) to managers, workers, officials, consumers, and citizens of a host country. An expatriate manager must never lose sight of the fact that the cultural upbringing of the society's people causes their environment to appear natural to them. When companies undertake international operations, they are operating in multiple, diverse environments. Further, they face regulation both by host-country governments and by international agencies that are overseeing their operations (see Figure E-3).

Operating in diverse foreign environments creates a disadvantage for the foreign firm: the cost of doing business at a distance. The profit equation for a domestic firm is revenues minus all operating costs and taxes. The foreign firm's profit equation includes additional *costs of doing business at a distance* such as the following:

- Need to acquire knowledge of local economic, social, legal, and cultural conditions.
- International communication requirements—planning, directing, controlling, and reporting activities—with miscommunication possible along the international communication circuit.
- Cultural communication gaps in both language and nonverbal cues.
- Need for complex managerial skills: the high cost of preparing expatriate managers or training host-country managers.
- Adaptation to local requirements concerning material supplies, labor, and distribution.

Cultural Risk, Political Imperatives, and Competitive Requirements

Finally, in multinational operations, every business function is constrained by social and political imperatives as well as by competitive requirements. In other words, even when MNCs are acting entirely legally, the normal conduct of international business incites many issues between MNCs, their home country, and the host countries in which they operate abroad.

Why is this the case? Because they must bear *additional costs of doing business at a distance,* multinationals face a disadvantage compared with domestic firms in a host country. Because of their *internal transfer capability* (capability to transfer funds, proprietary technology, and so forth across national boundaries but within the system

FIGURE E-3

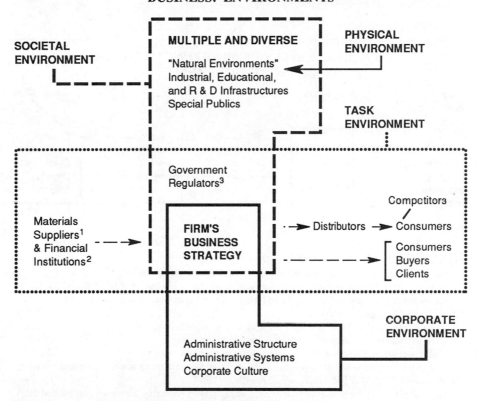

ADDITIONAL COMPLEXITIES OF INTERNATIONAL
BUSINESS: ENVIRONMENTS

Compared with domestic business, international business operations face

[1] Additional regulation of the International Trade System by: General Agreements on Tariffs & Trade

[2] Additional regulation of the International Monetary System by: International Monetary Fund, World Bank
   Additional complexity in the International Financial System by: National and Regional Currencies

[3] Additional regulation in the International Political System by: United Nations, UNESCO

of subsidiaries), multinationals have revenue or cost advantages when compared with domestic firms. Given these two conditions, it is rational for multinationals to pursue a *global maximizing strategy*—making decisions that maximize worldwide profits for the company. At the same time, such decisions are a zero-sum game: they are advantageous for some subsidiaries in the system and disadvantageous for others. For example, new facilities will be built at some subsidiaries but not at others; advanced technology and management skills will be distributed unequally; some subsidiaries will show greater than average profit and others will show less. (See exercises below for further examples.) Any government that hosts a disadvantaged subsidiary is likely to be displeased by the impacts. In short, issues arise between companies and countries when a multinational company implements a global maximizing strategy and a host (or a home) country has the objective of developing social and economic conditions (see Figure E-4).

FIGURE E-4

INTERNATIONAL BUSINESS FUNCTIONS AND ISSUES WITH GOVERNMENTS

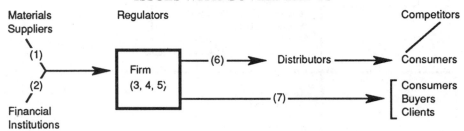

Business Function
    Issue

(1) INTERNATIONAL PURCHASING
    Raw materials can be acquired from within the firm or from other firms.
    In either case, if the acquisition crosses national boundaries, it is a matter of International Trade.
    Countries regulate International Trade with political motives as well as economic motives.

(2) INTERNATIONAL FINANCE
    Interest rates move with the economy in which a company is located.
    Foreign exchange rates can affect the profitability of a venture.
    Host countries can impose controls on sending funds out of the country.
    Host countries can protest that a prestigious foreign company can use up scarce capital in the country.

(3) INTERNATIONAL RESEARCH AND DEVELOPMENT
    Centralized research and development is economically more profitable but rouses charges that the company is not improving the level of knowledge in the host country.

(4) INTERNATIONAL PRODUCTION
    Issues with host country
        Use of a mature, easy-to-use technological process leaves the country vulnerable to nationalization of its foreign plant and equipment.
        But use of a new, difficult-to-use technological process rouses charges that the company is not fulfilling its role as a corporate citizen by transferring needed technology to the host country.
    Issues with home country
        Home-country unions fight foreign production because the country is exporting jobs.

(5) CULTURAL MANAGEMENT
    Problem of trade-off between
        Control of foreign operations by means of standardized reporting procedures
        Cultural sensitivity to local conditions and need to communicate with local managers and workers

(6) INTERNATIONAL DISTRIBUTION
    Need to adapt to local business customs and transportation systems

(7) INTERNATIONAL MARKETING
    Trade-off between
        Economic considerations of profit from standardized products
        Cultural responsiveness to local needs & wants and government regulations

MULTINATIONAL CORPORATIONS AND HOST-COUNTRY GOVERNMENTS: CONTRIBUTIONS, CRITIQUES, AND ISSUES

This book focuses on those environmental problems that arise when business operations transcend national boundaries.

We recognize that there is a problem to be overcome when discussing this topic. Many authors have political or ideological bias when discussing the topic of MNCs. Most writings tend to either strongly favor or strongly oppose MNCs. Our environmental approach aims to go beyond rhetoric. How?

First, we recognize both sides of the story:

- Multinational corporations face complexities in foreign operations; every business function is more problematic.

- Host-country governments face complexities in the operation of their countries due to the presence of international business and multinational corporations.

- Both corporations and countries have objectives and means for obtaining these objectives.

- Both parties tend to look on their objectives and means as being logical, reasonable, and efficient. Both parties can and have looked on the others' objectives as being illogical, unreasonable, inefficient, and even exploitative or corrupt.

Second, we present both sides of the picture:

- Statements of positions of contributions of MNCs
- Statements of positions criticizing MNCs

Third, we reframe the topic in terms of *issues that consider the logic and objectives of both companies and countries.*

EXERCISES

The following entries have been used as the basis of class exercises. They are especially effective when used as debates between small teams formed within the class. Due to the potential length of each discussion, it is helpful to schedule these exercises as occasional events throughout the term.

1. Marketing practices of multinationals
   Pro: Multinationals are meeting the wants and needs of the consumers.
   Con: Multinationals exhibit marketing malpractice that they would never get away with in their home country. Multinationals create needs and wants that are contra-developmental to developing nations.

Issue: What are standards of environmental protection and consumer pro-
            tection that obtain when a company from a high level of socio-
            economic development is selling products to a country at a much lower
            level of socioeconomic development?

2. Relation of multinationals to information

Pro: Multinationals have vastly improved the global communication
            system.

Con: News services located in major industrial nations edit world events
            into "news" that imparts far more information about the industrial
            nations than the developing nations.

Issue: What is balanced reporting that allows global perception of problems
            and prospects of all nations?

3. Relation of MNCs to host countries regarding unemployment problems

Pro: High-tech equipment both transfers modern skills and allows paying
            high wages to some persons in a poor country; high wages increase
            the buying power of some consumers, yielding a trickle-down effect.

Con: Capital-intensive technology has various impacts:
            It creates technological unemployment.
            Income inequity increases due to "aristocratic" class of multi-
            national workers.
            It disrupts family and community ties.

Issue: What is the level of technology appropriate to a host country's level
            of development? What level of technology plus planned worker educa-
            tion improves the skills levels of workers and can slowly be trans-
            ferred elsewhere in the economy?

4. Relation of MNCs to host countries regarding the transfer of technology

Pro: Without the multinationals, advanced technology would be available
            in the host country only decades later, at great cost to the country
            of reinventing the technology.

Con: Multinationals retain a technology gap for their own profit; delay of
            transfer of technology or scattered location of technology is essen-
            tial to maintain company's relative bargaining power with host
            countries.

Issue: What is a balanced plan for countries to acquire needed technology:
            Allowing the presence of foreign-owned technology?
            Licensing (buying the use of) technology?
            Modifying the licensed technology for local use?

5. MNC financial flows and capital controls of host countries

Pro: Multinationals have a responsibility to their shareholders.
            Profits are taken out of the country by means of various linkages
            among the headquarters and the subsidiaries, but the company first
            had to invest in its technology and its foreign plant and other assets.

Con: Multinationals defraud small countries by secret financial flows that obviate capital and financial flows imposed by countries. Taking opportunities that profit from such flows is an unfair source of competitive advantage of MNCs with regard to local firms in the host country.

Issue: What are the long-term economic and social benefits to the country as well as to the company in terms of
Development of infrastructure?
Improving skills levels of workers?
Training local executives who can be used elsewhere?

6. Administrative practices of multinationals

Pro: Multinationals transfer advanced administrative and managerial techniques by their operations abroad and by centralized administrative training centers that train many persons from underdeveloped as well as developed countries. Foreign operations are increasingly headed by host-country nationals.

Con: Multinationals create administrative dependency in which decisions taken at corporate headquarters may adversely affect the host country (from Steven Hymer).

Issue: What is a balanced industrial regulatory policy that sets out a clear, if tough, package of rights and obligations of companies, yet is competitive with alternative country sites for industry?

7. Overall impact of multinationals on the world economy

Pro: Multinational operations improve the efficiency of global allocations of real and financial resources and increase the availability of products and services.
Multinationals help to develop less-developed nations (development theory, see Chapter 8).

Con: Multinational operations continue patterns of unequal exchange developed in the old international division of labor (the dependencia view of André Gundar Frank).

Issue: What is the impact of the new international division of labor: stages of production within an industry performed by firms from different countries?

ENDNOTES

1. J. L. Bower, "Planning and Control: Top down or bottom up?" *Journal of General Management* (1974).

APPENDIX
Classification of Countries by Economic Performance

Two widely used quantitative measures of economic performance are *gross national product* (the value of all goods and services produced worldwide by companies headquartered in a nation) and *gross domestic product* (the value of all goods and services produced by firms within the geographical borders of a country, irrespective of the legal headquarters of the firms). There are several kinds of problems in classifying countries by comparing single quantitative measures, whether GNP/capita or GDP/capita.

- Monetization of transactions within a country

Both GNP per capita and GDP per capita measure only monetized transactions that are formally recorded. As shown by a UNESCO study of purchasing power in various countries, a study too expensive to be replicated, the problem is that the poorer the country, the more nonmonetized transactions exist. Two major kinds of nonmonetized transactions are the informal sector and the illegal sector.

Even in industrialized, developed countries, there is a huge (untaxed) informal sector of barter transactions. The dentist checks the teeth of the auto mechanic, and the mechanic checks the dentist's Volvo. This sector is estimated at 40 percent of the formal GDP of the United States. Extensive gray markets exist in planned economies. In societies where the vast majority of transactions are between kin or village residents, the GDP is vastly underestimated.

The size of the illegal sector in certain South American countries relative to the formal GDP is probably the largest in the world. Drug-related activities in Peru, for example, are estimated as one quarter of Peru's GDP.

- Diversity within a country

The category low-income countries corresponds generally to the UNESCO rubric of least-developed countries. India is an anomaly in this list because the diversity of regional economic developments in India permits the analyst to state that India is at all levels of economic development.

- Sectoral development

Lower-middle and upper-middle-income countries do not distinguish between less-developed countries and newly industrialized countries. To discriminate between these two categories, data on annualized average growth in GNP per capita is more telling than the overall figures of GNP. Newly industrialized countries have higher growth rates. Another measure of economic development, industrial sector as a percentage of GDP, reinforces this picture. From this perspective, countries like Greece and Spain (First World) are closer to countries like Romania and Bulgaria (Second World) and to countries like Korea and Taiwan (Third World) than to other First-World countries. Further, the sectoral structure (percentages of the economy in the agricultural, industrial, and service sectors) of industrialized countries is quite different from oil-exporting countries, despite the similarities in overall GNP per capita figures.

This discussion of appropriate measures of economic development has pointed out pitfalls in the classification of countries. The conclusion is that a combination of measures of economic development and performance is necessary to get an adequate picture.

GNP PER CAPITA

	(a) In 1986 Dollars	*(b) Average Annual Growth (%) 1965–1986*
Low-income countries	200	1.6
1. Ethiopia	120	0.0
2. Bhutan	150	0.0
3. Burkina Faso	150	1.3
4. Nepal	150	1.9
5. Bangladesh	160	.4
6. Malawi	160	1.5
7. Zaire	160	−2.2
8. Mali	180	1.1
9. Burma	200	2.3
10. Mozambique	210	..
11. Madagascar	230	−1.7
12. Uganda	230	−2.6
13. Burundi	240	1.8
14. Tanzania	250	−0.3
15. Togo	250	0.2
16. Niger	260	−2.2
17. Benin	270	0.2
18. Somalia	280	−0.3
19. Central Afr. Rep.	290	−0.6
20. India	290	1.8
21. Rwanda	290	1.5
22. China	300	5.1
23. Kenya	300	1.9
24. Zambia	300	−1.7
25. Sierra Leone	310	0.2

	(a) In 1986 Dollars	(b) Average Annual Growth (%) 1965–1986
26. Sudan	320	−0.2
27. Haiti	330	0.6
28. Pakistan	350	2.4
29. Lesotho	370	5.6
30. Ghana	390	−1.7
31. Sri Lanka	400	2.9
32. Mauritania	420	−0.3
33. Senegal	420	−0.6
34. Afghanistan	..	..
35. Chad	..	..
36. Guinea	..	..
37. Kampuchea, Dem.	..	..
38. Lao, PDR	..	..
39. Vietnam	..	..
Lower-middle-income countries		
40. Liberia	460	−1.4
41. Yemen, PDR	470	..
42. Indonesia	490	4.6
43. Yemen Arab Rep.	550	4.7
44. Philippines	560	1.9
45. Morocco	590	1.9
46. Bolivia	600	−0.4
47. Zimbabwe	620	1.2
48. Nigeria	640	1.9
49. Dominican Rep.	710	2.5
50. Papua, New Guinea	720	0.5
51. Ivory Coast	730	1.2
52. Honduras	740	0.3
53. Egypt, Arab Rep.	760	3.1
54. Nicaragua	790	−2.2
55. Thailand	310	4.0
56. El Salvador	820	−0.3
57. Botswana	840	8.8
58. Jamaica	840	−1.4
59. Camcroon	910	3.9
60. Guatemala	930	1.4
61. Congo, Peo. Rep.	990	3.6
62. Paraguay	1,000	3.6
63. Peru	1,090	0.1
64. Turkey	1,110	0.1
65. Tunisia	1,140	3.8
66. Ecuador	1,160	3.5
67. Mauritius	1,200	3.0
68. Colombia	1,230	3.0

	(a) In 1986 Dollars	(b) Average Annual Growth (%) 1965–1986
69. Chile	1,320	−0.2
70. Costa Rica	1,480	1.6
71. Jordan	1,540	5.5
72. Syrian Arab Rep.	1,570	3.7
73. Lebanon	..	..
Upper-middle-income countries		
74. Brazil	1,810	4.3
75. Malaysia	1,830	4.3
76. South Africa	1,850	0.4
77. Mexico	1,860	2.6
78. Uruguay	1,900	1.4
79. Hungary	2,020	3.9
80. Poland	2,070	..
81. Portugal	2,250	3.2
82. Yugoslavia	2,300	3.9
83. Panama	2,330	2.4
84. Argentina	2,350	0.2
85. Korea, Rep. of	2,370	6.7
86. Algeria	2,590	3.5
87. Venezuela	2,920	0.4
88. Gabon	3,080	1.9
89. Greece	3,680	3.3
90. Oman	4,980	5.0
91. Trinidad & Tobago	5,360	1.6
92. Israel	6,210	2.6
93. Hong Kong	6,910	6.2
94. Singapore	7,410	7.6
95. Iran, Islamic Rep.	..	..
96. Iraq	..	..
97. Romania	..	..
High-income oil-exporting countries		
98. Saudi Arabia	6,950	4.0
99. Kuwait	13,890	−0.6
100. United Arab Emirates	14,680	..
101. Libya	..	..
Industrial market countries		
102. Spain	4,860	2.9
103. Ireland	5,070	1.7
104. New Zealand	7,460	1.5
105. Italy	8,550	2.6
106. United Kingdom	8,870	1.7
107. Belgium	9,230	2.7
108. Austria	9,990	3.3

	(a) In 1986 Dollars	*(b) Average Annual Growth (%) 1965–1986*
109. Netherlands	10,020	1.9
110. France	10,720	2.8
111. Australia	11,920	1.7
112. Germany, Fed. Rep.	12,080	2.5
113. Finland	12,160	3.2
114. Denmark	12,600	1.9
115. Japan	12,840	4.3
116. Sweden	13,160	1.6
117. Canada	14,120	2.6
118. Norway	15,400	3.4
119. United States	17,480	1.6
120. Switzerland	17,680	1.4
Centrally planned economies		
121. Albania	..	..
122. Angola	..	..
123. Bulgaria	..	..
124. Cuba	..	..
Romania*	6,358	..
Poland*	6,890	..
Bulgaria*	7,222	..
Hungary*	8,260	..
125. Czechoslovakia*	9,717	..
126. German Dem. Rep.*	11,860	..
127. Korea, Dem. Rep.	..	..
128. Mongolia	..	..
129. USSR	..	..

Sources:* GNP/capita in 1987; reported in *New York Times* (May 15, 1989): 25, citing Research Project on National Europe, L.W. International Financial Research, Inc., Commerce Department, Central Intelligence Agency. Otherwise, *World Development Report, 1988* (World Bank, 1988), 110, 111.

Bibliography

Adler, Nancy. "Cross-Cultural Management Research: The Ostrich and the Trend." *Academy of Management Review* 8, no. 2 (April 1983).

———. "Preface." *International Studies of Management and Organization* 13, no. 4 (Winter 1982/83): 3–6.

Amsalem, Michel A. *Technology Choice in Developing Countries: The Impact of Differences in Factor Costs.* Washington, DC: International Finance Corporation—The World Bank, 1983.

Anderson, James N. D. *The World's Religions.* London: Inter-Varsity Fellowship of Evangelical Unions, 1950.

Arensberg, Conrad, and Arthur Niehoff. *Introducing Social Change, A Manual for Americans Overseas.* Chicago: Aldine, 1964.

Baal, J. van. *Symbols for Communication: An Introduction to the Anthropological Study of Religion.* Aasen, Neth.: Van Gorcum, 1971.

Banks, Arthur S., and Robert B. Textor. *A Cross-Policy Survey.* Cambridge, MA: M.I.T. Press, 1963.

Barrett, David B. *World Christian Encyclopedia.* Oxford: Oxford University Press, 1983.

Bartlett, Christopher A. "Multinational Organization: Where to After the Structural Stages?" Paper presented at the 1981 Annual Meeting of the Academy of International Business, Montreal.

Behrman, Jack N. "The Multinational Enterprise and Nation States: The Shifting Balance of Power." In *The Multinational Enterprise in Transition*, edited by Ashok Kapoor and Philip D. Grub. Princeton, NJ: Darwin Press, 1972.

Bellah, Robert N., ed. *Religion and Progress in Southeast Asia.* New York: Free Press, 1965.

Borthwick, Bruce M. "The Islamic Sermon as a Channel of Political Communication." *Middle East Journal* (Summer 1967): 299–313.

Bower, J. L. "Planning and Control: Top Down or Bottom Up?" *Journal of General Management* (1974).

Bowles, Richard. *Social Impact in Small Communities*. Toronto: University of Toronto Press, 1980.

Brewer, Thomas. "Political Risk Assessment for Foreign Direct Investment Decisions: Better Methods for Better Results." *Columbia Journal of World Business*, 16, no. 1 (1981).

Bustamante, Jorge. "Maquiladoras: A New Face of International Capitalism in Mexico's Northern Frontier." In J. Nash and M. P. F. Kelly, *Women, Men, and the International Division of Labor*, Albany: State University of New York, 1983.

Callahan, Joseph. "Mexico's Hidden Treasure: The Magical Maquiladoras." *Automotive Industries* (June 1987): 87.

Cavanagh, Gerald F. *American Business Values in Transition*. Englewood Cliffs, NJ: Prentice-Hall, 1976.

Clapham, M. *Multinational Enterprises and Nation States*. London: The Athlone Press, 1975.

Clark, Burton. *The Distinctive College: Antioch, Reed, and Swarthmore*. Chicago: Aldine, 1970.

Cockroft, James D., André Gundar Frank, and Dale L. Johnson. *Dependence and Underdevelopment: Latin America's Political Economy*. Garden City, NY: Anchor Books, 1972.

Cohen, Benjamin J. *The Question of Imperialism*. New York: Basic Books, 1973.

Colson, Elizabeth. "Ancestral Spirits and Social Structure Among the Plateau Tonga." *International Archives of Ethnography* 97, Part I (1954).

Copeland, Lennie, and Lewis Griggs. *Going International: How to Make Friends and Deal Effectively in the Global Marketplace*. New York: Random House, 1985.

Craig, William L. "Application of the Trading with the Enemy Act of Foreign Corporations Owned by Americans: Reflections on *Fruehauf v. Massardy*." *Harvard Law Review* 83 (January 1970): 585.

Critchfield, Richard. "The Plight of the Cities: Djakarta—the First to Close." *Columbia Journal of World Business* 6 (July–August 1971): 89–93.

David, Kenneth. "Hierarchy and Equivalence in Jaffna, North Sri Lanka." In *The New Wind: Changing Identities in South Asia*, edited by Kenneth David. World Anthropology Series, Proceedings of the IXth International Congress of Anthropological and Ethnological Sciences. The Hague: Mouton, 1977.

————. "Epilogue: What Shall We Mean by Changing Identities." In *The New Wind: Changing Identities in South Asia*, edited by Kenneth David. World Anthropology Series, Proceedings of the IXth International Congress of Anthropological and Ethnological Sciences. The Hague: Mouton, 1977.

————. "Hidden Powers: Cultural and Socioeconomic Accounts of Jaffna Women." In *The Powers of Tamil Women*, edited by Susan Wadley. Syracuse: Syracuse University Press, 1979.

————. "Home Government Policy and International Competitive Performance of Third World Corporations: A Study of Indian and Korean Service Industries." In *Political Risks in International Business*, edited by Thomas L. Brewer. New York: Praeger, 1984.

————. "Planning the Project." In Thomas L. Brewer, Kenneth David, and Linda Lim, *Investing in Developing Nations: A Guide for Executives*. New York: Praeger, and Washington, DC: Overseas Private Investment Corporation, 1986.

————. "Managing Cultural Problems." In Thomas L. Brewer, Kenneth David, and Linda Lim, *Investing in Developing Nations: A Guide for Executives*. New York: Praeger, and Washington, DC: Overseas Private Investment Corporation, 1986.

————. "International Competitiveness in Construction and Computer Software: The Case of South Korea and India." In *The Pacific Challenge in International Business*, edited by W. Chan Kim and Philip K.Y. Young. Ann Arbor: UMI Research Press, 1987.

————. "Inter-Organizational Learning." Paper presented at the Strategic Management Association meetings, San Francisco, October 1989.

Davis, Shelton H. *Victims of the Miracle: Development and the Indians of Brazil*. Cambridge, UK: Cambridge University Press, 1977.

Davis, Tim R. V. "Managing Cultures at the Bottom." In *Gaining Control of the Corporate Culture*, edited by Ralph H. Kilman, et al. London: Jossey-Bass, 1986.

Deal, Terrence E., and Allan Kennedy. *Corporate Cultures: The Rites and Rituals of Corporate Life*. Reading, MA: Addison-Wesley, 1982.

Dean, Vera Micheles. *The Nature of the Non-Western World*. New York: Mentor Books, 1956.

De la Torre, Jose, and Brian Toyne. "Cross-National Managerial Interaction: A Conceptual Model." *Academy of Management Review* 3, no. 3 (July 1978): 462–475.

Deutsch, Karl W. *Nationalism and Social Communication*. Cambridge, MA: M.I.T. Press, 1953.

Dos Santos, Theotonio. "The Crisis of Development Theory and the Problems of Dependence in Latin America." In *Underdevelopment and Development in the Third World Today*, edited by Henry Bernstein. Baltimore: Penguin Books, 1972.

Doz, Yves L., and C. K. Prahalad. "How Multinational Corporations Cope with Host Government Intervention." *Harvard Business Review* (March–April 1980): 149–157.

Edelman, Murray. *Political Language*. New York: Academic Press, 1977.

Eiteman, David K., and Arthur I. Stonehill. *Multinational Business Finance* 3d ed. Reading, MA: Addison-Wesley, 1982.

Emmanuel, Arghiri. *L'Echange Inégal*. London: NLB, 1969.

———. *Appropriate or Underdeveloped Technology?* Chichester, UK: Wiley, 1982.

Evans-Pritchard, E. E. "The Notion of Witchcraft Explains Unfortunate Events." *Witchcraft, Oracles, and Magic Among the Azande*. Oxford: Clarendon Press, 1937.

Evered, R. "The Language of Organizations: The Case of the Navy." In *Organizational Symbolism*, edited by L. Pondy, P. Frost, G. Morgan, and T. Dandridge. Greenwich, CT: JAI Press, 1983.

Farmer, Richard N., and Barry M. Richman. *Comparative Management and Economic Progress*. Homewood, IL: Irwin, 1965.

Fayerweather, John. *International Business Management, A Conceptual Framework*. New York: McGraw-Hill, 1969.

———. "Nationalism and the Multinational Firm." In *The Multinational Enterprise in Transition*, edited by Ashok Kapoor and Philip D. Grub. Princeton, NJ: Darwin Press, 1972.

Fernandez-Kelly, Maria Patricia. *For We Are Sold, I and My People: Women and Industry in Mexico's Frontier*. Albany: State University of New York, 1983.

Fillol, Thomas. *Social Factors in Economic Development, The Argentine Case*. Cambridge, MA: M.I.T. Press, 1961.

Fleary, Lynn. "Business makes a run for the border." *Fortune* (August 18, 1986).

Frank, André Gundar. "The Development of Underdevelopment." *Imperialism and Underdevelopment, A Reader*. New York: Monthly Review Press, 1970.

Geertz, Clifford. "The Integrative Revolution: Primordial Sentiments and Civil Politics in the New States." In *Old Societies and New States: The Quest for Modernity in Asia and Africa*, edited by Clifford Geertz. New York: The Free Press, 1963.

Gephart, Robert P. "Status Degradation and Organizational Succession: An Ethnomethodological Approach." *Administrative Science Quarterly* 23, no. 4 (November 1978): 553–581.

Gillin, John P. *Social Change in Latin America Today*. New York: Vintage Books, 1961.

Gilpin, Robert. *U.S. Power and the Multinational Corporation*. New York: Basic Books, 1975.

Gleason, Henry A. *An Introduction to Descriptive Linguistics*. New York: Holt, 1955.

Godelier, Maurice. *Rationality and Irrationality in Economics*. New York: Monthly Review Press: 1972.

———. "The Concept of the 'Tribe': A Crisis Involving Merely a Concept or the Empirical Foundations of Anthropology Itself." In *Perspectives in Marxist Anthropology*, translated by Robert Brain. Cambridge, UK: Cambridge University Press, 1977.

———. "The Concept of Social and Economic Formation: The Inca Example," In *Perspectives in Marxist Anthropology*, translated by Robert Brain. Cambridge, UK: Cambridge University Press, 1977.

Gregory, Kathleen L. "Native-View Paradigms: Multiple Cultures and Culture Conflicts in Organizations." *Administrative Science Quarterly* 28 (1983): 359–376.

Hagen, Everett E. *On the Theory of Social Change*. Homewood, IL: Dorsey Press, 1962.

Hahlo, H. R., J. G. Smith, and R. W. Wright, eds. *Nationalism and the Multinational Enterprise*. Dobbs Ferry, NY: Oceana Publications, 1973.

Hall, Edward T. *The Silent Language*. New York: Doubleday, 1959.

Hirsch, Paul, and J. Andrews. "Ambushes, Shootouts, and Knights of the Round Table: The Language of Corporate Takeovers." In *Organizational Symbolism*, edited by L. Pondy, P. Frost, G. Morgan, and T. Dandridge. Greenwich, CT: JAI Press, 1983.

Hobson, J. A. "The Economic Taproot of Imperialism." In *Economic Imperialism, A Book of Readings*, edited by Kenneth Boulding and Tapan Mukerjee. Ann Arbor: University of Michigan Press, 1972.

Hodge, Robert W., et al. "A Comparative Study of Occupational Prestige." In *Social Stratification in Comparative Perspective*, edited by Reinhard Bendix and Seymour M. Lipset. New York: Free Press, 1966.

Hofstede, Geert. *Culture's Consequences: International Differences in Work-Related Values*. London: Sage, 1980.

———. "Do American Theories Apply Abroad?" *Organizational Dynamics* 10, no. 1 (Summer 1981): 63–80.

———, and Michael Harris Bond, "The Confucius Connection: From Cultural Roots to Economic Growth." *Organizational Dynamics* 16, no. 4 (Spring 1988): 5–24.

Huntington, Samuel P. "Transnational Organizations in World Politics." *World Politics* 25, no. 3 (April 1973): 340.

Hymer, Stephen. "The Efficiency (Contradictions) of Multinational Corporations." In *Multinational Corporations: A Radical View*. Cambridge, MA: Harvard University Press, 1979.

Inkeles, Alex, and Peter H. Rossi. "National Comparisons of Occupational Prestige." *American Journal of Sociology* (January 1956).

Iwata, Ryushi. *Japanese-Style Management: Its Foundations and Prospects*. Tokyo: Asian Productivity Organization, 1982.

Jacobson, Harold K. *Networks of Interdependence: International Organizations and the Global Political System*. New York: Knopf, 1979.

Jennings, Eugene E. *Routes to the Executive Suite*. New York: McGraw-Hill, 1971.

Kakar, Sudhir. "Authority Patterns and Subordinate Behavior in Indian Organizations." *Administrative Science Quarterly* 16 (1971).

———. "The Theme of Authority in Social Relations in India." *Journal of Social Psychology* 84, no. 1 (June 1971): 93–110.

Katona, George, Burkhard Strumpel, and Ernest Zahn. *Aspirations and Affluence, Comparative Studies in the United States and Western Europe*. New York: McGraw-Hill, 1971.

Kluckhohn, Clyde. *Mirror for Man, The Relation of Anthropology to Modern Life*. New York: McGraw-Hill, 1949.

Kobrin, Stephen J. "The Environmental Determinants of Foreign Direct Investment: An Ex-Post Empirical Analysis." *Journal of International Business Studies* (Fall 1976): 29.

Korzenny, Betty Ann. "Cross-Cultural Issues in the Process of Sending U.S. Employees of Multinational Corporations for Overseas Service." Paper presented at the annual meetings of the Speech Communications Association, San Antonio, Texas, 1979.

Kumar, Krishna. "Social and Cultural Impacts of Transnational Corporations: An Overview." In *Transnational Enterprises: Their Impact on Third World Societies and Cultures*, edited by Krishna Kumar. Boulder, CO: Westview Press, 1980.

Lerche, Charles O., and Abdul A. Said. *Concepts of International Politics* 2d ed. Englewood Cliffs, NJ: Prentice Hall, 1970.

Lester, Robert C. *Theravada Buddhism in Southeast Asia*. Ann Arbor: University of Michigan Press, 1972.

Levi-Strauss, Claude. *The Savage Mind*. Chicago: The University of Chicago Press, 1966.

Linden, Eugene. "Playing with Fire." *Time* (September 18, 1989).

Lomnitz, Larissa. "History of a Mexican Urban Family." *Journal of Family History* 3, no. 4 (1978): 391–409.

Louis, Meryl R. "Sourcing Workplace Cultures: Why, When, and How." In *Gaining Control of the Corporate Culture*, edited by Ralph H. Kilman, et al. London: Jossey-Bass, 1986.

Magee, Stephen. "Information and the Multinational Corporation: The Appropriability Theory of Foreign Direct Investment." In *International Financial Management*, edited by Donald Lessard. Boston: Warren, Gorham, and Lamont, 1979.

Martin, Joanne. "Stories and Scripts in Organizational Settings." In *Cognitive Social Psychology*, edited by A. Hasdorf and A. Isen. New York: Elsevier, 1982.

Martin, Joanne, and Caren Siehl. "Organizational Culture and Counter-Culture: General Motors and Delorean." Research Paper Series, no. 633, Graduate School of Business, Stanford University, 1981.

——. "Organizational Culture and Counterculture: An Uneasy Symbiosis." *Organizational Dynamics* (Autumn 1983): 52–64.

Masters, Roger D. "World Politics as a Primitive Political System." In *International Politics and Foreign Policy: A Reader in Research and Theory*, edited by James N. Rosenau. New York: Free Press, 1969.

McClelland, David. *The Achieving Society*. New York: Irvington, 1961.

Mesthene, Emmanuel G. "Symposium: The Role of Technology in Society—Some General Implications of the Research of the Harvard University Program on Technology and Society." *Technology and Culture* 10, no. 4 (October 1969): 500.

Michael, Donald N. "Technology and the Management of Change in a Culture Context." Paper given at Conference on the Problems of Modernization in Asia, Honolulu, 1970.

Middleton, John. "The Cult of the Dead: Ancestors and Ghosts." *Lugbara Religion: Ritual and Authority Among an East African People*. London: Oxford University Press, 1960.

Moch, Michael, and Anne S. Huff. "Chewing Ass Out: The Enactment of Power Relationships Through Language and Ritual." Presentation to the Academy of Management meetings, Detroit, 1981.

Mukerji, D. P. "Mahatma Gandhi's Views on Machines and Technology." *International Social Science Bulletin* 6, no. 3 (1954): 441.

Mumford, Lewis. *Technics and Civilization*. New York: Harcourt, Brace, 1934.

Murra, John. "The Economic Organizations of the Inca State." Unpublished thesis, University of Chicago, 1956.

Myrdal, Gunnar. *Asian Drama, An Inquiry into the Poverty of Nations*. New York: Twentieth Century Fund, 1968.

Nahavandi, A., and A. Malekzadeh. "Acculturation in Mergers and Acquisitions. *Academy of Management Review* 13, no. 4 (1988): 79–90.

Nair, Kusum. *Blossoms in the Dust: The Human Factor in Indian Development*. New York: Praeger, 1962.

Nayar, Baldev Raj. *National Communication and Language Policy in India*. New York: Praeger, 1969.

Negandhi, Anant. "Cross-Cultural Management Studies: Too Many Conclusions, Not Enough Conceptualization." *Management International Review* 14, no. 6 (1974/76): 59–65.

Organski, A. F. K. *World Politics*. New York: Knopf, 1964.

Packard, Vance. *The Status Seekers*. New York: Pocket Books, 1961.

Peaslee, A. L. "Education's Role in Development." *Economic Development and Cultural Change* 17, no. 3 (April 1969): 293–318.

Pei, Mario. *The Story of Language* rev. ed. Philadelphia: J. B. Lippincott, 1965.

Pettigrew, Andrew M. "Strategic Aspects of Management of Specialist Activity." *Personnel Review* 4 (1975): 5–13.

Peters, Thomas, and Robert H. Waterman, Jr. *In Search of Excellence*. New York: Harper & Row, 1982.

Phalon, Richard, "Hell Camp." *Forbes* (January 1984): 56–58.

Pirsig, Robert M. *Zen and the Art of Motorcycle Maintenance*. New York: Bantam Books, 1974.

Platig, E. Raymond. "International Relations as a Field of Inquiry." In *International Politics and Foreign Policy: A Reader in Research and Theory*, edited by James N. Rosenau. New York: Free Press, 1969.

Pober, Madeline. "Tokyo Woes: Orienting Yourself to Japan." *Savvy* (April 1984): 82.

Pondy, Louis. "Leadership Is a Language Game." In *Leadership: Where Else Can We Go?*, edited by M. McCall and M. Lombardo. Durham, NC: Duke University Press, 1978.

Pye, Lucien W. *Politics, Personality, and Nation Building: Burma's Search for Identity*. New Haven: Yale University Press, 1962.

Raju, M. K., and C. K. Prahalad. *The Emerging Multinationals-Indian Enterprise in the ASEAN Region*. Madras, India: M. K. Raju Consultants, 1980.

Ramond, Charles. "Predicting Demand for Consumer Products in Foreign Countries." Paper given at the meeting of the Academy of International Business, Toronto, December 1972.

Redfield, Robert. *The Little Community: Peasant Society and Culture*. Chicago: The University of Chicago Press, 1960.

Ricks, D., M. Fu, and J. Arpan. *International Business Blunders*. Cincinnati: Grid, 1974.

Robinson, Richard D. "The Developing Countries, Development, and the Multinational Corporation." *Annals of the American Academy of Political and Social Science* 403 (September 1972): 39.

Robinson, Thomas W. "National Interests." In *International Politics and Foreign Policy: A Reader in Research and Theory*, edited by James N. Rosenau. New York: Free Press, 1969.

Robock, Stephan H., and Kenneth Simmonds. *International Business and Multinational Enterprise* 3d ed. Homewood, IL: Irwin, 1983.

Rohlen, Thomas P. "Spiritual Education in a Japanese Bank." *American Anthropologist* 75, no. 5 (October 1973): 1542–1562.

Sahlins, Marshall. "The Original Affluent Society." *Stone Age Economics*. London: Tavistock, 1974.

Sathe, Vijay. *Culture and Related Corporate Realities*. Homewood, IL: Irwin, 1985.

Schein, Edgar G. "Is Organizational Change Possible?" Paper presented at the American Management Association meetings, 1981.

Schneider, Benjamin. "Organizational Climates: An Essay." *Personnel Psychology* 28, no. 4 (Winter 1975): 447–479.

Scotton, Carol. "Language Policies. National Development, and Communication." Revision of paper prepared for Seminar on Development, Stanford University Institute of Mass Communications, June 1974.

———. "The Role of Norms and Other Factors in Language Choice in Work Situations in Three African Cities (Lagos, Kampala, Nairobi)." In *Language in Sociology*, edited by Rolf Kjolseth and Albert Verdoodt. Louvain, Belgium: Editions Peeters, 1976.

———. "Neighbors and Lexical Borrowing: A Study of Two Ateso Dialects." *Language* 49, no. 4 (1983): 871–889.

Sheth, Jagdish N. "Cross-Cultural Influences on Buyer-Seller Interaction/Negotiation Process." *Asian Pacific Journal of Management* 1, no. 1 (September 1983): 46–55.

Shrikant, Manesh. "Management of the External Competitive Context." D.B.A. thesis, Harvard University, 1979.

Siehl, Caren. "Cultural Sleight-of-Hand: The Illusion of Consistency." Unpublished doctoral dissertation, Stanford University, 1984.

Slater, Robert. *World Religions and World Community*. New York: Columbia University Press, 1968.

Soderstrom, Edward Johnathon. *Social Impact Assessment*. New York: Praeger, 1981.

Spiro, Melford E. "Ghosts, Ifaluk, and Teleological Functionalism." *American Anthropologist* 54, no. 4 (October–December 1952): 497–503.

Stern, Jonathan P. "Specters and Pipe Dreams." *Foreign Policy* (Winter 1982): 31.

Stobaugh, Robert Jr. "How to Analyze Foreign Investment Climates." *Harvard Business Review* (September–October 1969): 73.

Stone, John. "Canada, Quebec Nationals, Cree Indians, and the James Bay Hydroelectric Project." Paper for Seminar, Environments of International Business, Michigan State University, June 1983.

Tandon, Prakash. "Maturing of Business in India." *California Management Review* (Spring 1972).

Tiano, Susan. "Maquiladora, Women's Work, and Unemployment in Northern Mexico." Women in International Development working paper #43. East Lansing: Michigan State University, 1984.

Trice, H., and J. Beyer. "Studying organizational cultures through rites and ceremonials." *Academy of Management Review* 9 (1984): 653–659.

Tugendhat, Christopher. *The Multinationals*. New York: Random House, 1972.

Vernon, Raymond. "Foreign Trade and Investment: Hard Choices for Developing Countries." In *The Economic and Political Consequences of Multinational Enterprise: An Anthology*, edited by Raymond Vernon. Cambridge: Harvard University Press, 1972.

Webber, Ross A. *Culture and Management, Text and Readings in Comparative Management*. Homewood, IL: Irwin, 1969.

Weber, Max. *The Protestant Ethic and the Spirit of Capitalism*, translated by Talcott Parsons. New York: Scribner's, 1958.

Weick, Karl. *The Social Psychology of Organizing* 2d ed. Reading, MA: Addison-Wesley, 1979.

Whorf, Benjamin Lee. *Language, Thought, and Reality*. New York: Wiley, 1956.

Wilkins, Alan. "Organizational Stories as an Expression of Management Philosophy: Implications for Social Control in Organizations." Doctoral dissertation, Graduate School of Business, Stanford University, 1978.

———, and Joanne Martin. "Organizational Legends." Research Paper No. 521, Graduate School of Business, Stanford University, 1979.

X, Malcolm. *The Autobiography of Malcolm X, As Told to Alex Haley*. New York: Ballantine, 1973.

Yoshino, M. Y. *Japan's Managerial System, Tradition and Innovation*. Cambridge, MA: M.I.T. Press, 1968.

Index